Frame Shifting for Teachers

Learn how you can successfully address persistent teaching dilemmas by reframing how you think about and respond to them. The authors show how adopting habits of mind, including curiosity and an asset-based teaching approach, is necessary for tackling teaching challenges more effectively and equitably. Chapters explain how you can then apply frame shifting by considering your dilemma in three domains—relationships, classroom management, and curriculum and instruction. Practical examples, exercises, and discussion questions throughout the book will help you apply the concepts to your own teaching situation. In addition, a bonus online study guide contains reproducible templates, additional examples, suggested answers, and more. Appropriate for teachers to read independently or through book studies and PLCs, the book will leave you with new strategies for changing your beliefs and reactions, and ultimately improving how you approach and reach your students.

Brianna L. Kennedy is Professor of Education in the School of Education at the University of Glasgow. She studies the marginalization and belonging of students from nondominant social backgrounds. As a former middle school teacher, she prioritizes the bridging of theory, research, and practice. Dr. Kennedy taught in the Los Angeles Unified School District from 1998 to 2005.

Amy S. Murphy is Clinical Associate Professor in the Department of Theory and Practice at the University of Georgia. Her work focuses on justice-oriented teacher education, culturally responsive classroom management, and young adolescents. A former teacher of ten years in Florida, she maintains her connection to schools through a close school–university partnership in which she supports pre-service and in-service educators.

Also Available from Routledge Eye On Education

(www.routledge.com/k-12)

What Great Teachers Do Differently, 3rd Edition: Nineteen Things That Matter Most
Todd Whitaker

Classroom Management from the Ground Up
Todd Whitaker, Madeline Whitaker Good, Katherine Whitaker

Identity Affirming Classrooms: Spaces That Center Humanity
Erica Buchanan-Rivera

75 Quick and Easy Solutions to Common Classroom Disruptions
Bryan Harris and Cassandra Goldberg

Passionate Learners: How to Engage and Empower Your Students
Pernille Ripp

Case Studies on Diversity and Social Justice Education, 3rd edition
Paul Gorski and Seema Pothini

Frame Shifting for Teachers

Developing a Conscious Approach to Solving Persistent Teaching Dilemmas

Brianna L. Kennedy and Amy S. Murphy

NEW YORK AND LONDON

Designed cover image: © Getty Images

First published 2024
by Routledge
605 Third Avenue, New York, NY 10158

and by Routledge
4 Park Square, Milton Park, Abingdon, Oxon, OX14 4RN

Routledge is an imprint of the Taylor & Francis Group, an informa business

© 2024 Brianna L. Kennedy and Amy S. Murphy

The right of Brianna L. Kennedy and Amy S. Murphy to be identified as authors of this work has been asserted in accordance with sections 77 and 78 of the Copyright, Designs and Patents Act 1988.

All rights reserved. No part of this book may be reprinted or reproduced or utilised in any form or by any electronic, mechanical, or other means, now known or hereafter invented, including photocopying and recording, or in any information storage or retrieval system, without permission in writing from the publishers.

Trademark notice: Product or corporate names may be trademarks or registered trademarks, and are used only for identification and explanation without intent to infringe.

Library of Congress Cataloging-in-Publication Data
Names: Kennedy, Brianna L., author. | Murphy, Amy S., 1977- author.
Title: Frame shifting for teachers : developing a conscious approach to solving persistent teaching dilemmas / Brianna L. Kennedy and Amy S. Murphy.
Description: First edition. | New York : Routledge, 2024. | Includes bibliographical references and index.
Identifiers: LCCN 2023050508 | ISBN 9781032294896 (hbk) | ISBN 9781032281568 (pbk) | ISBN 9781003301806 (ebk)
Subjects: LCSH: Teachers--United States--Psychology. | Teacher-student relationships--United States. | Classroom management--United States. | Curriculum planning--United States. | Self-actualization (Psychology) | Curiosity. | Teachers--Training of--United States.
Classification: LCC LB2840 .K456 2024 | DDC 371.1001/9--dc23/eng/20240207
LC record available at https://lccn.loc.gov/2023050508

ISBN: 978-1-032-29489-6 (hbk)
ISBN: 978-1-032-28156-8 (pbk)
ISBN: 978-1-003-30180-6 (ebk)

DOI: 10.4324/9781003301806

Access the Support Material: www.routledge.com/9781032281568

Typeset in Palatino
by SPi Technologies India Pvt Ltd (Straive)

Contents

List of Key Figures	x
List of Figures	xi
List of Tables	xiii
Focus on Culture Sections	xvi
Support Material	xviii
Author Biographies	xxiii

Part I   Foundations   1

1 Introduction   7
   Grounding Case   7
   Ms. Nash's Next Steps: An Introduction to the
      Three Domains of Teaching   9
   Articulating Ms. Nash's Dilemma Using the Basics
      of the Frame Shifting Approach   13
   The Role of Culture in Ms. Nash's Dilemma   17
      How To Use This Book   18
         Part I: Foundations   19
         Part II: The Domains of Teaching   19
         Part III: Putting It All Together   20
         Supporting Materials   20
         Suggestions for How to Use This Book
            Individually or In a Group Setting   21
   For Discussion and Practice   22
   References   22

2 Strengthening Foundational Habits of Mind   23
   Habit of Personal Attribution   26
      Distal and Proximal Characterizations   26
      External and Internal Attributions   29
   Habit of Asset Identification   33
   Habit of Deliberate Interpretation   39
      Observation of Empirical Facts   43

From Observation to Interpretation ... 45
From Interpretation to Judgment ... 50
From Judgment to Decision ... 52
Engaging the Habits of Mind to Describe
  Ms. Nash's Dilemma ... 55
Practicing the Habits of Mind: Why Don't the
  Caregivers Care Enough to Show Up? ... 57
  Engaging the Habit of Personal Attribution
    With the Practice Dilemma ... 58
  Engaging the Habit of Asset Identification
    With the Practice Dilemma ... 58
  Engaging the Habit of Deliberate Interpretation
    With the Practice Dilemma ... 59
Engaging the Habits of Mind to Describe the
  Back-to-School Night Dilemma ... 61
Conclusions About Habits of Mind ... 62
For Discussion and Practice ... 65
References ... 67

3 Frame Shifting ... 69
Identifying Your Current Dilemma Framing ... 73
Shifting the Frame Among the Domains of
  Teaching ... 76
  Frame Shifting to the Domain of Classroom
    Management ... 79
  Developing Dilemma Statements and Focus
    Questions in the Domain of Relationships ... 82
  Developing Dilemma Statements and Focus
    Questions in the Domain of Curriculum and
    Instruction ... 86
Practicing Frame Shifting With Examples From
  Different Educational Levels ... 89
For Discussion and Practice ... 97
References ... 98

Part II The Domains of Teaching	**99**
4 Frame Shifting to the Domain of Relationships	**103**
Improving Teacher–Student Relationships	105
Warmth and Friendliness	107
Getting to Know Students Well	110
Instructional Agency and Warm Demanding	112
High Academic Expectations Coupled With Academic Support	116
Caregiver Communication and Community Life	119
Teacher–Class Relationships	123
Improving Student–Student Relationships by Creating Classroom Communities	125
Helping Students Get to Know Each Other	127
Building a Class Culture to Support Collaborative Teams	130
Continuing to Provide Appropriate Structure and Boundaries	131
Key Takeaways: Teacher Moves to Address Dilemmas Related to Relationships	132
For Discussion and Practice	135
References	138
5 Frame Shifting to the Domain of Classroom Management	**143**
Rules	147
Routines	151
Establishing and Maintaining Rules and Routines	156
Teacher Verbal Behaviors	158
Teacher Nonverbal Behaviors	167
Navigating Classroom Management Tensions	178
De-Escalation	180
Time-Outs	185
Restorative Practices	185

Key Takeaways: Teacher Moves to Address Dilemmas Related to Classroom Management	188
For Discussion and Practice	191
References	193

6 Frame Shifting to the Domain of Curriculum and Instruction — 197

Curriculum	201
Explicit Curriculum	202
Privileged Knowledge and the Hidden Curriculum	211
Making Curriculum Matter to Students	214
Instruction	227
Instructional Design	230
Instructional Sequences	236
Instructional Formats	237
Steps or Components of Instructional Formats or Activities	248
Key Takeaways: Teacher Moves to Address Dilemmas Related to Curriculum and Instruction	249
For Discussion and Practice	254
References	256

Part III Putting It All Together — 259

7 Practicing Engaging the Habits of Mind — 263

Sample Case: Group Projects in Mr. Lee's Class	265
Engaging the Habit of Personal Attribution with Mr. Lee's Dilemma	267
Engaging the Habit of Asset Identification With Mr. Lee's Dilemma	272
Engaging the Habit of Deliberate Interpretation With Mr. Lee's Dilemma	280
Developing Empirical Observations	284
From Observation to Interpretation	287
From Interpretation to Judgment	292
From Judgment to Decision	294
Engaging All of the Habits of Mind to Describe Mr. Lee's Dilemma	295
For Discussion and Practice	299

8 **Practicing Frame Shifting to the Three Domains of Teaching** **301**
   Frame Shifting Mr. Lee's Dilemma 305
      How Mr. Lee Initially Framed His Dilemma:
         Domain of Curriculum and Instruction 305
      Frame Shifting Mr. Lee's Dilemma to the
         Domain of Classroom Management 320
      Frame Shifting Mr. Lee's Dilemma to the
         Domain of Relationships 326
      Review of Mr. Lee's Case 330
   For Discussion and Practice 332

Glossary 333
Key Figures 341
Recommended Readings About Cultural Differences
   in the Classroom 343

Key Figures

1	Three Domains of Teaching	341
2	Illustration of the Process of Narrowing the Dilemma Description to a Focus Question	341
3	Framing the Dilemma	342
4	Using the Zoomed In Frame as a Focus for Generating Dilemma Statements, Focus Questions, and Teacher Moves Within Each Domain	342

Figures

2.1	Focusing on Proximal Dilemmas	28
2.2	Steps in the Habit of Deliberate Interpretation	40
2.3	Where Ms. Nash's Dilemma Statement was Originally Positioned	44
2.4	Engaging the Habit of Asset Identification When Caregivers Do Not Attend Back to School Night	59
2.5	Applying the Habit of Deliberate Interpretation to the Dilemma of Caregiver Absence	60
3.1	Ms. Nash's Current Dilemma Frame Zoomed in on the Domain of Classroom Management	74
3.2	Focus Questions Ms. Nash Identified in the Domain of Classroom Management Using the Zoomed In Frame	81
3.3	Focus Questions Ms. Nash Identified in the Domain of Relationships Using the Zoomed In Frame	85
3.4	Focus Questions Ms. Nash Identified in the Domain of Curriculum and Instruction Using the Zoomed In Frame	90
3.5	Focus Questions Ms. Nash Generated in All Three Domains of Teaching Using the Frame Shifting Approach	93
4.1	Teacher Moves Ms. Nash Identified in the Domain of Relationships Using the Zoomed In Frame	134
5.1	Teacher Moves Ms. Nash Identified in the Domain of Classroom Management Using the Zoomed In Frame	189
6.1	Transforming Ms. Nash's Original Warm-Up Activity to Include Students' Funds of Knowledge and Develop Higher Order Thinking	224
6.2	Relationships Between Terms Used to Describe Instruction	228

6.3	Connecting Shulman's Model of Pedagogical Reasoning and Action to Addressing Teaching Dilemmas	234
6.4	Teacher Moves Ms. Nash Identified in the Domain of Curriculum and Instruction Using the Zoomed In Frame	251
7.1	Using Empirical Observations to Identify Different Plausible Interpretations in Mr. Lee's Case	291
8.1	Mr. Lee's Current Dilemma Frame Zoomed in on the Domain of Curriculum and Instruction	310
8.2	Teacher Moves Generated by Mr. Lee's Frame Shifting	331

Tables

1.1	Ms. Nash's Original Driving Question and Dilemma Statement	15
2.1	Comparison Between Deficit Thinking and Asset-Based Thinking	35
2.2	Comparison of Teacher Conclusions in Response to Deficit- Versus Asset-Based Approaches to Students	36
2.3	Example of How New Empirical Clues Lead to New Interpretations and Judgments	42
2.4	Examining a Different Plausible Interpretation in Ms. Nash's Dilemma	46
2.5	Judgments Resulting from Interpretations	50
2.6	Different (More Generous) Judgments Resulting From Different Interpretations	51
2.7	Ms. Nash's Different Interpretations Lead to Different Judgments	52
2.8	Examples of How Different Judgments Lead to Different Decisions	53
2.9	How Ms. Nash Changed Her Original Driving Question and Dilemma Statement after Developing all Three Habits of Mind	56
2.10	Teachers' Original Driving Question and Dilemma Statement Regarding Caregiver Absence at Back to School Night	57
2.11	Revising the Original Driving Question and Dilemma Statement after Developing all Three Habits of Mind	61
2.12	Review of the Three Habits of Mind	64
3.1	Indicators of the Domain of Relationships	74
3.2	Indicators of the Domain of Classroom Management	75

3.3	Indicators of the Domain of Curriculum and Instruction	75
3.4	Ms. Nash's Driving Question and Dilemma Statement After Applying the Habits of Mind	76
3.5	Guiding Questions for Reframing Using the Frame of Classroom Management	78
3.6	Ms. Nash's Additional Dilemma Statements and Focus Questions in the Domain of Classroom Management	79
3.7	Guiding Questions for Reframing to the Domain of Relationships	82
3.8	The Dilemma Statements and Focus Questions Ms. Nash Generated When Frame Shifting to the Domain of Relationships	84
3.9	Guiding Questions for Reframing to the Domain of Curriculum and Instruction	87
3.10	The Dilemma Statements and Focus Questions Ms. Nash Generated When Frame Shifting to the Domain of Curriculum and Instruction	90
3.11	Reframing Ms. Nash's Dilemma	92
4.1	Guiding Questions for Reframing to the Domain of Relationships	104
4.2	Ms. Nash's Dilemma Statements and Focus Questions in the Domain of Relationships	104
4.3	Example "Check-In" Questions by Subject	129
5.1	Guiding Questions for Reframing Using the Frame of Classroom Management	145
5.2	Ms. Nash's Dilemma Statements and Focus Questions in the Domain of Classroom Management	146
5.3	Evaluating Classroom Rules	149
5.4	Comparing the Two Types of Redirection	165
5.5	The SIMMER Down Method for De-Escalating Conflicts	180
5.6	Affective Statements	187

6.1	Guiding Questions for Reframing to the Domain of Curriculum and Instruction	198
6.2	The Dilemma Statements and Focus Questions Ms. Nash Generated When Frame Shifting to the Domain of Curriculum and Instruction	201
6.3	Example Showing the Difference Between Explicit and Hidden Curricula	202
6.4	Scenarios Connecting Classroom Dilemmas to Curricular Positions	206
6.5	Examples of Brianna's and Amy's Current Frames of Reference	216
6.6	Overview of Selected Instructional Formats	239
7.1	Mr. Lee's Original Driving Question and Dilemma Statement	267
7.2	Mr. Lee's Initial Observation	285
7.3	Comparison Between Mr. Lee's Initial and Revised Observation Statements	287
7.4	Examining Different Plausible Interpretations of Mr. Lee's Observations	290
7.5	Mr. Lee's Different Interpretations Lead to Different Judgments	293
7.6	Examples of How Different Judgments Lead to Different Decisions in Mr. Lee's Dilemma	296
7.7	How Mr. Lee Changed His Original Driving Question and Dilemma Statement after Developing all Three Habits of Mind	298
8.1	Mr. Lee's Driving Question and Dilemma Statement after Engaging the Habits of Mind	306
8.2	Mr. Lee's Additional Dilemma Statements and Focus Questions in the Domain of Curriculum and Instruction	317
8.3	Mr. Lee's Dilemma Reframed to the Domain of Classroom Management	324
8.4	Mr. Lee's Dilemma Reframed to the Domain of Relationships	329

Focus on Culture Sections

Focus on Culture 1	Challenging Inequitable Systems through Proximal Dilemmas	28
Focus on Culture 2	Maintaining High Expectations for All Students	39
Focus on Culture 3	How Teachers' Frames of Reference and Biases Influence Their Interpretations	48
Focus on Culture 4	How Teacher Mastery of the Interdependent Domains of Teaching Benefit Students from Marginalized Backgrounds	71
Focus on Culture 5	Culturally Based Communication and Teacher–Student Relationships	107
Focus on Culture 6	Demonstrating Authentic Care with Students	115
Focus on Culture 7	Rightful Presence as a Classroom Pillar to Support Equity and Justice	117
Focus on Culture 8	Developing Authentic Teacher Solidarity With Families	119
Focus on Culture 9	Considerations for Rules and Routines When There are Cultural Differences Between Teacher and Students	152
Focus on Culture 10	Cultural Differences in Verbal and Nonverbal Behaviors	166
Focus on Culture 11	Culturally Responsive Classroom Management	174
Focus on Culture 12	Diversity Pedagogical Content Knowledge	209

Focus on Culture 13	Rethinking "Cultural Capital": Community Cultural Wealth	220
Focus on Culture 14	Understanding the Three Tenets of Culturally Relevant Pedagogy	225
Focus on Culture 15	Using Cooperative Learning Structures to Support Language Learning	242

Support Material

The book is also accompanied by a Study Guide. To access it, please go to www.routledge.com/9781032281568 and click on the link that says Support Material. A link to the Study Guide will appear.

For Chapter 1

Exercises
- 1.1 Identifying Your Dilemma
- 1.2 Considering the Three Domains of Teaching Within Your Dilemma
- 1.3 Identifying Your Driving Question and Dilemma Statement

For Chapter 2

Exercises
- 2.1 Building Teacher Efficacy
- 2.2 Developing the Habit of Personal Attribution
- 2.3 Developing the Habit of Asset Identification
- 2.4 Practicing Plausible Interpretation
- 2.5 Developing the Habit of Deliberate Interpretation
- 2.6 Revising Your Original Driving Question and Dilemma Statement

Extended Examples
- Table 2.1 Comparison Between Deficit Thinking and Asset-Based Thinking
- Table 2.2 Comparison of Teacher Conclusions in Response to Deficit- Versus Asset-Based Approaches to Students
- Table 2.5 Judgments Resulting from Interpretations

- **Table 2.6** Different (More Generous) Judgments Resulting From Different Interpretations
- **Table 2.8** Examples of How Different Judgments Lead to Different Decisions

Suggested Answers
- **Exercise 2.4** Practicing Plausible Interpretations
- **Discussion Activity 2b**

For Chapter 3

Exercises
- **3.1** Identifying the Domain of Teaching in Which Your Dilemma is Placed
- **3.2** Developing Dilemma Statements and Focus Questions in the Domain of Classroom Management
- **3.3** Developing Dilemma Statements and Focus Questions in the Domain of Relationships
- **3.4** Developing Dilemma Statements and Focus Questions in the Domain of Curriculum and Instruction
- **3.5a** Reframing a Primary School Dilemma (with Possible Answers)
- **3.5b** Reframing a Primary School Dilemma (with Possible Answers)
- **3.6a** Reframing a Middle School Dilemma (with Possible Answers)
- **3.6b** Reframing a Middle School Dilemma (with Possible Answers)
- **3.7a** Reframing a High School Dilemma (with Possible Answers)
- **3.7b** Reframing a High School Dilemma (with Possible Answers)
- **3.8a** Reframing a Post-Secondary Dilemma (with Possible Answers)
- **3.8b** Reframing a Post-Secondary Dilemma (with Possible Answers)
- **3.9** Focus Questions Within Each Domain

Suggested Answers
- **Discussion Activity 1** Dilemma Statements
- **Discussion Activity 2** Identifying the Primary Domain of Teaching
- **Discussion Activity 3** Sample Answer for (A) Above

For Chapter 4

Exercises
- **4.1** Evaluating the Quality of Student–Student Relationships
- **4.2** Identifying Teacher Moves in the Domain of Relationships

Suggested Answers
- **Discussion Activity 7**

For Chapter 5

Exercises
- **5.1** Evaluating Your Classroom Rules
- **5.2** Anticipating What and When to Precorrect
- **5.3** Using Prosody
- **5.4** Evaluating Your Uses of Verbal and Nonverbal Behaviors
- **5.5** Identifying Teacher Moves in the Domain of Classroom Management

For Chapter 6

Exercises
- **6.1** Exploring the Role of Curricular Positions in Your Dilemma
- **6.2** Evaluating Your Pedagogical Content Knowledge
- **6.3 (Extended Version)** Exploring Students' Experiences with Explicit Curriculum
- **6.4 (Extended Version)** Exploring Students' Experiences with Hidden Curriculum
- **6.5** Identifying Teacher Moves in the Domain of Curriculum and Instruction

Suggested Answers
- Exercise 6.3 (Extended Version) Exploring Students' Experiences with Explicit Curriculum
- Exercise 6.4 (Extended Version) Exploring Students' Experiences with Hidden Curriculum
- **Discussion Activity 3**

For Chapter 7

Here we provide two additional cases along with exercises to provide readers with practice in developing the habits of mind.

- **Extended Material** Considering Mr. Lee's Core Dilemma Within Different Educational Levels
  - Table 7.8 Applying Mr. Lee's Dilemma Across Education Levels
- **Developing the Habits of Mind Together**
  - Case 2 Talking Over One Another in Ms. Cohen's Whole-Class Discussion
  - Exercises 7.1–7.9 (including a discussion of possible responses)
- **Developing the Habits of Mind Independently**
  - Case 3 Disruptive Use of Technology in Ms. Ortega's Spanish II Class
  - Exercises 7.1–7.9
- **Additional Discussion and Practice**

Suggested Answers
- Handout A Ms. Cohen's Steps in the Habit of Deliberate Interpretation
- Exercises 7.1–7.9 for Ms. Ortega's Case
- Handout A Ms. Ortega's Steps in the Habit of Deliberate Interpretation

For Chapter 8

Here we continue to build on Cases 2 and 3 presented in the Study Guide materials for Chapter 7 as readers practice frame shifting to different domains of teaching.

- **Extended Material** Frame Shifting Mr. Lee's Dilemma Across Educational Levels
  - **Table 8.6** Example from the Domain of Classroom Management: Precorrection Across Educational Levels
  - **Table 8.7** Example from the Domain of Relationships: Teambuilding Across Educational Levels
- **Frame Shifting Together**
  - **Case 2** Practicing Frame Shifting with Ms. Cohen's Dilemma
  - **Exercises 8.1–8.7** (including a discussion of possible responses)
- **Frame Shifting Independently**
  - **Case 3** Practicing Frame Shifting with Ms. Ortega's Dilemma
  - **Exercises 8.1–8.7**
- **Additional Discussion and Practice**

Suggested Answers
- **Exercises 8.1–8.8** for Ms. Ortega's Case
- **Figure 8.3** Teacher Moves Generated by Ms. Cohen's Frame Shifting
- **Handout 10** Collection of Teacher Moves Generated by Frame Shifting (Ms. Ortega)

Author Biographies

Brianna L. Kennedy is Professor of Education in the School of Education at the University of Glasgow. She studies the inclusion and exclusion of students from nondominant social backgrounds with a particular focus on educational and school policy and classroom teaching. As a former middle school teacher, she prioritizes the bridging of theory, research, and practice, and she investigates and develops appropriate inquiry approaches to do so. She has developed additional lines of research in qualitative inquiry and the scholarship of teaching and learning. In each of these three lines of research, she prioritizes the reimagining and reworking of education and schooling to enact social justice. Dr. Kennedy came to Glasgow in 2023 after holding tenured faculty positions at Utrecht University in the Netherlands and at the University of Florida in the United States. She taught in the Los Angeles Unified School District from 1998-2005. Her hobbies include making art, running in the forest, and having adventures with her wonderful rescue dog, Sam.

Amy S. Murphy is Clinical Associate Professor in the Department of Theory and Practice at the University of Georgia. Her work focuses on justice-oriented teacher education pedagogies, culturally responsive classroom management, and young adolescents. She is an embedded professor at a local middle school where she teaches university courses onsite, coaches teacher candidates, and provides professional learning to in-service teachers. She also collaborates with local school district leaders to offer induction support to teachers in their first three years of teaching. Dr. Murphy came to academia after teaching 7th - 9th graders for ten years in Florida. She enjoys hiking the North Georgia mountains with her dogs, trying out new recipes, and playing cribbage.

Part I

Foundations

Teaching is hard—perhaps the hardest career that there is if you do it well. But we choose to teach anyway, certainly not for the income or status, but because we want to make a difference. We want to connect with students intellectually and emotionally, help them learn and develop, and see them become all that they can be. Despite these good intentions, we also have bad days, even bad years, experiences that make us wonder if it's worth it. Even the most content of teachers can face situations that seem impossible to improve. If you are a teacher who has a persistent teaching dilemma, then this book is for you. We don't promise to solve your dilemma or to give you a few quick tips to make things better. Instead, we will offer you an approach that may take some time to develop but that we think will help you successfully tackle a whole range of dilemmas throughout your teaching career.

Who We Are and What We Believe

Before we get started, you may be wondering who we are and why we think we are qualified to write a book about teaching. You're probably especially wondering this if you are a veteran teacher, someone who has been around awhile, watched the reform movements come and go, and developed your own ideas about what works for your kids. Good questions. We are both former classroom teachers who have collectively taught for over 20 years in urban schools in the US. Brianna taught public elementary and middle school in high-poverty schools in Los Angeles with students from marginalized racial, ethnic, and linguistic backgrounds. She also taught alternative education with children who had been expelled from school and had many of her own persistent teaching dilemmas to work through in order to offer these students, who had been so failed by the school system, the best education possible. Amy also taught in a diverse public school in Florida that was affiliated with the local university. She always looked for ways to engage students from marginalized backgrounds, as well as those who were disaffected from school by using innovative instructional design. She developed these innovations in collaboration with colleagues and university faculty, which began her own journey into academia. She continues this work now as a faculty member who collaborates closely with school leaders and teachers in a local school–university partnership.

Now, in addition to being former full-time K-12 teachers, we also work as academics who develop expertise not only through our teaching practice but also through our research. We prioritize staying grounded in primary and secondary schools, and we believe that our most important work is the work that helps real teachers and real students in real schools. We currently work in teacher preparation and professional development in a variety of settings, and we engage in scholarship in ways that our schedules and positions did not allow when we worked as full-time teachers.

We believe that good teaching benefits all students but that students from marginalized backgrounds—those who face persistent and systemic disadvantages, especially due to race, ethnicity, immigration status, linguistic background, sexual orientation, gender identity, socioeconomic status, or other social group memberships—particularly need good schools in order to flourish (Milner, 2013). Because these students are systematically disadvantaged by social institutions, they depend on school to be an equalizer. We prioritize the rethinking and reorganization of schooling to diminish or erase the ways that schools currently separate or further disadvantage students in these groups. We write and teach and research for the sake of developing good teaching in all classrooms, with a particular focus on students from marginalized groups and backgrounds.

We are motivated by, and committed to, the creation of safe, constructive educational communities that actively include and build upon the assets of all students. We believe that in order to do that, educators need to be able to identify and challenge the ways that current school organization or teaching practice might marginalize certain groups even when educators have the best of intentions (Lewis & Diamond, 2015). Throughout this book, we offer examples and applications from international contexts that focus on the roles of social group membership in teaching and learning and suggest ways to increase inclusivity and reduce marginalization at the school and classroom levels. We describe teaching practice in relation to the US education structure and provide a description of this structure for international readers in the online Study Guide.

Overview

In this part, we begin with a description of a professional development trajectory with one teacher who we worked closely with, who we will call Teresa Nash, a middle school teacher in the midwestern United States. Ms. Nash's teaching dilemma will serve as a case to ground our discussions and provide examples for the key concepts we present throughout the book.[1] We then present the main ideas of the **frame shifting** approach. By the end of this part, the reader will have all of the key concepts necessary for using this approach to address persistent teaching dilemmas.

Chapter 1 gives an overview and presents vocabulary and processes we describe throughout the book. We introduce you to the three **domains of teaching** in order to ground our discussion of teaching dilemmas (Key Figure 1), and we ask you to identify and articulate the dilemma that you will work on as you read the book. We also introduce Key Figure 2 which illustrates the process of educators moving from their dilemma to solutions by defining terms. In Chapter 2, we establish the foundational beliefs necessary for making frame shifting work. We name these beliefs **habits of mind** and show how the engagement of each habit will be necessary for setting the reader up for success with frame

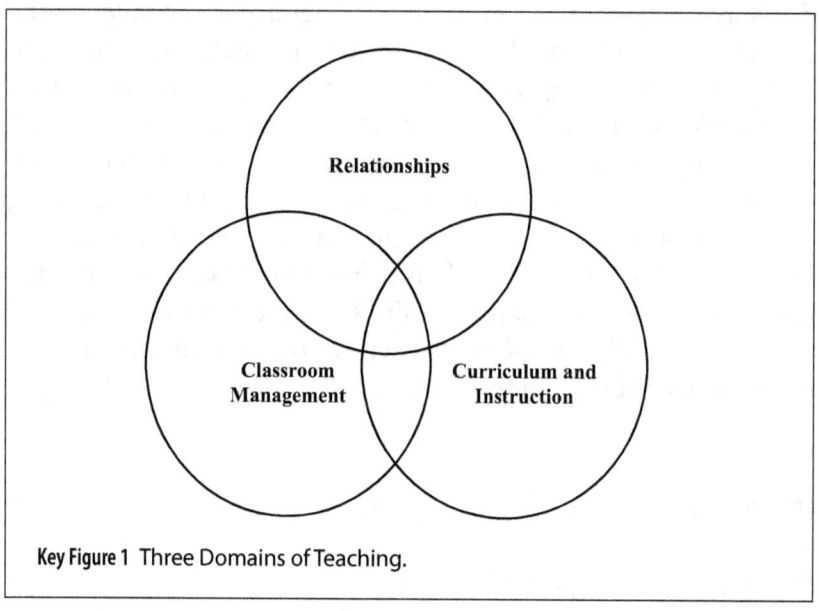

Key Figure 1 Three Domains of Teaching.

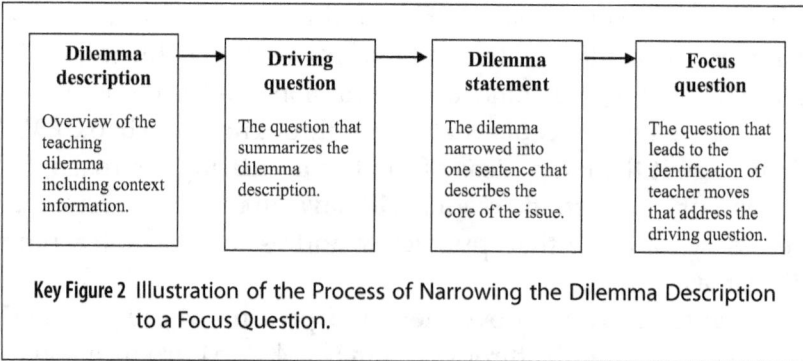

Key Figure 2 Illustration of the Process of Narrowing the Dilemma Description to a Focus Question.

shifting, which we present in Chapter 3. We begin Chapter 3 by defining and describing each of the three domains of teaching and discuss their **interdependence**. We ask the reader to identify the domain in which their teaching dilemma is positioned. Next, we define frame shifting and show how a shift from one domain of teaching to another can yield new possibilities for addressing persistent dilemmas. By the end of Part I, you should be able to:

- Explain and elaborate on both key figures and apply them to your own dilemma.
- Name and explain the three habits of mind and evaluate how well you engage them.
- Articulate a driving question and dilemma statement that reflect your use of all three habits of mind.
- Identify the domain of teaching in which you first placed your dilemma, frame shift it to all domains, and list the focus questions you generate in doing so.

Note

1 We thank Teresa Nash for her willingness to let us use this example and for her admirable commitment to good teaching. We have fictionalized parts of her story to improve readability. She has read this portrayal and approved its content and use.

1

Introduction

In this chapter we introduce you to Ms. Nash, a teacher who we met while facilitating a professional learning community (PLC) with a small group of teachers at her school, all of whom wanted to focus on improving their classroom management. Here is Ms. Nash's story.

Grounding Case

Ms. Nash was a second-year sixth grade physical science teacher at a public middle school in a mid-size town in the midwestern United States where the largest employer was a research university. She was a White woman in her early 30s who laughed easily at people's jokes and had a healthy, self-deprecating sense of humor. She grew up in a middle-class family that valued higher education, and she earned a PhD in the natural sciences before deciding to become a teacher. A provisional certification enabled her to begin teaching before she had completed a teacher training program.

The children enrolled in the local schools consisted of two main groups: White, middle- and upper-income children and children of highly skilled immigrants who taught or did research at the university or worked in the town's largest industry sector, and low-income, mostly Black (but some White) children whose caregivers worked in the service sector that supported the university or industry sector, or who were otherwise under- or unemployed. Neighborhoods in the town were residentially segregated among these groups, and this segregation resulted in the local schools in the poor parts of town receiving low rankings in the state scoring system. In response to these low rankings, the district created magnet programs at low-performing schools to attract higher-scoring White and upper-income children from across town to boost the school rankings. Although Ms. Nash's school received one overall grade based on the performance of the entire student population, the students in the magnet program remained organizationally segregated from those in the main program. Teachers in the school disliked the segregation and unequal financial investment in the two programs but ultimately accepted it. Many staff members considered students in the magnet programs as more deserving of the investments and viewed students in the main program as less intellectually engaged and more behaviorally challenged.

Ms. Nash was initially hired to teach in the magnet program for students identified as highly gifted, but in her second year she was assigned one class of students from the main program. Shortly after starting the school year with this group, Ms. Nash experienced challenges with getting the students organized and focused. She joined the PLC with us for support and assistance in the fall of that year. While Ms. Nash prioritized student agency and encouraged students to voice their opinions during class discussions, she admitted she needed additional help with her classroom management. When it was her turn to share with the group what she hoped to get out of the PLC, she expressed, "I don't know what I'm doing wrong, but the kids come in loud and rowdy. They move from seat to seat, some wandering aimlessly, well past the point when the bell rings, even though I have an

> **Exercise 1.1** *Identifying Your Dilemma*
> 1) Jot down ideas about any persistent challenges you face as a teacher that you would ultimately like to improve. You might consider a particular student who does not follow your instructions, a group of students who talk instead of doing their work, persistently unequal outcomes among different ethnic groups of students, or anything else you can think of.
> 2) Choose one of those dilemmas that you would like to think about as you read this book. Why do you think this dilemma exists? What strategies have you already used to try to solve it? What happened? How do you explain those results?

assignment on the board waiting for them. In my other classes, the kids just come in, sit down, and get to work, and that's what I want to happen with this group as well. I've tried using seating charts. I've tried different attention getters. I've tried other classroom management techniques, but nothing seems to work with this class. I don't understand why it's not happening, but I've really had enough!" Now that you have heard from Ms. Nash, complete Exercise 1.1. All exercises are also provided in the online Study Guide where you will have more space to respond.

Ms. Nash's Next Steps: An Introduction to the Three Domains of Teaching

As we talked further with Ms. Nash, we asked her details about the three **domains of teaching** as they occurred during the transition into class. We first explained that the three domains of teaching simultaneously take place at every moment during classroom interactions. That means that if we capture any snapshot of classroom teaching, we can identify what is happening in all three domains. These domains are: **relationships**, **classroom management**, and **curriculum and instruction**. We define the domain of relationships as sustained patterns of interaction between the teacher and the whole class, the teacher and each individual student, and the students themselves. Classroom management consists of the rules, routines, and teacher behaviors that structure teaching and learning. Curriculum includes the content taught both explicitly and implicitly in the classroom through physical materials, verbal exchanges, and classroom activities. Instruction means the activities designed and used to support the students' learning of the curriculum. When discussing the domains in Ms. Nash's PLC we relied upon Key Figure 1, which we also build and draw upon throughout the book. In Key Figure 1, you see how the three domains overlap. That is because they are **interdependent** and affect one another. We further explain the domains and their interdependence in Chapter 3 and in Part II.

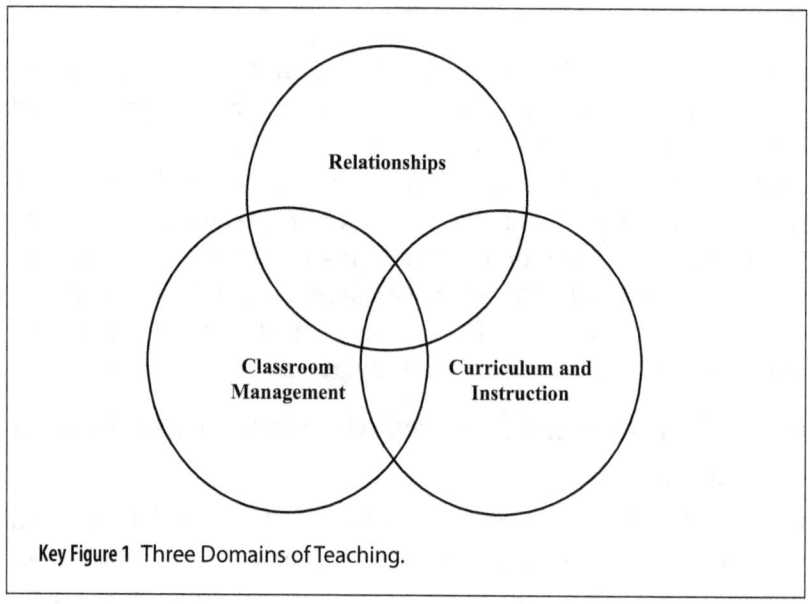

Key Figure 1 Three Domains of Teaching.

When describing the relationships in her classroom, Ms. Nash expressed that she cared deeply about her students but that she didn't know if they really knew that. She tried to encourage them to work hard and care about science by accepting and building upon their answers and contributions in class. She gave them space and freedom to choose their seats, work at their own pace, and follow their own intrinsic motivation because she believed this approach would best foster their development without stifling their individuality or their spirits. She thought her students basically liked each other, although she did not know how well they really got along outside of class and she did not see them working together in mutually beneficial ways toward the academic goals she set for them during class. She was sometimes surprised when they made fun of each other because she could find their jokes and personal slights to be quite cruel. When we asked her about her knowledge of students' lives outside of class, Ms. Nash said that she did not know much about what they liked or how they spent their time. Because she was so busy as a second-year teacher creating lessons and grading assignments, she had never been to any of their extracurricular activities and did not know whether they were involved in school activities beyond the classroom. She tried to make connections with their caregivers through phone calls, but she usually only called when she struggled with a student's behavior. Oftentimes, caregivers did not answer the phone or the number did not work, and Ms. Nash did not understand why.

When we turned to the domain of classroom management, Ms. Nash let out a deep sigh and said,

> This is absolutely the hardest for me. I just can't get them settled and focused. No matter what I do, they just don't do the assignment. Everything seems to take forever, so much longer than I planned that we just don't seem to get to the important parts of the lesson. I want to do creative activities that they find interesting and that help them think critically and deeply, like right now we are working on a unit where they design and build model solar cars. But they're so busy playing with the materials that they never actually get the cars put together. I use strategies like attention getters to get the whole group to be quiet, but those only work for a short time, if at all. Sometimes it seems like those attempts even make things worse. It's like each person needs individual attention and direction to complete the assignment, but there is only one of me, so it's impossible. I really want to figure out how to make this work, but it seems much

easier to just put it all away and read from the textbook instead. At least that way, they might sit still, be quiet, and have some work to show for it at the end of the period. I don't want to resort to this, but I'm at a loss for how to make this work.

We could feel Ms. Nash's discouragement and empathize with her desires as she talked about her classroom management.

We noticed that Ms. Nash had already described some of her curricular and instructional decisions and preferences when talking about her classroom management, but we asked her more about this third and final domain. In terms of curriculum, she stated that she was responsible for teaching standards upon which the students would be tested at the end of the school year, but she expressed that the standards were stated in broad enough ways that she had a bit of freedom to fill in particular content. She wanted the students to be interested and she tried to choose material she thought they would like, although she said she did not always know what that was.

Ms. Nash approached her science instruction from direct, lived experience in the field. She believed scientific understanding required authentic explorations of the content and provided such experiences for her students. For example, students built solar ovens out of pizza boxes in her classes while learning the engineering cycle. She tried to choose instructional activities that she thought the students would find fun and thought-provoking, but many of the activities that she used with the gifted classes did not seem to engage this class in the same way and she was not sure why. Students in the main program seemed to struggle more to get focused during group work, so much so that Ms. Nash shied away from using it as an instructional strategy even though she believed that, in theory, it could be a powerful way for children to learn. She explained that she was on the verge of giving up on hands-on learning and group work in this class. This dilemma created an internal conflict for

Ms. Nash: she wanted to provide engaging and authentic curriculum and instruction for her students, but she did not know how to manage it with this class. Now, we turn back to the classroom dilemma you identified in #2 of Exercise 1.1. Consider how the three domains of teaching play a role in this dilemma as you complete Exercise 1.2.

> **Exercise 1.2** *Considering the Three Domains of Teaching Within Your Dilemma*
> 1) When you experience your dilemma, what is occurring in the domain of relationships?
> 2) When you experience your dilemma, what is occurring in the domain of classroom management?
> 3) When you experience your dilemma, what is occurring in the domain of curriculum and instruction?

Articulating Ms. Nash's Dilemma Using the Basics of the Frame Shifting Approach

As we continue the narrative of Ms. Nash's case, we will introduce and illustrate basic concepts and foundational principles of frame shifting. In describing her case, we will refer to the **dilemma description**, the **driving question**, the **dilemma statement**, and the **focus question**. We also use these terms throughout the book. Key Figure 2 illustrates the relationship between these terms, with the broad dilemma description being narrowed down and workshopped to ultimately lead to a specific focus question positioned within one domain of teaching. The focus questions you generate by frame shifting will help you identify teacher moves to ultimately solve your dilemma. Moving through the process illustrated in Key Figure 2 will allow you to break the dilemma down into separate but related parts that can be examined in a new way, which is the crux of the frame shifting approach.

> **Key Terms**
>
> *Dilemma description*: Overview of the teaching dilemma including context information and all other information relevant to the dilemma.
>
> *Driving question*: The question that summarizes the dilemma description and drives the teacher to persist toward a solution. The frame shifting approach is designed to answer the driving question.
>
> *Dilemma statement*: The narrowing down of the dilemma into one sentence that describes the core of the issue.
>
> *Focus question*: A question that derives from the dilemma statement and leads to the identification of teacher moves that address the driving question.

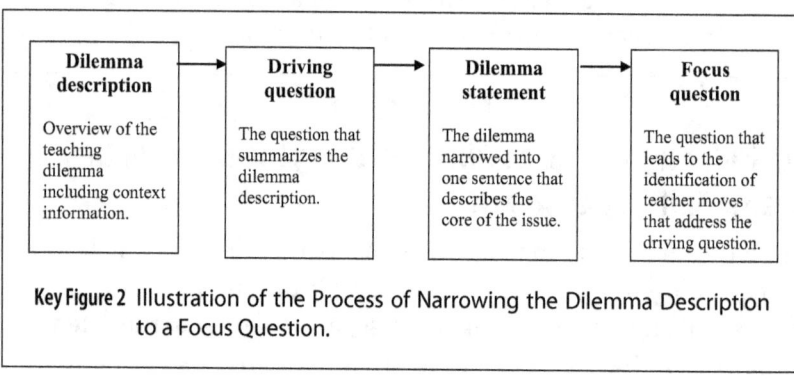

Key Figure 2 Illustration of the Process of Narrowing the Dilemma Description to a Focus Question.

The dilemma description includes information about the context and details about the problem the teacher is having. Everything Ms. Nash has told us so far (and that you have completed in Exercises 1.1 and 1.2) is her dilemma description. Next, we guided her and the other PLC members through an activity during which they would identify their driving question. The driving question summarizes the part of the dilemma that the teacher really wants to understand and solve. It is the question that is motivating the reader to read this book and that the frame shifting approach is designed to answer. We return to the driving question and solve it bit by bit as we work through the frame shifting approach. In Ms. Nash's case, she knew she had many issues to tackle, but they all had to do with one thing she was most curious about and most needed to solve, which she stated as her driving question: "What will make the students quiet and efficient in finishing the warm-up so we can smoothly transition into the lesson?"

The driving question can have multiple causes and the dilemma description gives us clues about these. At this beginning step in the frame shifting approach, we try to narrow down the possible causes of the dilemma into one or more dilemma statements. In our PLC, we asked the teachers to narrow each of their dilemmas to one dilemma statement that addressed the core of the issue. To help Ms. Nash identify a dilemma statement, we referred to her driving question and asked, "What's really the problem? Why do you think the students aren't quiet or efficient? What's happening in class instead of the efficient warm-up time that you would like to see?" Ms. Nash then narrowed her dilemma description to the dilemma statement: *Students enter the classroom in an unruly manner and are not interested in working on the posted assignment* (see Table 1.1). We looked forward to working with her to see how her development of the habits of mind might change some of the language she used in her dilemma statement. For Exercise 1.3, practice writing your own driving question and dilemma statement for the classroom dilemma you identified in Exercise 1.1. Keep in mind the information you described in Exercise 1.2 related to the three domains of teaching.

Before turning the dilemma statements into focus questions in the PLC, we planned a subsequent meeting to look at how teachers' beliefs were reflected in their driving questions and dilemma statements. We refer to these beliefs as **habits of mind**

TABLE 1.1 *Ms. Nash's Original Driving Question and Dilemma Statement*

Ms. Nash's Original Driving Question	Ms. Nash's Original Dilemma Statement
The question that summarizes your dilemma description and that you will try to answer using frame shifting.	The narrowing down of the dilemma into one sentence that describes the core of the issue that you would like to improve.
"What will make the students quiet and efficient in finishing the warm-up so we can smoothly transition into the lesson?"	*Students enter the classroom in an unruly manner and are not interested in working on the posted assignment.*

> **Exercise 1.3** *Identifying Your Driving Question and Dilemma Statement*
>
> 1) Write your driving question in the left-hand column of the table below (see Table 1.1 for an example of how Ms. Nash did this). You will return to this as you continue to read and complete activities throughout the book.
> 2) Ms. Nash's dilemma had to do with the entire context around students entering class, but she narrowed her dilemma statement to: *Students enter the classroom in an unruly manner and are not interested in working on the posted assignment.* Narrow your dilemma to one dilemma statement that you will initially focus on as you read this book and write it in the right-hand column of the table below.
>
> | Your Driving Question | Your Dilemma Statement |
> |---|---|
> | The question that summarizes your dilemma description and that you will try to answer using frame shifting. | The narrowing down of the dilemma into one sentence that describes the core of the issue that you would like to improve. |
> | | |

and define and discuss them in the next chapter. We suspected that after learning about these beliefs that are fundamental to the frame shifting process, the PLC participants would want to revise their driving question and dilemma statement before proceeding so that we could enter the process of shifting frames across the three domains of teaching from an optimal starting point that maximizes chances for success. As we proceed through the next parts of the book, we will return to Ms. Nash and her dilemma to explain and elaborate on our main points. The distinctions between the terms presented so far are probably a bit unclear now. They will become clearer as we unpack their definitions and importance and as you practice them at the end of the chapters and as we go along.

The Role of Culture in Ms. Nash's Dilemma

A discussion of how teachers think about and respond to classroom dilemmas cannot be divorced from a consideration of the ways in which race, culture, and other social groupings affect teaching and learning. It is important to consider how our cultural backgrounds inform our ideas about teaching, such as what we deem as "appropriate" student behavior. According to culturally responsive classroom management experts Carol Weinstein, Mary Curran, and Saundra Tomlinson-Clarke (2003), successful teaching requires teachers to acknowledge that culture impacts both students' and teachers' behaviors and that schools are places where power structures may include or exclude students according to their backgrounds. We will examine these issues throughout the book as we discuss teaching dilemmas as powerful opportunities for implementing approaches that can lead to social change.

As Ms. Nash described her dilemma, we could not help but note that although she did not directly name her students' racial identities and cultural practices as being relevant to the classroom, we immediately saw that they were. Differing expectations about time, movement, volume, collaboration, and respect between Ms. Nash and her mostly Black students fueled Ms. Nash's dilemma as well as her feelings of hopelessness about her classroom management. Differing **frames of reference** and life experiences led to differences in the topics and the ways of working that students and teachers found interesting and relevant, which affected curriculum and instruction. Organizational discrimination that occurred as a result of the tracked system that grouped students essentially by race into "haves" and "have nots" at the school also contributed to her students' lack of respect for the system itself as well as for her as a representative of the system. As we move into the subsequent parts of the book, we will consider how differences between teachers and students that result from cultural backgrounds, social positions, power structures, and hierarchies can influence and even cause teaching dilemmas. We will address these issues throughout the book, particularly in sections named *Focus on Culture*.

How To Use This Book

In this book, we present an approach to addressing teaching dilemmas that asks teachers to train their minds so that it becomes natural and instinctive to engage and enact these ideas. That's why the book relates teacher moves to **habits of mind** and includes exercises that encourage you to take multiple perspectives. These habits of mind and the topics developed throughout the book apply to all levels of education, although we gear most examples to primary and secondary education. Our teacher educator colleagues and other faculty members in postsecondary institutions will likely recognize the relevance of habits of mind and **frame shifting** for their own teaching as well. If you belong to this group, you may best relate to the examples throughout the book and Study Guide that address postsecondary contexts.

Each chapter of this book can stand alone. However, we have designed the book to develop a comprehensive approach that requires the understanding of each previous chapter in order to fully apply the new material discussed, and the material and exercises build upon each other across chapters. Therefore, we encourage you to read the book from beginning to end, or at least to skim through the main ideas of each chapter before moving on to the next. We know that as a teacher you do not have a lot of time, and maybe also not a lot of extra energy. But we also know that if you are attracted to this book because you have exhausted your own ideas and attempts to address a teaching dilemma, then it will be worth it to read, consider, and digest each chapter's material in order to fully understand the approach we are offering. If you only look at pieces of the book without grasping the entire approach and its usefulness, you might be tempted to dismiss it as just another thing that won't work. We encourage you to give the ideas presented here a fair chance by reading the whole book. Here is an overview of how the book is organized.

Part I: Foundations

In Chapters 1–3, we lay the foundation for the rest of the book. In this introductory chapter, we have already described a case dilemma based on our professional development work with a classroom teacher. We used Ms. Nash's case to introduce you to the **domains of teaching**, which we further develop in Part II (Chapters 4–6). We will return to the case study throughout the book to illustrate key points. In Chapter 2, we discuss the teacher beliefs, or **habits of mind**, that play a key role in how teachers view and characterize classroom dilemmas and affect whether you will find success with our approach to addressing these dilemmas.

In Chapter 3, we explain the **interdependence** of the three domains of teaching as well as the importance of teachers' mastery of all three domains particularly when teaching marginalized and underserved student groups. Then, we use the concept of interdependence to present **frame shifting**. We use the metaphor of a picture frame to define an outline that gives focus to an object and separates what is included in a field of vision from that which is around, outside, or beyond it. Frame shifting allows the teacher to focus on how each of the three domains of teaching may affect the dilemma and may also provide strategies for a solution. If you find yourself stuck in your own way of thinking about your dilemma, the combination of adopting the habits of mind presented in Chapter 2 and employing the frame shifting approach presented in Chapter 3 may allow you to challenge how you think about your dilemma and consider new possibilities.

Part II: The Domains of Teaching

Next, we turn our attention to defining teaching practice. When we say "teaching," we assume we all mean the same thing, but what *is* teaching, actually? In this part, we further develop the definitions of the three **domains of teaching** presented above. This framework of examining teaching within three domains provides a structured way of thinking about the concrete teacher moves that can both cause and solve classroom dilemmas. This framework will be critical in the reframing process that we first present in Chapter 3 and then apply in these chapters. Chapter 4 explains **relationships**; Chapter 5 examines **classroom management**; and Chapter 6 addresses **curriculum and instruction**. In each of these chapters, we expand on the definition of each domain by describing its relevance to teaching, briefly synthesizing knowledge about how teachers have succeeded in the domain, and discussing the roles of culture and cultural responsiveness as they relate to each domain.

Part III: Putting It All Together

In the final part, we apply the ideas explained in the previous chapters to addressing classroom dilemmas. We present a set of three cases in which we meet teachers facing new teaching dilemmas and walk through all of the key concepts we have discussed. We use the **gradual release of responsibility model** of instruction (Fisher & Frey, 2021) to organize Part III, with the first case presented in the book and the second and third practice cases presented in the online Study Guide. With the first case, we talk through each of the steps involved in applying the habits of mind; in the second case, we provide prompts to stimulate the reader's thinking as you practice the steps, followed by a description of sample responses to these prompts; and for the third case, we present exercises for readers to try independently, with suggested answers at the end. Chapter 7 guides the reader through developing and applying the **habits of mind** to the three new cases. We use this same organizational structure in Chapter 8 as we return to the three cases and practice shifting the frame to each of the three **domains of teaching** to generate new teacher moves.

Supporting Materials

Throughout the book, we have included key terms in bold the first time they appear in each new section. The terms are defined in the part of the book where they are discussed in depth and you can also find them in the glossary at the end of the book. The glossary also lists the page numbers of the text where each word is defined. Throughout many of the chapters and at the end of each, there are exercises and questions for discussion. Just as you have seen throughout this chapter, exercises provided within the text are labeled as "Exercises" and intended to engage you with practicing the content being discussed. There is an online Study Guide that accompanies the book and there you can find suggested answers for selected activities as well as all of the exercises reproduced at full-page length so that you have more space for writing your answers and can use them multiple times. The online Study Guide can be accessed at www.routledge.com/9781032281568. At the end of the book, we also include reproductions of key figures and a list of suggested readings to help you dig deeper into issues related to culture, diversity, and social justice, which complement the content discussed in the *Focus on Culture* sections throughout the book. We sometimes refer to tables or figures you have seen previously or in other chapters. If you need to quickly find a particular table or figure, check the List of Tables or the List of Figures at the front of the book right after the Contents page. There you can also find a list of the *Focus on Culture* sections.

Suggestions for How to Use This Book Individually or In a Group Setting

We imagine that readers can engage with this book in a variety of formats. Of course, you can pick it up and work individually on your teaching dilemma. In that case, we would encourage you to consider using video observations of your practice so that you can go back and study the particular things you are working on. Video recordings may also help you notice things you did not see or consider before. Ideally, you would be able to partner with a colleague or coach as you work through your individual dilemma.

Another format we can imagine is a group of teachers working together in the context of a PLC. You might each have your own driving question but meet together to work through each chapter, perhaps with each person taking the lead for a different chapter and using the provided resources to guide the activities of each meeting. We also hope this book will be taken up in school–university partnerships and collaborations, which could include courses for pre-service teachers, support for professional development schools, or individual collaborations between faculty members and practicing educators. This book has relevance for all of these possible uses, and the resources provided are intended to offer flexibility for meeting structures and groupings as well as duration and intensity.

For Discussion and Practice

1. When you consider Ms. Nash's case dilemma, what other information do you think might be important to know? Why might that information be important?
2. Discuss with colleagues persistent teaching dilemmas you each have had. Explain to them the three domains of teaching and see if you can identify what was happening in each of the three domains of teaching when these dilemmas were occurring.
3. Share your current dilemma with at least one colleague and explain what is happening in each of the three domains of teaching during your dilemma.
4. Explain to your colleague your driving question and dilemma statement and clarify how these are different than your dilemma description.

References

Fisher, D., & Frey, N. (2021). *Better learning through structured teaching: A framework for the gradual release of responsibility* (3rd ed.). ASCD.

Weinstein, C., Curran, M., & Tomlinson-Clarke, S. (2003). Culturally responsive classroom management: Awareness into action. *Theory Into Practice*, 42(4), 269–276. https://www.jstor.org/stable/1477388

2
Strengthening Foundational Habits of Mind

In this chapter, we introduce core concepts that will help you identify your beliefs about your teaching dilemma. Some beliefs may prevent you from making progress whereas others may help to clarify aspects of your dilemma. Strengthening these foundational beliefs is the first step in successful frame shifting. We discuss beliefs early in the book because in our experience, when educators describe persistent dilemmas they often describe attempting solutions that have not worked for them. The very nature of having teaching dilemmas, especially if they are persistent, can contribute to educators feeling a low sense of **teacher efficacy** to improve the situation. You may believe that finding a solution simply is not possible or you may dismiss suggestions made by others. We have often heard educators say, "That won't work with *my* kids," or "I've tried that, but it didn't work." We believe they have tried their best with the tools they have, but we also want to ask them (and you) to suspend conclusions about certain strategies and approaches in order to consider how a shift in beliefs might be necessary to support progress toward addressing your teaching dilemma.

We describe the three teacher beliefs we focus on in this book as **habits of mind**. This term has been popularized in contemporary education by Arthur Costa and Bena Kallick in their book series that describes important habits of mind for teaching, learning, and leading in schools. They define a habit of mind as a mental discipline that "is practiced so it becomes a habitual way of working toward more thoughtful, intelligent action," especially when specific answers are not yet known (Costa & Kallick, 2008, p. xvii). We agree with their assertion that teachers should first develop and adopt certain mental dispositions before they select and evaluate strategies for their teaching. Often, the development of effective mental dispositions requires conscious attention and practice for mastery. In this chapter, we describe in detail specific habits of mind necessary for frame shifting and give you opportunities to become conscious about these habits and to practice them.

> **Key Terms**
>
> *Habits of Mind*: The beliefs and ways of thinking that play a key role in how teachers view, characterize, and respond to classroom dilemmas.

We start with the assumption that every teacher has both implicit and explicit beliefs and operates according to those beliefs, even if the educator does not state them and/or is not aware of the role their beliefs play in their teacher moves (Kohn, 2006). An awareness of one's beliefs, or habits of mind, allows teachers to be intentional about how they respond both internally and externally to student behaviors that challenge them and helps them consider multiple possible interpretations of both student and teacher behaviors. For example, a teacher who perceives disrespect and gets annoyed at students who constantly raise their voices in the hallways may respond differently if they understand and appreciate that loud talking may indicate social camaraderie in students' lives outside of school. In this case, if the teacher can ask questions about their own explicit and implicit beliefs about behaviors, they can potentially shift their interpretation of loud talking from being a sign of disrespect and bad manners to being a culturally normative indicator of positive social interaction.

In this chapter, we further explore the critical role of **interpretation** and other habits of mind that we define as foundational skills teachers need in order to shift how they frame their classroom dilemmas. We introduce three separate but related habits of mind. First, we will work toward identifying the part of your dilemma that is within your control, and we will address beliefs about your ability to deal with the dilemma successfully. We call this adoption of ownership over the dilemma the **Habit of Personal Attribution**. Next, we will define positions related to beliefs about students, families, and communities and explore the enactment of an asset-focused disposition that will be most productive for effective frame shifting. We name this the **Habit of Asset Identification**. Engaging these first two habits of mind will be essential for succeeding with the third habit. In the third and final habit of mind, we will break down the process of diagnosing the source of your dilemma in order to allow for new framing to occur. We call this the **Habit of Deliberate Interpretation**.

Key Terms

- *Habit of Personal Attribution*: Focusing teaching dilemmas within the realm of the educator's control.
- *Habit of Asset Identification*: Basing the deliberation about a dilemma on the assets and positive attributes (as opposed to deficits) of students, caregivers, or their communities.
- *Habit of Deliberate Interpretation*: Breaking down the process of diagnosing the source of one's dilemma by exploring alternative interpretations before making judgments or drawing conclusions. The steps in the habit of deliberate interpretation are *observation, interpretation, judgment, conclusion.*

The goals of developing and engaging these habits is twofold. First, we want to use them to workshop your initial **driving question** and **dilemma statement** in order to prepare for **frame shifting**. Second, we want to lay the foundation for ways of thinking that we will continue to draw upon throughout the description of frame shifting in Part II and that can support successful approaches to all of your teaching challenges in the future. As we describe each of the three habits of mind, we will return to Ms. Nash's dilemma description, driving question, and dilemma statement to see how engaging each habit might influence the way she is thinking about and describing the dilemma. The cultural backgrounds and positioning of both students and teachers affect every habit presented in this chapter just as they affect every interaction that occurs in the classroom, and we home in on these issues in the *Focus on Culture* sections.

Habit of Personal Attribution

To begin, we need to develop the **Habit of Personal Attribution**, which focuses on the part of the dilemma that is within the realm of the teacher's control and positions the responsibility for solving the dilemma with the teacher. This habit of mind first addresses how you define the dilemma and then examines where the responsibility for solving the problem is placed.

Distal and Proximal Characterizations

When you first define a dilemma, you determine the extent to which it sits within your control to address. Teachers can only effectively **frame shift** dilemmas that they have the power and position to make progress on. Using the following two characterizations of how a dilemma might be positioned can be helpful here: **distal** and **proximal**. A distal dilemma is beyond an educator's control to address, whereas a proximal dilemma is within an educator's close and direct sphere of influence. This distinction is important because positioning a dilemma distally, or choosing a distal dilemma to try to improve, will cost time and energy that will then be insufficient to completely solve the dilemma (Aguilar, 2014). For the individual educator, resources are better spent on proximal dilemmas, those over which we have some control.

> **Key Terms**
> *Distal*: A dilemma caused by circumstances or conditions beyond the educator's control.
> *Proximal*: A dilemma, or consequence of a distal dilemma, that is within the educator's control to change.

Some dilemmas are distal through and through, meaning that the educator is better off accepting that they are incapable of solving the dilemma themselves and thus should work within the situation rather than spend resources on it. An example of a distal dilemma is poverty. Poverty is distal because addressing poverty requires complex interventions that address housing policies, school districting, economic development and redistribution, wage regulations, and other issues beyond an educator's control. While an individual educator or team of educators can advocate for poverty relief, these educators are unlikely to solve the core problem of poverty on their own. However, these educators can invest time and resources in understanding the specific impacts of poverty on their school community and mitigating those impacts at the school and classroom levels.

While the dilemma of poverty itself is distal, the impacts of poverty might be situated at the proximal level since poverty causes more micro-level dilemmas that an individual teacher can address. For example, proximal dilemmas rooted in the distal problem of poverty may be that students do not come to school in clean clothes or they come to school hungry. Educators can respond to these dilemmas by keeping extra sets of clean clothes available at school for students who do not have them or educators might collaborate with a local grocery store to supply granola bar snacks nearing the expiration date. Neither of these strategies

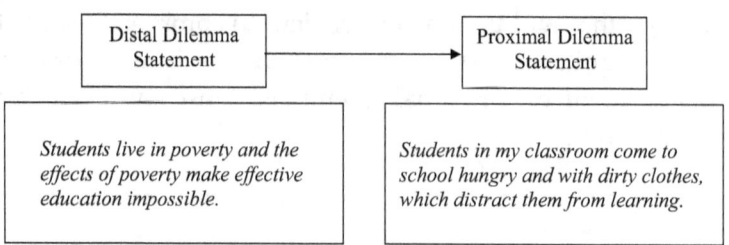

Figure 2.1 Focusing on Proximal Dilemmas.

solves poverty, but both of them mitigate the immediate, physical effects of poverty on the students' experiences at school. In this example, the teachers have repositioned the distal focus on the problem of poverty to a proximal focus on students' needs for snacks or clean clothes during school time. Whereas some dilemmas legitimately fall outside of educators' spheres of influence to solve, many other dilemmas that educators position as distal can be repositioned to be proximal (see Figure 2.1 for an example).

> **Focus on Culture 1: Challenging Inequitable Systems through Proximal Dilemmas**
>
> A good example of using a **proximal** characterization for a dilemma would be a teacher's approach to addressing racism, sexism, gender identity discrimination, or any other kind of institutionalized bias. The social factors maintaining an inequitable status quo are **distal**, as is the status quo itself when we focus on an entire society. However, teachers do have a degree of control over their daily interactions with students, the classroom culture and climate, instructional activities, and ways of choosing the **explicit** and **hidden curriculum**, which can all minimize microaggressions related to societal discrimination that occur in the classroom (Gorski & Pothini, 2024). Improving classroom climate and instruction are proximal targets that also empower the teacher to make change within their own sphere of influence. We discuss examples of how teachers can challenge an inequitable status quo through each **domain of teaching** in Part II.

External and Internal Attributions

In addition to positioning dilemmas as **distal** or **proximal**, teachers may use the Habit of Personal Attribution to identify whether they have attributed the problem to an external or internal source when they (often implicitly) describe who is responsible for addressing the dilemma. Assigning an **external attribution** means positioning the responsibility for solving the problem as outside of, or beyond, the educator. With an external attribution, the teacher is dependent on people or circumstances outside of, or external to, themselves in order to solve the dilemma. Conversely, an **internal attribution** positions the responsibility for solving the problem as within the educator. For example, if the dilemma statement includes blame of student or parent attitudes or behaviors, which also overlaps with the next habit of mind we will discuss, then the teacher may have adopted an external attribution because students or parents would need to change before the dilemma could resolve. This situation is related to having a distal dilemma because in both cases the teacher has little power to make a difference. When teachers identify a dilemma that is distal, that dilemma will be dependent upon a shift in forces beyond a teacher's control to solve. If that teacher tries to position a distal dilemma internally, such as solving poverty, that is a set-up for burn-out since the teacher will not be able to solve that problem within their own context. It is also possible that a teacher may identify a proximal dilemma but attribute its solution to external forces. In the second step of the **Habit of Personal Attribution**, we want to move the attribution of addressing proximal dilemmas to internal forces, those that reside within the teacher.

> **Key Terms**
>
> *External Attribution:* Positioning the responsibility for solving the dilemma outside of, or beyond, the educator and/or expressing a sense of hopelessness about being able to solve it.
> *Internal Attribution:* Positioning the responsibility for solving the dilemma within the educator and expressing efficacy at being able to solve it.

An external attribution of a proximal dilemma often results from the educator having a low sense of self-efficacy about being able to succeed at positively impacting a particular situation. Psychologist Albert Bandura (1977) defined self-efficacy as individuals' feelings that they can influence what happens to them and have the power to do so. This is similar to having a sense of **personal agency**, which you will see in Chapter 4. The related term **teacher efficacy** refers to a teacher's sense of confidence and responsibility for motivating and teaching all students (Tschannen-Moran & Woolfolk Hoy, 2001). If an educator has a low sense of efficacy as it relates to the dilemma being addressed, then the educator is unlikely to view the dilemma as proximal or solvable and is likely to engage in **deficit thinking**, which we will talk about below when discussing the next **habit of mind**.

> **Key Terms**
>
> *Teacher Efficacy*: A teacher's sense of confidence and responsibility for motivating and teaching all students.

When a teacher has a high sense of self-efficacy, even if the teacher does not know precisely how to address a particular situation, the teacher is more likely to place the responsibility for solving the dilemma within themselves. Educators with internal attributions take what Corbett and colleagues (2002) called an "It's My Job" approach, meaning that these teachers adopt the perspective that the barriers students face to learning academic content are the teachers' responsibilities to address. These researchers identified this approach when they conducted a study in two diverse public-school districts in the US, each enrolling approximately 10,000 students, with over 25% living in poverty. They noted that in over 1000 surveys, the vast majority of educators agreed with the statement that all students could succeed, but some educators added a deficit-based caveat to the end of the sentence such as "if they are willing to try" (p. 19) or "but some don't because of their families" (p. 25). The "It's My Job" teachers completed the sentence with "and it's my job to make sure they do." These teachers committed to having no excuses for not persisting in addressing barriers to student progress that were within their control. Even if they did not achieve success with a student, they continued to try. This approach reflects an internal attribution for addressing dilemmas.

If you experience low teacher efficacy, you may benefit from reviewing the knowledge, dispositions, and skills you already have that can help you address your dilemma (see Exercise 2.1). For example, when we first started working with Ms. Nash and she described the situation she wanted to change in her classroom—students' inattention during the transition into class—she expressed exasperation and hopelessness about being able to make a change. She did not see how a change could come nor did she believe she had the tools to make that change. That is to say, her teacher efficacy was low. In addition to facing initial low teacher efficacy, Ms. Nash often heard her colleagues express deficit thinking and witnessed their actions that resulted from it. It was common at her school to send students out of class for small behavioral infractions and to blame students for their own failure without considering how teachers could improve their own practices to improve students' learning experiences. The combination of her colleagues' negativity and Ms. Nash's low teacher efficacy resulted in a predicament in which she could not imagine how she could effectively solve the problem.

However, we pointed out to Ms. Nash that she had extensive knowledge about her subject area and even though she had not completed her teaching certification, she was gathering knowledge about teaching from various sources. She had the desire to be an excellent teacher and was willing to learn new skills in order to do so. She brought curiosity, open-mindedness, and persistence to the situation. Then, we asked Ms. Nash how she could build upon this foundation to gather more resources that would help bolster her teacher efficacy. Together, we identified several practitioner-focused sources for knowledge about teaching, such as trade journals and the National Science Teachers Association. Ms. Nash also mentioned collaborations she had with other

Exercise 2.1 *Building Teacher Efficacy*

Directions

Consider which of the following you already have and/or can draw upon as you approach your dilemma:

Dispositions	Knowledge	Skills	Resources
☐ Curiosity	☐ Content area	☐ Collaboration	☐ More skilled colleagues
☐ Optimism	☐ Student developmental levels	☐ Learning new things	☐ School and district leaders
☐ Persistence	☐ Students' personal and learning needs	☐ Practices of reflection	☐ Community, parent, and/or university partners
☐ Courage	☐ Student activities and interests	☐ Insightfulness	☐ Trade journals
☐ Commitment	☐ Community strengths and resources	☐ Attention to detail	☐ Professional organizations
☐ Openness	☐ Parent and family backgrounds, values, and approaches	☐ Building connections with students and families	☐ Professional development opportunities
☐ Friendliness	☐ Other:_____	☐ Other:_____	☐ Other:_____
☐ Honesty			
☐ Willingness to learn			
☐ Self-reflection			
☐ Other:_____			

teachers in her district who shared ideas with her about how they had addressed their own teaching dilemmas in the past. Identifying these resources bolstered Ms. Nash's teacher efficacy so that she felt more confident in adopting an internal attribution in addressing her dilemma.

After focusing on developing her teacher efficacy, we asked Ms. Nash to consider how she could engage the Habit of Personal Attribution in her dilemma. The dilemma was occurring within her classroom, so it was proximal, but we noticed in her **driving question** that she had placed the responsibility for solving the problem not on herself but on her students: "What will make the students quiet and efficient in finishing the warm-up so we can smoothly transition into the lesson?" In this phrasing of the driving question, the students needed to change their behavior in order for the dilemma to be solved. Ms. Nash was placing the responsibility for the dilemma, and thus the power to change it, on her students. Her original driving question and **dilemma statement** are proximal but reflect an external attribution. After we have discussed all three habits of mind, we will consider how engaging them might help Ms. Nash revise her driving question and dilemma statement, thereby sharpening her focus for **frame shifting**.

The Habit of Personal Attribution involves proximal and internal, rather than distal and/or external, positioning of dilemmas. We note that it is also in this habit of mind that teachers can regain a sense of power and control over solving the persistent dilemmas that nag them. Practice developing this habit of mind related to your dilemma by completing questions in Exercise 2.2.

Habit of Asset Identification

Because educators' beliefs impact their judgments and responses to challenging situations, it is important when facing persistent dilemmas to consider how we think about and position students. That is the purpose of the **Habit of Asset Identification**. As you read about this habit, consider Ms. Nash's **dilemma description** in which she saw students as loud, rowdy, not wanting to get to

> **Exercise 2.2** *Developing the Habit of Personal Attribution*
> **Directions**
> Consider these questions in developing personal attribution.
>
> *Diagnosing a distal approach*
> - Am I dependent on a change in policy or some other part of the situation that I cannot impact before I would be able to solve the dilemma?
> - What else is preventing me from solving the dilemma?
>
> *Adopting a proximal position*
> - What part of the dilemma can I affect in the classroom?
>
> *Diagnosing an external attribution*
> - When I think about how I have described my dilemma up until now, who has the power to solve it?
> - Who do I think is responsible for solving the dilemma?
> - Have I given up on, or already dismissed, my ability to solve the dilemma because I do not have the knowledge or skills to solve it?
>
> *Adopting an internal attribution*
> - What personal characteristics do I have that might help me solve the dilemma?
> - What additional knowledge or skills might I need to develop? How can I do that?
> - What material resources do I have that might help me solve the dilemma?
> - How can others in my immediate environment help me?

work, and just generally pushing her to her limit. You may also want to look back at the notes you made at the end of Chapter 1 regarding your own teaching dilemma. To understand this **habit of mind**, we need to define the terms **deficit thinking** and **asset-based thinking**. Deficit thinking identifies causes for dilemmas as residing within students and families and/or within their communities and being due to something that is inherently wrong with them (Kennedy & Soutullo, 2018; Valencia, 1997, 2010). Asset-based thinking identifies the strengths or good qualities that students, families, and communities have that can be brought to bear to solve a dilemma and can help us shift negative perceptions about certain traits to be more neutral or positive. Table 2.1 provides one example, with additional examples provided in the Study Guide. The Habit of Asset Identification involves the move from deficit thinking to asset-based thinking.

> **Key Terms**
> *Deficit Thinking*: Identifying the cause for the dilemma as due to something that is wrong with students, caregivers, or communities.
> *Asset-Based Thinking*: Identifying characteristics, dispositions, or resources of students, caregivers, and communities as beneficial and necessary for resolving the dilemma.

Sometimes deficit thinking and the need for the Habit of Asset Identification can be easy to identify. In each of the examples in Table 2.1, the educator identifies something that is wrong with the student and there is an element of blame toward the student for the named shortcoming. We mentioned above that blame can be an indicator of **external attribution**. Here we point out that comments that imply blame are also reliable clues that show the presence of deficit thinking. Deficit thinking may be difficult to notice at first, but when you practice listening carefully, you will start to hear it, perhaps from your colleagues' descriptions of their classroom experiences or even in the way you think about your own experiences. In Table 2.2, we explore how a teacher taking a deficit

TABLE 2.1 *Comparison Between Deficit Thinking and Asset-Based Thinking*

Example of Deficit Thinking	Moving to Asset-Based Thinking
1. Kayla is always interrupting me when I'm speaking to the class as a group. She does not have respect for adults.	Kayla has strong opinions and leadership skills and isn't afraid to speak up.

TABLE 2.2 *Comparison of Teacher Conclusions in Response to Deficit- Versus Asset-Based Approaches to Students*

Examples of Deficit Thinking	Teacher's Conclusion Resulting from Deficit Thinking	Moving to Asset-Based Thinking	Teacher's Conclusion Resulting from Asset-Based Thinking
1. Kayla is always interrupting me when I'm speaking to the class as a group. Kayla does not have respect for adults.	I need to teach Kayla respect by being stricter and more consistent with punishing her lack of respect.	Kayla has strong opinions and leadership skills and isn't afraid to speak up.	I need to help Kayla use her skills to be an effective leader in different situations.

view of each of the students named in Table 2.1 would come to different conclusions and make different moves to address that student than a teacher taking an asset view. In these examples, the teacher taking an asset-based perspective is also likely to have a more open and friendly approach with the student involved, which may facilitate the effectiveness of any move the teacher attempts. Notice that deficit thinking and external attribution work hand in hand. That is how these first two habits are related and why both are necessary to master before moving on to the third one. (Extended versions of Tables 2.1 and 2.2 that include additional examples are available in the online Study Guide).

Sometimes deficit thinking can be more nuanced. It can even masquerade as sympathy and compassion. For example, a teacher might know that a child is facing a tough set of circumstances and as a result decide not to assign the student challenging academic tasks. Or the educator might leave the student alone rather than checking to see if the student needs help with an assignment. While these decisions may seem helpful, they may also reveal deficit thinking because the teacher assumes a weakness or inability in the student to handle a particular academic challenge. Scholar, educator, and activist Gloria Ladson-Billings (2007) refers to this teacher behavior as the "'You-Poor-Dear' Syndrome" (p. 319). In working through her dilemma, Ms. Nash particularly recognized how the You-Poor-Dear Syndrome might have been playing a role. She allowed excessive amounts of time for students to make transitions and complete activities not only because she was unsure how to raise and reinforce her expectations but also because she did not want the children to feel pressured or "stupid." Upon closer examination, she determined that tightening her **routines** and raising her expectations and requirements would better build upon her students' assets as curious individuals eager to succeed. On the other hand, a teacher's decision to leave a student alone during emotionally challenging tasks or situations in which the child might feel put on the spot might be a sign of the teacher's cultural responsiveness or emotional intelligence. So, in determining how you are using the Habit of Asset Identification, carefully consider the context and circumstances by asking yourself about the assumptions you are making about the student in determining your course of action.

When Ms. Nash considered whether engaging the Habit of Asset Identification might mean that she had further rethinking and revising to do related to her dilemma, she noticed that she had used some deficit-focused language in her original **dilemma statement**. Her dilemma statement was: *Students enter the classroom in an unruly manner and are not interested in working on the posted assignment.* She could now see that she had evaluated students as not interested in working when she knew that she had seen them quite engaged and diligent during other parts of the class. This realization made her further wonder how she could recover and build upon those assets. In addition to providing a useful lens for viewing the connection between teachers' beliefs about students and their resulting teacher moves, a timely and effective use of the Habit of Asset Identification can help educators develop the other habits of mind as well because it provides or restores a positive and motivating view of students.

The questions in Exercise 2.3 can help you in developing this habit of mind. The first set of yes/no questions asks you to evaluate your current beliefs. If your answers to any of these questions is no, you might get stuck in your ability to make progress with your dilemma. If this is the case, we encourage a deeper dive

> **Exercise 2.3** *Developing the Habit of Asset Identification*
>
> **Directions**
>
> Consider these questions in adopting a focus on assets.
>
> *Evaluating your current beliefs about students:*
> - Do I fully believe that no student really wants to fail if they believe they can succeed?
> - Do I sometimes lower my expectations for some students out of "pity?"
> - Do I fully believe that every student wants to make their caregiver or other significant adults proud if they believe that is possible?
> - Do I fully believe that every caregiver loves their child?
>
> *Diagnosing deficit thinking:*
> - When I think about my dilemma, what do I think is wrong with the students?
> - How is my cultural or social position shaping my perspective about what might be wrong with the students?
> - What assumptions am I making based on cultural stereotypes?
> - When I think about my dilemma, what do I think is wrong with the students' caregivers for situations outside of school?
>
> *Identifying assets:*
> - What strengths do I notice in my students?
> - What strengths do I notice in caregivers and in students' communities?
> - How could I build upon students' and caregivers' strengths to solve my dilemma?

into answering the questions listed under "identifying assets." Some of the teacher moves related to relationships discussed in Chapter 4 can help you get to know students, families, and communities better so that their assets are more noticeable for you.

> **Focus on Culture 2: Maintaining High Expectations for All Students**
>
> Students from marginalized backgrounds who face inequities or bias due to social group membership can particularly elicit teacher sympathy, which teachers might then translate into low expectations. Culturally responsive pedagogy (discussed again in Chapters 4 and 6) requires that teachers maintain high expectations in order to support student success, which is key for accomplishing educational equity (Delpit, 2012; Ladson-Billings, 2017). Failing to challenge students or allowing them to produce work that is not high quality, rigorous, or reflective of **higher order thinking** is based on **deficit thinking** since it presumes that students cannot reach this high bar. We can draw a similar conclusion about educators' decisions regarding student placements in homogeneous remedial groupings or lower educational tracks, especially in national contexts where students are tracked at early ages and sorted into different secondary schools by track. Sometimes students are also complicit in an unspoken agreement between educators and students to exchange behavioral compliance for easy work that requires little effort. Haberman (1991) situated this exchange within the "pedagogy of poverty" and recognized that teachers need highly effective instructional strategies that support high expectations and motivate students to meet those expectations.

Habit of Deliberate Interpretation

Although each of the **habits of mind** targets a separate specific skill, the three habits of mind work together. The **Habit of Personal Attribution** and the **Habit of Asset Identification** provide a basis for engaging the last habit of mind, the **Habit of Deliberate Interpretation**. It is important that teachers continue to focus on **proximal** issues, have an **internal attribution**, and build upon students' **assets** in order to succeed at the process we describe next. In this third and final habit of mind, we evaluate the judgments we have made in the **dilemma description, driving question,** and **dilemma statement,** because judgments often leave us with little room left to have a positive impact on the dilemma. For example, if we judge something as bad, that evaluation may signify the end of the possibilities for change because there is nothing left to do. By engaging the Habit of Deliberate Interpretation, we try to notice and repair where we might have made negative judgments so far with our dilemma. We examine if we can produce a more useful interpretation of facts by peeling back these judgments and re-examining **empirical** evidence.

As part of ongoing reflection about their practice, educators engage in quick rounds of identifying and diagnosing progress or problems, followed by identifying and selecting among options for furthering progress. Experienced teachers do this set of thought actions nearly instinctively, making the word "habit" particularly appropriate in describing this mental process. In this section, we focus on this process by slowing it down and breaking it into its constituent parts, or steps. Those steps include **observation, interpretation, judgment,** and **decision** (see Figure 2.2). We call this the Habit of Deliberate Interpretation to emphasize the importance of being intentional when we are interpreting, judging, and ultimately responding to persistent dilemmas. In the rapid pace of teaching, it is easy to make swift judgments about dilemmas that arise and to act accordingly. Developing this habit of mind requires us to approach dilemmas with deliberate thought and action.

First let's consider the steps of observation and interpretation. An observation is a straightforward, empirical description of a

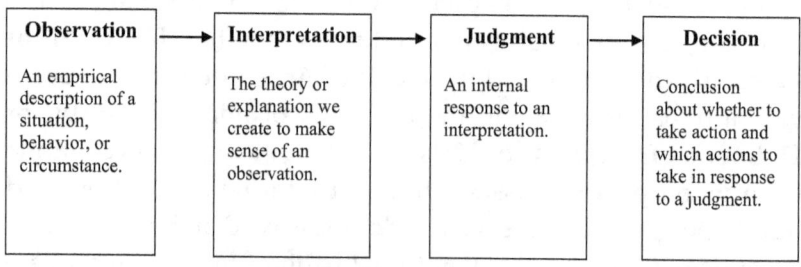

Figure 2.2 Steps in the Habit of Deliberate Interpretation.

situation, behavior, or circumstance. An observation is distinct from an interpretation because it involves the taking in of empirical facts prior to making sense of them. Observations are things you can see or hear that do not yet involve interpretation or judgment. An interpretation is an inference that results from a sense-making process about the observation. Here are some examples. You might observe puddles of water on the street outside when you wake up in the morning; then you might infer, or interpret, that it rained during the night. You might observe a child laying underneath the monkey bars at the playground and crying; then you might interpret that the child fell off the monkey bars and is surprised or injured. Now let's connect these first two thought actions with the next step in the chain, **judgment**, as illustrated in Figure 2.2. Oftentimes, there is a judgment or emotional reaction attached to the interpretation. So, you might conclude that the caregiver of the child at the playground was not paying careful enough attention and become angry at the caregiver's negligence. Here is another example: You *observe* a student in the back of the class with their head on their desk. You *interpret* that the student is tired. You *judge* that the student has not prioritized your class by getting enough sleep to be able to keep their head up.

Key Terms

Observation: Empirical description of a situation, behavior, or circumstance.

Interpretation: The theory or explanation we create to make sense of an observation.

Judgment: Internal response to an interpretation.

Decision: Conclusion about whether to take action and which actions to take in response to a judgment.

This distinction between observation, interpretation, and judgment is particularly important for understanding how the Habit of Deliberate Interpretation works and how to strengthen it. In life both inside and outside the classroom, we often leap from a first encounter with an experience to judgment without checking first whether or not our interpretations are correct. In the Habit of Deliberate Interpretation, we have to create enough space between the first encounter, or the observation, and the interpretation to imagine different interpretations. Then, we engage the skills of curiosity and investigation to form these new interpretations (Toshalis, 2015).[1] Differences in interpretation between teacher and student as well as harsh judgments by teachers may fuel conflicts, so one essential exercise we suggest before addressing a dilemma is to check the interpretation by first suspending judgment. For example, you might ask yourself whether the student's head is on their desk because they are, indeed, tired. You could explore your interpretation to see whether or not it is true by walking over and checking with the student. Imagine that, in doing so, the student raised their head only to reveal tears on their cheek. This new observation would probably lead to a different interpretation, such as that the student is upset, and then to a different judgment, such as that the student needs space or tenderness or to talk to a confidante. This process is shown in Table 2.3.

Usually we move from observation to judgment nearly instantaneously, without even realizing it. In the Habit of Deliberate Interpretation, we are slowing down that process and breaking it into steps so that we can take each step consciously. Engaging this habit will likely require identifying a judgment you have made seemingly automatically and learning to work backwards through the process of Deliberate Interpretation in order to be able to start with the empirical facts and reinterpret them. Next, we explore how teachers can intentionally move through each of the steps

TABLE 2.3 *Example of How New Empirical Clues Lead to New Interpretations and Judgments*

Observation (Clue)	Interpretation	Judgment
Student's head on desk.	Student is tired.	Student doesn't prioritize sleep.
Student's head on desk with tears.	Student is upset.	Student needs space/tenderness.

of the Habit of Deliberate Interpretation when facing challenging dilemmas, which, again, will ultimately empower the teacher to be able to make more and different teacher moves when **frame shifting**. As we explain how this process works, we lay out the connections between each step in a chronological way. You may first articulate the judgment, but you have already moved swiftly through observation and interpretation to arrive there, probably without realizing it. The development of this habit requires more conscious attention to these first steps in this chain.

Observation of Empirical Facts

Our **judgments**, and the decisions we based from them (the final two steps in determining a given teacher move), result from what started as an **observation**. To examine this process in more detail, we need to confirm that when we discuss an observation, we are not unwittingly describing a judgment or interpretation. We need to be sure that we are starting with a description of **empirical** and neutral facts and that we are describing specifically what we see and hear when we think there is a problem in the classroom and doing so without interpreting any of those facts. The attribute of curiosity can be particularly useful here. You are a detective who will try to figure out a case, but first you have to collect the clues. If you interpret "what happened" too soon, you may create an incorrect theory about it (Kennedy & Thornberg, 2018). Consider these questions to help you make an empirical observation:

- What specifically do I see during the dilemma?
- What specifically do I hear?
- What happens right before the dilemma?
- What happens right after?

> **Key Terms**
>
> *Empirical*: Facts that are directly experienced using our senses, such as the actions we see and the words that we hear.

44 ♦ Foundations

After we explained the **Habit of Deliberate Interpretation** and asked Ms. Nash to practice moving backwards from judgment to observation, she noticed that her original **dilemma statement** contained judgments and that she would need to revise it in order to be able to begin from a more neutral position. Remember from Chapter 1 that in Ms. Nash's **dilemma description**, she expressed exasperation that the students come in loud and rowdy, wandering aimlessly, and not starting the posted assignment. She had articulated her initial dilemma statement as: *Students enter the classroom in an unruly manner and are not interested in working on the posted assignment.* Notice how this statement includes subjective judgment about the students' behavior as "unruly" and that they "are not interested in working." She thought this was what she was observing, but then we pointed out that "unruly" is not something you see or hear. First you see or hear certain sounds, words, or movements, then you interpret those sounds and movements, and then you judge them as "unruly." Similarly, you cannot see or hear a lack of interest in working. You can only interpret and judge something you see or hear as a lack of interest. Essentially, Ms. Nash has skipped the important step of making an objective observation and then interpreting it and went straight to judgment (see Figure 2.3).

When we reminded Ms. Nash about how the **Habit of Personal Attribution** requires teachers to have an **internal**

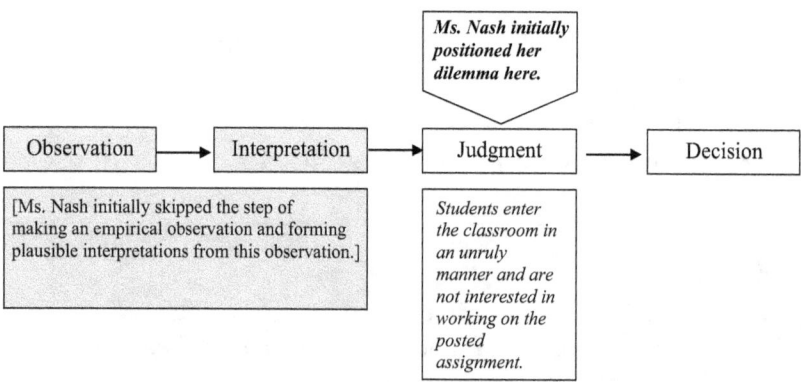

Figure 2.3 Where Ms. Nash's Dilemma Statement was Originally Positioned.

attribution of responsibility for addressing the dilemma, she saw how her leap to judgment also pushed the locus of control back to the students. If the students are unruly, then it is up to the students to fix the problem by changing their behavior. Engaging the Habit of Personal Attribution helped Ms. Nash stay on track as she learned the Habit of Deliberate Interpretation. Assuming we now have a neutral observation, or collection of clues, we can move on to seeing how observation leads to interpretation.

From Observation to Interpretation

The move from **observation** to **interpretation** involves a process of critical thinking called **induction** (Kennedy & Thornberg, 2018). Induction is the process detectives use to come up with a theory or explanation of what happened at a crime scene by looking at all of the available clues when they investigate a crime. As more or different clues become available, different theories or conclusions become possible. We suggest that adopting the **Habit of Deliberate Interpretation** requires teachers to look for additional clues related to causes for the dilemma and then to explore various possible interpretations of those observations through the process of induction.

> **Key Terms**
>
> *Induction*: A process of critical thinking in which we develop different theories or conclusions as we are presented with new information.

Focusing on the process of induction helps us disentangle our interpretations and judgments from an **empirical**, neutral description of what we observe. When we asked Ms. Nash to separate observation from interpretation and to explore different possible interpretations, she said: "I observe the students coming into the room, some after the tardy bell rings, sitting in whichever desk they choose, and then either staring at the board or talking to a classmate. I interpret that the students are chatty or distracted or do not want to work." This distinction Ms. Nash was able to make between her observation and her interpretation was a helpful one. Developing the Habit of Deliberate Interpretation allowed her to see other ways to interpret the same behaviors. She made this shift by noticing other clues that she had neglected before. She noticed how students looked around in slightly confused ways at the remaining empty seats when they first entered the classroom. She also listened more carefully to their complaints that they did not understand the warm-up prompts. Previously, in arriving too quickly at interpretations of too few observations, she had dismissed these complaints as a way for students to procrastinate on getting to work.

After considering these additional clues, she slowed down her interpretation process and decided to take students' comments at face value, which meant that students had no guidance about where to sit or did not understand what they were supposed to do and so did nothing or talked to their friends. Relying on additional clues, Ms. Nash reformulated her interpretation of students' delayed transition to classwork from laziness or a lack of motivation, to confusion. Making the distinction between observation and interpretation allowed Ms. Nash to observe new clues and then draw different inferences about the reasons for the dilemma (see Table 2.4). As she made this change, Ms. Nash was able to point out how she was engaging the **Habit of Personal Attribution**. She remarked that her first plausible interpretation contained an **external attribution** because it focused on what the students have control over, but when she considered additional

TABLE 2.4 *Examining a Different Plausible Interpretation in Ms. Nash's Dilemma*

Observation (Clue)	Plausible Interpretation (Theory/Explanation)	A Different Plausible Interpretation
Students come into the room, some after the tardy bell rings, sitting in whichever desk they choose, and then either staring at the board or talking to a classmate.	*Students are chatty or distracted or do not want to work.*	*Students do not know where to sit and do not understand what they are supposed to do with the opening task.*

clues, she could make a different interpretation that allowed her to adopt an **internal attribution**. This change went along with new feelings of confidence and **teacher efficacy**, and these positive feelings also encouraged her to continue to engage the **Habit of Asset Identification** as she saw her students as allies in their learning process. This is an example of how the **habits of mind** work together. We will see this again when we practice these skills in Chapter 7.

In Exercise 2.4, we list five observations, the first two related to everyday life and the last three based on classroom life. In the

---

Exercise 2.4 *Practicing Plausible Interpretation*

Directions

Practice the Habit of Deliberate Interpretation by considering how additional information that may not be immediately known may lead to a different interpretation of the observation.

Observation (Clue)	Plausible Interpretation (Theory/Explanation)	A Different Plausible Interpretation
1. A car speeds by you and swerves briefly into oncoming traffic before returning to the proper lane.	The driver is distracted or intoxicated and briefly lost control of the car.	
2. Your cell phone suddenly turns off.	You have had it longer than three years, so it has stopped working.	
3. A student in your class does not respond when you ask if anyone has any questions.	The student understands all of the material and directions.	
4. A student in your class speaks up defensively when you redirect her behavior.	The student does not like to be caught doing something wrong.	
5. A student is late to your class nearly every day.	The student spends too much time talking to friends between classes.	

---

second column, we list plausible interpretations of these observations. We have left the third column blank for you to practice identifying a different plausible interpretation based on the same observation or "clue." To complete this column, consider how additional information, or clues that may not immediately come into view, may lead to a different interpretation of the observation. You can find suggested answers in the online Study Guide.

Applying this exercise to classroom dilemmas can allow you to think differently about the evidence you observe or might encourage you to ask different questions about what you observe, which can introduce new possibilities for successfully solving a persistently troubling issue. How we respond to situations we observe depends on the conclusions we make from our inductive process, so using the Habit of Deliberate Interpretation results in new possible, more effective, responses. One key skill in identifying different plausible interpretations involves identifying, or perhaps even imagining the existence of, additional clues to make sense of the observation just as Ms. Nash did when she returned to her **dilemma description** to identify other empirical facts that were occurring in class before, during, and after her dilemma. Her different interpretations then led to different **judgments** as well as different possibilities for how she could respond. We explore this move from interpretation to judgments in the next section.

Focus on Culture 3: How Teachers' Frames of Reference and Biases Influence Their Interpretations

An individual's interpretation of evidence often involves their **frames of reference**, assumptions, stereotypes, and biases. By frames of reference, we mean the objects and patterns that are most familiar to you. In the previous exercises, we referred to a car speeding by and a cell phone turning off. If we had written this chapter before the invention of cars or cell phones or for audiences unfamiliar with these technologies, those objects would not be part of our shared frame of reference and the examples would make no sense. Another example might refer to moving the clean clothes from the washing machine to the dryer and adding fabric softener. But for an audience where owning a dryer is not a common experience, or in communities where dryers are economically out of reach, avoided due to environmental concerns, or inaccessible due to infrastructural limitations, this example would not tap into a shared frame of reference. We automatically use our frames of reference when we **interpret** and make **judgments** about **observations**. For example, Ms. Nash interpreted her students' behavior at the beginning of class as unruly based on her image of what it meant to "do school," which was shaped by her White, middle class, highly educated background. We will return to frames of reference in Chapter 6 and will discuss how they are also relevant when considering dilemmas related to **curriculum and instruction**.

Teachers also respond to according to their own stereotypes and biases about students even when they do not realize they have biases. Research has shown, for instance, that teachers in the US are more likely to respond more negatively to the misbehavior of Black students than White students even when the teachers do not believe they are being biased (Okonofua & Eberhardt, 2015). Not realizing that bias plays a role in their responses, teachers may then blame students for requiring harsh discipline rather than examining the teachers' own decisions about punishment.

We naturally lean toward the interpretation of evidence that most aligns with what (and how) we know about the world. In the example from the previous tables in which the student speaks up defensively and the teacher interprets the student's behavior to have a certain meaning or to reflect a certain attitude, that teacher's interpretation might differ depending on the ethnic background or gender of the student and the teacher's internalized stereotypes about students from that background and/or that gender. When the teacher is from the culture of power in society and also has the power in the classroom to reward and sanction certain behaviors, these

> differences between teachers and students may lead to consequences that reinforce this power differential, reduce student engagement, and worsen students' chances for success (Gregory & Roberts, 2017; Weinstein et al., 2003). Thus, the Habit of Deliberate Interpretation is a particularly important **habit of mind** for teachers to exercise when there are cultural differences between themselves and their students. Further, it can empower teachers to engage their curiosity and to use tools of investigation to question and explore their previous interpretations and judgments related to culturally shaped expectations and behaviors.

From Interpretation to Judgment

Let's next focus on the difference between an **interpretation** and a **judgment**. An interpretation occurs when you make sense of an **observation**. You see something and then create a story that explains the thing you see, just like the detective identifies a suspect based on a theory or an explanation for a certain clue or set of clues. That story is an interpretation. We respond to interpretations with internalized judgments, which we often arrive at quickly and unconsciously. If we look back at our initial set of plausible interpretations, they lead to particular judgments. Table 2.5 and subsequent tables show one example from outside

TABLE 2.5 *Judgments Resulting from Interpretations*

Observation	Plausible Interpretation	Judgment
1. A car speeds by you and swerves briefly into oncoming traffic before returning to the proper lane.	The driver is distracted or intoxicated and briefly lost control of the car.	*The driver is an irresponsible lawbreaker.*
2. A student in your class does not respond when you ask if anyone has any questions.	The student understands all of the material and directions.	*The student is a fast, independent learner who does not need as much teacher support as some of the other students.*

the classroom and one example from inside the classroom, with all of the examples from Exercise 2.4 addressed in the online Study Guide. You have probably already guessed that when we change the interpretation and create a different story to explain the clues, it also changes the judgment. So, when we adopt different plausible interpretations, we might instead come to the judgments shown in Table 2.6.

As you can see, the **Habit of Deliberate Interpretation** impacts our judgments about our observations. In each example, the new interpretation leads to a more generous judgment, which matters in the classroom because our judgments impact how we respond to students, whether it's in our attitude toward the student or the tangible ways we treat them. Ms. Nash found that once she explored alternative interpretations of her students' behaviors at the beginning of class—that students did not know where to sit and did not understand what they were supposed to do with the opening task—her judgment shifted to her own instruction and classroom management and away from the perceived misbehavior of her students. This move was reinforced by her engagement of the **Habit of Personal Attribution** which helped her to place the responsibility for solving the dilemma on herself rather than on her students. Continuing Table 2.4, we can

TABLE 2.6 *Different (More Generous) Judgments Resulting From Different Interpretations*

Observation	Different Plausible Interpretation	Different Judgment
1. A car speeds by you and swerves briefly into oncoming traffic before returning to the proper lane.	*The driver has just received word of an emergency, is rushing to the scene, and swerves to avoid a pothole.*	*The city really should repair the streets so that emergencies like this do not cause further accidents.*
2. A student in your class does not respond when you ask if anyone has any questions.	*The student hesitates to ask questions because the student does not want to feel stupid.*	*The student needs more help, but the teacher needs to be sure that the help is offered in a private, discreet manner.*

TABLE 2.7 Ms. Nash's Different Interpretations Lead to Different Judgments

Observation	Plausible Interpretation	Judgment	Different Plausible Interpretation	Different Judgment
Students come into the room, some after the tardy bell rings, sitting in whichever desk they choose, and then either staring at the board or talking to a classmate.	Students are chatty or distracted or do not want to work.	*Students are disrespectful and lazy.*	Students did not know where to sit and did not understand what they were supposed to do with the opening task.	*Students do not understand the instructional activity and classroom management procedures.*

now examine how Ms. Nash's interpretations shaped her judgments in Table 2.7.

From Judgment to Decision

Next, we look at the final link in the steps of developing the **Habit of Deliberate Interpretation** as shown in Figure 2.2. New **judgments** often lead to different **decisions**. Decisions are conclusions about whether to take action and which actions to take in response to a judgment. In Table 2.8, we return to our examples and list possible decisions resulting from both the original judgments (Table 2.5), as well as those resulting from the new judgments (Table 2.6) based on different plausible **interpretations**. In this table the decisions are italicized to allow you to quickly contrast how the decisions differ based on the interpretation and judgment. When you compare and contrast the different decisions and actions, you see how developing the Habit of Deliberate Interpretation results in different diagnoses for the cause of the dilemma and different actions being taken. These actions then may have quite different outcomes, some of which will make the dilemma worse and some will make the dilemma better. For example, tightening sanctions for tardiness in response to the student who is late is likely to increase the student's anxiety and lead to a sense of desperation which could then lead to

Strengthening Foundational Habits of Mind ◆ 53

TABLE 2.8 *Examples of How Different Judgments Lead to Different Decisions*

Observation	Plausible Interpretation	Judgment	Decision	Different Plausible Interpretation	Different Judgment	Different Decision
1. A car speeds by you and swerves briefly into oncoming traffic before returning to the proper lane.	The driver is distracted or intoxicated and briefly lost control of the car.	The driver is an irresponsible lawbreaker.	You call the police and report the erratic driving. You believe the police should arrest the driver.	The driver has just received word of an emergency, is rushing to the scene, and swerves to avoid a pothole.	The city really should repair the streets so that emergencies like this do not cause further accidents.	You pull over and stay out of the driver's way. When you get home, you call to report the pothole to the city.
2. A student in your class does not respond when you ask if anyone has any questions.	The student understands all of the material and directions.	The student is a fast, independent learner who does not need as much teacher support as some of the other students.	You leave the student alone during independent work time.	The student hesitates to ask questions because the student does not want to feel stupid.	The student needs more help, but the teacher needs to be sure that the help is offered in a private, discreet manner.	You assign a skilled and kind peer to sit near the student. You check in with him discreetly and ask the peer to assist with particularly difficult tasks.

disengagement. Initiating caregiver contact and enlisting a colleague for help, on the other hand, could convey a sense of support for the student and could solve the problem that is causing the tardiness. So, investigating observations in order to revise interpretations and formulate more accurate ones can make a significant difference. The Habit of Deliberate Interpretation is critical for identifying effective responses to education dilemmas. The questions in Exercise 2.5 can help you in developing this habit of mind as you assess your observations, interpretations, judgments, and decisions related to your dilemma.

Exercise 2.5 *Developing the Habit of Deliberate Interpretation*
Directions
Consider these questions in developing the habit of deliberate interpretation.

Reflecting on your starting point:
- What feelings do I have about the dilemma?
- What judgments am I making that cause these feelings?
- How is my cultural or social position affecting my interpretation and judgment of the dilemma?
- What assumptions am I making based on cultural stereotypes?

Observation of empirical facts:
- What information about the dilemma can I actually observe with my senses?
- Is my observation empirical (neutral and focused specifically on what I see and hear without interpretation or judgment)?
- Which part of my framing of the dilemma results from my observation and which part results from my interpretation?
- What other important information might exist that I have not yet observed or paid attention to?

From observation to interpretation:
- How could I interpret the information I observe differently?
- How do these new interpretations make me feel about my ability to effect change with this dilemma?

From interpretation to judgment:
- What new judgments might result from these new interpretations?
- How are these judgments different than the ones I had before?

From judgment to decision:
- What new conclusions can I identify now?
- How are these conclusions different than the ones I was coming to before?

Engaging the Habits of Mind to Describe Ms. Nash's Dilemma

After working through all three **habits of mind** with Ms. Nash, we returned to her **dilemma description, driving question**, and **dilemma statement**. Recall that her original driving question was: "What will make the students quiet and efficient in finishing the warm-up so we can smoothly transition into the lesson?" Her original dilemma statement was: *Students enter the classroom in an unruly manner and are not interested in working on the posted assignment*. When considering the **Habit of Personal Attribution**, Ms. Nash had noticed that both her driving question and her dilemma statement had placed the responsibility for solving the problem on her students. Her **external attribution** appeared in the phrase "make the students." Here, even though the teacher is positioned as making the students do something, the focus is still on students changing their behavior rather than how the teacher might be able to prevent or improve the situation. When she considered what she had learned when developing the **Habit of Asset Identification**, she further realized that in her dilemma statement, she was taking a deficit orientation toward students' behaviors. She had presumed that the ultimate cause of the disruptive situation was that students did not want to do the work. She wanted to be sure that her revised driving question and statement of the dilemma allowed her to see students' strengths more clearly and to build on them. Engaging the Habit of Personal Attribution allowed her to also consider how her instruction, and not just the behavior of the students, might be related to the dilemma. She became even more convinced of this when we shifted the frame from the domain of **classroom management** to the domain of **curriculum and instruction**, as we explain in Chapter 3.

As she continued to work through a revision of her driving question and dilemma statement, Ms. Nash engaged the **Habit of Deliberate Interpretation**. She realized that her original dilemma statement included the words "unruly" and "not interested," which not only expressed **deficit thinking** and attributed the problem as external to Ms. Nash but also conveyed **judgments** rather than **empirical observations**. She needed to focus on empirical observations in order to be able to see different ways to **interpret** what was happening in her classroom. She decided to change her dilemma statement to the following more neutral description of her challenge: *Students do not enter the classroom quickly and do not start working on the posted assignment.* Table 2.9

TABLE 2.9 *How Ms. Nash Changed Her Original Driving Question and Dilemma Statement after Developing all Three Habits of Mind*

	Before Applying Habits of Mind	After Applying Habits of Mind
Driving Question	"What will **make the students** quiet and efficient in finishing the warm-up so we can smoothly transition into the lesson?"	"How do **I structure** the transition into class so students quietly and quickly finish the warm-up and we smoothly transition into the lesson?"
Dilemma Statement	*Students enter the classroom in an **unruly manner** and are not **interested** in working on the posted assignment.*	*Students **do not enter the classroom quickly** and **do not start working** on the posted assignment.*

shows how Ms. Nash adjusted her driving question and dilemma statement after engaging all three habits of mind. These revisions are key for setting her up to embark on the next step of **frame shifting**, which we will see when we return to her dilemma in Chapter 3.

Practicing the Habits of Mind: Why Don't the Caregivers Care Enough to Show Up?

Now that we have learned all three **habits of mind** and seen how they have transformed Ms. Nash's **driving question** and **dilemma statement**, let's practice engaging them using the following **dilemma description** that one teacher shared with us:

> We are mandated to plan a Back to School Night each fall, but the caregivers just don't come. They also don't come to meetings that are specifically about their child unless we contact them multiple times. Sometimes administrators even encourage us to go to their homes first in order to get caregivers to make an appearance at school. They just don't seem to think that school is important. Sometimes I really wonder if some of them care about their kids' success at all.

When asked to use this dilemma description to identify the driving question, the teacher stated: "What will make the caregivers care more and show up to school meetings?" The related dilemma statement was: *Caregivers don't care about their children's education* (see Table 2.10).

TABLE 2.10 *Teachers' Original Driving Question and Dilemma Statement Regarding Caregiver Absence at Back to School Night*

Original Driving Question	Original Dilemma Statement
"What will make the caregivers care more and show up to school meetings?"	*Caregivers don't care about their children's education.*

Engaging the Habit of Personal Attribution With the Practice Dilemma

When you engage the **Habit of Personal Attribution,** you can ask the questions in Exercise 2.2 to determine whether the dilemma is proximal and **internally attributed.** Whether or not a problem is **distal** or **proximal** may also depend on the educator's network or sphere of influence. For example, designing an effective reorganization of Back to School Night might be a distal dilemma for one single teacher but a proximal dilemma for an administrative team at the school or district level. If teachers face this distal dilemma, they can engage in the type of exercise we described above in relation to the distal dilemma of poverty, where they identify how best to mitigate the impact of the dilemma on their own students. They can then be sure they are adopting an internal attribution by considering what personal characteristics and professional skills and tools they already have that can impact the dilemma (see Exercise 2.1).

Engaging the Habit of Asset Identification With the Practice Dilemma

The **Habit of Asset Identification** will set teachers up for success in their work with students and caregivers while they address this dilemma. The questions in Exercise 2.3 can guide this process, as they relate to educators' current beliefs about students and families. When we look closely at the dilemma statement, *Caregivers don't care about their children's education,* we see that there is an embedded belief that caregivers do not care about their children. When we engage the **Habit of Deliberate Interpretation** next, we will consider those **judgments** differently. But first, you will need to be able to suspend your beliefs about student and caregiver deficiencies and replace them, for example, with the belief that every caregiver loves their child and that every student wants to make their caregiver proud. We can see an illustration of this difference in Figure 2.4. These **asset-focused** beliefs might stretch you if you have collected a lot of evidence over your career that you think shows that caregivers actually do not care. Releasing the grip of those beliefs by engaging this habit is going to be critical for taking the next step. We will use the Habit

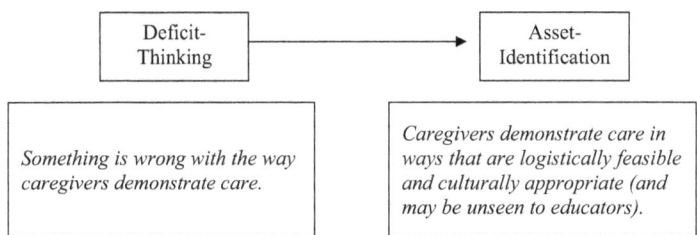

Figure 2.4 Engaging the Habit of Asset Identification When Caregivers Do Not Attend Back to School Night.

of Asset Identification to help us interpret this evidence differently, but that can only work if you are able to hold on to, and draw out, the assets that your students and their caregivers have.

Engaging the Habit of Deliberate Interpretation With the Practice Dilemma

When we go back to the original dilemma statement, *Caregivers don't care about their children's education*, we can identify that there is a **judgment** embedded here. This dilemma statement is not an **empirical observation** but rather a judgment that has already followed an **interpretation**. By slowing down our thinking, we can identify what we actually see and hear when the dilemma occurs. In other words, we make an empirical observation. We observe that caregivers do not attend. We literally do not see them there, so that is the empirical observation. In doing this, we can imagine a revision of the initial dilemma **statement** to one that is more focused on the observation. Figure 2.5 illustrates how the positioning of the dilemma statement moves from judgment to observation as we engage the Habit of Deliberate Interpretation.

From that observation, we can move to interpreting what we observe, being sure to engage the **Habit of Personal Attribution** and the **Habit of Asset Identification** by shifting from a **deficit-based** interpretation that blames caregivers to an **asset-based** interpretation. This asset-based focus helps us imagine different clues, or sets of circumstances, that could lead to this same observation, which helps us interpret these facts differently. For example, caregivers may have conflicting demands with multiple

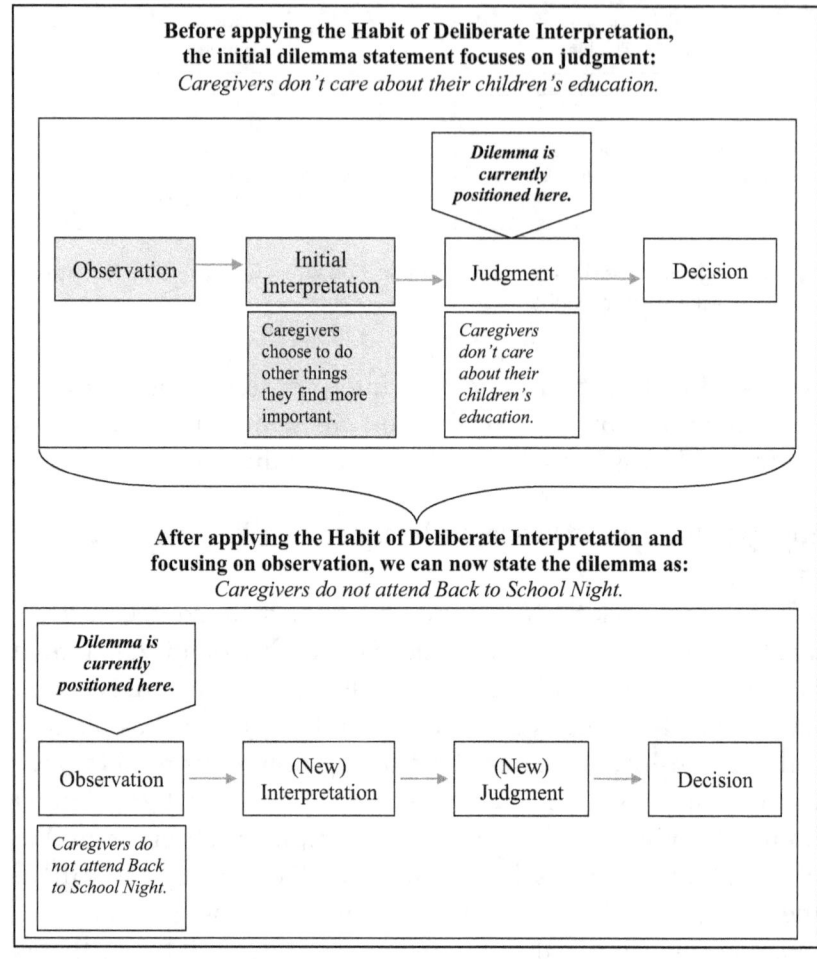

Figure 2.5 Applying the Habit of Deliberate Interpretation to the Dilemma of Caregiver Absence.

jobs, need to care for elders or young children, or have their own health concerns or limitations, or caregivers may come from a cultural background in which caregivers do not enter schools out of respect for the expertise of the professionals at school. We can then replace the initial interpretation that caregivers choose to do things they find more important with a new interpretation, which will then lead to a new judgment and a new decision about what to do. For example, we might interpret the evidence as caregivers not knowing about Back to School Night, or not understanding why it is important. Or we might actually question whether or not the event is actually important. A teacher might even interpret the evidence as a display of something they don't yet understand, judge that they should learn more, and decide to ask students and parents why there is such a low turnout. These would be actions resulting from a new interpretation and judgment of a neutral observation.

Engaging the Habits of Mind to Describe the Back-to-School Night Dilemma

After engaging all three **habits of mind** we can revise the **driving question** to: "How can I engage with caregivers about what their child is doing in my classroom?" We can then revise the **dilemma statement** to one that is more neutral such as: *Caregivers do not attend Back to School Night* (see Table 2.11). The original dilemma statement took a deficit-oriented and **externally attributed** approach to the dilemma that involved a judgment that left the teacher with no options for succeeding with the dilemma. But this revised driving question and dilemma statement put the solution for the dilemma back within reach. For example, teachers might decide to draw upon their multilingual abilities

TABLE 2.11 *Revising the Original Driving Question and Dilemma Statement after Developing all Three Habits of Mind*

	Before Applying Habits of Mind	After Applying Habits of Mind
Driving Question	"What will **make the caregivers** care more and show up to school meetings?"	"How **can I** engage with caregivers about what their child is doing **in my classroom?"**
Dilemma Statement	*Caregivers **don't care** about their children's education.*	*Caregivers **do not attend** Back to School Night.*

and social networks to find multiple ways to contact caregivers or they might leverage their instructional prowess by engaging in focus groups with their students about how to convey the information or experiences that Back to School Night is meant to convey to caregivers. Such an approach might involve building relationships with students and their families, which we discuss in Chapter 4. They might also redesign the Back to School Night experience itself, for instance by preparing a class assignment for students to give student-led classroom tours of bulletin boards and portfolio displays, or they might prepare Back to School Night family activities for students to lead. They may also consider how they could go to their students' communities rather than requiring caregivers to come to the school or change the schedule so that the event occurs on a weekend day instead of an evening.

These activities do not resolve caregivers' conflicting demands at home or reorganize the school-wide event—both **distal** dilemmas—but they can leverage students' own influence over their caregivers' attendance at Back to School Night or address other difficulties that make caregivers' attendance difficult. In taking these steps, educators show an **internal attribution** for who is responsible for solving the dilemma. They take action themselves. Now that you have seen how Ms. Nash engaged the habits of mind to revise her original driving question and dilemma statement (Table 2.9) and have seen the process again in this example (Table 2.11), try Exercise 2.6.

Conclusions About Habits of Mind

In this chapter, we discussed three **habits of mind** that will help you with identifying and addressing your teaching dilemmas. We discussed these habits and their related skills and beliefs by defining and comparing the concepts relevant to each one. Table 2.12 includes a review of each habit, including the positions that many teachers initially take when describing their persistent dilemmas (i.e., their default position), the foundational skills needed to shift those positions, and the key developments involved in moving from teachers' default positions to new positions as they master each habit.

Exercise 2.6 *Revising Your Original Driving Question and Dilemma Statement*

Go back to the driving question and dilemma statement that you formulated in Exercise 1.3.

1. *Habit of Personal Attribution*: Circle the words that can help you identify who currently has the power to solve your dilemma. Who is currently responsible for solving it?
2. *Habit of Asset Identification*: Circle any words that reflect deficit-based thinking.
3. *Habit of Deliberate Interpretation*: Circle any words that are interpretations and judgments.
4. Reword your driving question and dilemma statement in the table below by replacing the circled words. Use Tables 2.9 and 2.10 for inspiration and/or consider these tips:
   ◆ Revise the way you describe the characteristics, dispositions, or resources of students, caregivers, and communities as beneficial and necessary for resolving the dilemma.
   ◆ If your answers indicate a distal positioning or an external attribution, try stating it as proximal and internally attributed.
   ◆ Replace interpretations or judgments with empirical observations.

Your Revised Driving Question	Your Revised Dilemma Statement
The question that summarizes your dilemma description and that you will try to answer using frame shifting.	The narrowing down of the dilemma into one sentence that describes the core of the issue that you would like to improve.

TABLE 2.12 *Review of the Three Habits of Mind*

Habit of Personal Attribution

Frequent Default Position	*Shift Needed*	*Key Development*
Distal: A dilemma caused by circumstances or conditions beyond the educator's control.	**Proximal**: A dilemma within the educators' control to change.	Move from a distal positioning to a proximal positioning of the dilemma.

Frequent Default Position	*Foundational Belief Needed*	*Key Development*
External Attribution: Positioning the responsibility for solving the dilemma outside of the teacher.	**Internal Attribution**: Positioning the responsibility and capability for solving the dilemma within the teacher.	Move from an external to an internal attribution.

Habit of Asset Identification

Frequent Default Position	*Foundational Belief Needed*	*Key Development*
Deficit-Based Thinking: Identifying something lacking in students, caregivers, or communities as the reason for the dilemma.	**Asset-based Thinking**: Identifying student, caregiver, and community resources that can help solve the dilemma.	Move from deficit-based to asset-based descriptions of students, caregivers, and communities in defining and making observations about the dilemma.

Habit of Deliberate Interpretation

Frequent Default Position	*Foundational Skill Needed*	*Key Development*
A dilemma may originally be approached by starting with a **judgment**, or an internal response to an **interpretation**.	Use **observation** to describe a situation, behavior, or circumstance without interpretation or judgment.	Move from interpretations to observations in describing your dilemma. Explore alternative plausible interpretations before making judgments or drawing conclusions.

Although we have presented these developments in a rather black and white way, as either/or binaries, we understand that many teaching dilemmas have a number of causes and a number of possible solutions. We also understand that teaching is a complex and demanding endeavor and that teachers are often blamed for societal problems or held accountable for solutions that are beyond our control. We certainly do not want to make this situation worse. However, we believe that if educators can make the shifts in identifying and defining their dilemmas in the ways we have described, you may find a sense of hope to address nagging problems that may otherwise wear you down. We also believe that the key developments described above can lead to a sense of empowerment toward making substantial progress in meeting your own goals for your teaching.

For Discussion and Practice

Below you will see an imaginary conversation occurring between teachers in the teachers' lounge. Read the dialogue and then proceed with the activity.

Teacher 1: My students don't finish their homework because they don't get any help at home.[a]

Teacher 2: Well, you're lucky if that's your worst problem. Many of my students don't finish their homework because they have to take care of younger siblings or work in order to help their caregivers make ends meet.[b]

Teacher 3: I used to have problems with homework, too. But I finally just stopped giving it. No one can miss turning it in if there's nothing to turn in![c] My biggest challenge now, though, is covering all the content at the pace required to finish everything. Even if I can teach it fast enough, the students don't seem to learn it fast enough and without assigning homework, I just don't manage it.[d]

Teacher 4: I don't give homework either and I used to think that my students weren't learning enough, but then I shifted my expectations of what mastery should look like and began to design every assignment as a strategic formative assessment. I see more evidence of learning and can more quickly adjust my instruction when there's a problem, but I'm still working on creating assignments as assessments that are motivating and accurate while also introducing students to the types of words and tasks that the formal tests will ask of them. I find that part to be really hard.[e]

Teacher 1: Why don't you just use the assessments given to us by the district?

Teacher 4: I do use those but they only happen quarterly and I need feedback on nearly a daily basis. Plus, I have found that when I challenge myself to think of assignments as assessments, I leave out more of the boring and repetitive stuff and end up with assignments that students are more motivated to complete.

Teacher 5: That sounds great and I would like to do that, too, but with all of the paperwork we have to do and all of the grading that would involve, I simply don't have the time.[f]

1. To what extent does this dialogue resonate with what you yourself have thought, heard, or experienced?
2. During the conversation, each teacher mentioned a teaching dilemma, which has been labeled with a letter a–f in superscript at the end of the last sentence. Using Table 2.12 as a resource to help you, try the following:
    a. For each of the dilemmas a–f, identify the teacher's dilemma.
    b. Use the key terms from each habit of mind to characterize how the dilemma is worded (e.g., proximal, internal attribution, etc.). You can find suggested answers in the online Study Guide.
    c. Using Table 2.12, determine which key development(s), if any, you would need to make in order to revise each dilemma statement in keeping with all three habits of mind as Ms. Nash did in Table 2.9.
    d. Revise each dilemma statement accordingly, if necessary.
3. Which habits of mind do you think you already have? Why do you think so? How did you develop them?
4. Which habits of mind do you find most challenging? Explain.

Note

1 Some educators might recognize this distinction from the procedural steps involved in functional behavior assessments used to better understand and address students' challenging behaviors in school settings.

References

Aguilar, E. (2014, January 22). Spheres of control. *Education Week*. Retrieved from https://www.edweek.org/leadership/opinion-spheres-of-control/2014/01

Bandura, A. (1977). Self-efficacy: Toward a unifying theory of behavioral change. *Psychological Review, 84*(2), 191–215. https://doi.org/10.1037/0033-295X.84.2.191

Corbett, D., Wilson, B., & Williams, B. (2002). *Effort and excellence in urban classrooms: Expecting—and getting—success with all students*. Teachers College Press.

Costa, A. L., & Kallick, B. (Eds.). (2008). *Learning and leading with habits of mind*. ASCD.

Delpit, L. (2012). *Multiplication is for White people*. The New Press.

Gorski, P. C., & Pothini, S. G. (2024). *Case studies on diversity and social justice education* (3rd Ed.). Routledge.

Gregory, A., & Roberts, G. (2017). Teacher beliefs and the overrepresentation of Black students in classroom discipline. *Theory Into Practice, 56*(3), 187–194. https://doi.org/10.1080/00405841.2017.1336035

Haberman, M. (1991). The pedagogy of poverty versus good teaching. *Phi Delta Kappan, 92*(2), 81–87. https://doi.org/10.1177/003172171009200223

Kennedy, B. L., & Soutullo, O. (2018). "We can't fix that": Deficit thinking and the exoneration of educator responsibility for teaching students placed at a disciplinary alternative school. *Journal of At-Risk Issues, 21*(1), 11–23. https://eric.ed.gov/?id=EJ1187272

Kennedy, B. L., & Thornberg, R. (2018). Deduction, induction, and abduction. In U. Flick (Ed.), *The SAGE handbook of qualitative data collection* (pp. 49–64). SAGE. https://doi.org/10.4135/9781526416070

Kohn, A. (2006). *Beyond discipline* (10th Anniversary ed.). ASCD.

Ladson-Billings, G. (2007). Pushing past the achievement gap: An essay on the language of deficit. *The Journal of Negro Education, 76*(3), 316–323. Retrieved from http://www.jstor.org/stable/40034574

Ladson-Billings, G. (2017). The (R)Evolution will not be standardized. In D. Paris & H. S. Alim (Eds.), *Culturally sustaining pedagogies* (pp. 141–156). Teachers College Press.

Okonofua, J. A., & Eberhardt, J. L. (2015). Two strikes: Race and the disciplining of young students. *Psychological Science, 26*(5), 617–624. https://doi.org/10.1177/0956797615570365

Toshalis, E. (2015). *Make me! Understanding and engaging student resistance in school*. Harvard Education Press.

Tschannen-Moran, M., & Woolfolk Hoy, A. W. (2001). Teacher efficacy: Capturing an elusive construct. *Teaching and Teacher Education, 17,* 783–805. https://doi.org/10.1016/S0742-051X(01)00036-1

Valencia, R. R. (1997). *The evolution of deficit thinking*. Routledge. https://doi.org/10.4324/9780203046586

Valencia, R. R. (2010). *Dismantling contemporary deficit thinking*. Routledge. https://doi.org/10.4324/9780203853214

Weinstein, C., Curran, M., & Tomlinson-Clarke, S. (2003). Culturally responsive classroom management: Awareness into action. *Theory Into Practice, 42*(4), 269–276. https://www.jstor.org/stable/1477388

3
Frame Shifting

Once a teacher has engaged the three **habits of mind** discussed in Chapter 2 and revised their **driving question** and **dilemma statement** accordingly, they can then move on to determining in which **domain of teaching** their persistent dilemma lies, as this determination will shape an effective response. This is how we defined the three domains of teaching in Chapter 1 (see Key Figure 1):

> **Key Terms, Three Domains of Teaching**
>
> *Relationships*: Sustained patterns of interaction between the teacher and the whole class, the teacher and each individual student, and the students themselves.
>
> *Classroom Management*: Rules, routines, and teacher behaviors that structure teaching and learning.
>
> *Curriculum (Domain also includes Instruction)*: Content taught both explicitly and implicitly in the classroom through physical materials, verbal exchanges, and classroom activities.
>
> *Instruction (Domain also includes Curriculum)*: Activities designed and used to support the students' learning of the curriculum.

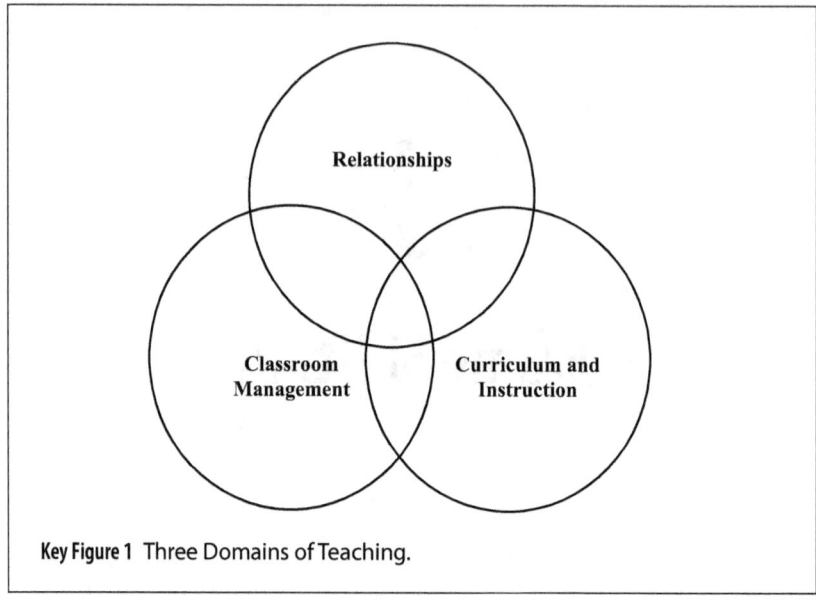

Key Figure 1 Three Domains of Teaching.

In this chapter we focus on how **frame shifting** works and will illustrate the key steps in the process using Ms. Nash's dilemma. In classrooms, the practices in each domain of teaching do not exist in isolation: All of the domains occur at the same time every minute that class is in session. Thinking of the domains in isolated ways can sharpen our focus on discrete teaching moves that impact our dilemmas, but we also need to zoom out to see how these domains relate to each other.

> **Key Terms**
>
> *Frame shifting*: The act of focusing on how each of the domains of teaching may affect a teaching dilemma and also provide strategies for a solution.

The concept of **interdependence** can assist in this zooming out process. Of course, you are familiar with the term interdependence outside of this context, but we are going to define it in a very specific way in relation to the three domains of teaching. For our purpose, interdependence refers to the impact that a teacher's approach in each domain has on the other domains (Kennedy-Lewis, 2012). For example, building and maintaining positive **relationships** with students (i.e., the relationship domain) affects, and is affected by, how a teacher approaches **curriculum and instruction** (i.e., the curriculum and instruction domain). Interdependence is represented in Key Figure 1 through the overlapping of the three circles showing each domain. Frame shifting provides an approach for exploring interdependence more precisely and systematically in addressing your dilemma.

Key Terms

Interdependence: The connected relationship that each domain of teaching has with each of the other domains. As a result of interdependence, a teacher's practices in each domain impacts the other domains. Also, a dilemma in one domain impacts, and is impacted by, issues related to the other domains.

Focus on Culture 4: How Teacher Mastery of the Interdependent Domains of Teaching Benefit Students from Marginalized Backgrounds

In a research study we conducted at an alternative school in which nearly the entire student body included youth from nondominant racial and ethnic backgrounds and youth living in poverty, we saw how teachers' implementations of all three domains of teaching affected their daily success even if they were particularly masterful in one of the domains (Kennedy, 2011; Kennedy-Lewis, 2012). That meant that teachers who knew their subject matter well and developed creative assignments for students (i.e., strong in the domain of **curriculum and instruction**) did not meet their daily goals if their **classroom management** did not support the lesson and if their **relationships** with students did not motivate the students to engage in the material. It also meant that teachers who had excellent rapport with students (i.e., strong in the domain of relationships) could succeed at keeping students quiet and

> maintaining a positive classroom climate but did not achieve student learning outcomes if the teacher was not also a master at curriculum and instruction. Teacher mastery of all three domains proved particularly critical in classrooms where students may not have experienced such mastery previously and were dependent on school for providing these experiences. In other words, these students from marginalized backgrounds may have been subjected to years of schooling in unstructured or underresourced environments, with temporary or underqualified teachers, with limited exposure to engaging and relevant school-related tasks, or with disaffected peers. These findings suggest that teachers who teach students from marginalized backgrounds in such circumstances may find particular relevance in examining the interdependence of the three domains of teaching related to their dilemmas.

In this chapter, we explain the approach of frame shifting to help you identify new solutions to your dilemma that you might not have previously considered. Remember from Chapter 1 that we defined a frame as an outline that gives focus to an object and separates what is included in a field of vision from that which is around, outside, or beyond it. Here we introduce Key Figure 3, which uses the graphic image of a frame to illustrate the frame shifting approach that we will unpack in this chapter and then continue to develop throughout the rest of the book. In Key Figure 3, the large rectangle represents the frame and includes the **driving question** which guides the teacher's inquiry as they persist towards finding a solution to their dilemma. Here, the frame is large enough to allow us to focus on the entire dilemma description, which includes everything going on at the time of the dilemma in all three domains of teaching, which are positioned within the frame. You can imagine that the habits of mind are also coexisting with the dilemma description, forming a sort of three-dimensional sphere around the figure. Keep in mind that the habits of mind are present and affect the entire situation.

What we will do in this chapter is describe the process in which we zoom the frame in more closely to examine each of the three

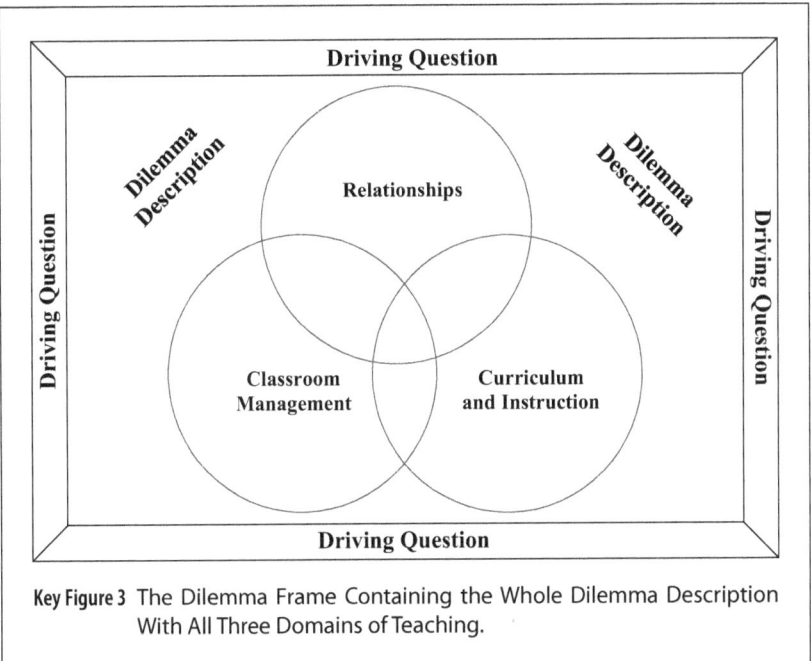

Key Figure 3   The Dilemma Frame Containing the Whole Dilemma Description With All Three Domains of Teaching.

domains of teaching one by one. The domains stay interlocking and the driving question remains, but the frame focuses in on one domain at a time (see Figure 3.1). This process allows us to look more closely at details we may not have previously considered when initially describing the dilemma. We suggest that teachers often implicitly or explicitly define, or frame, a persistent dilemma within one primary domain of teaching. Shifting the frame to focus on how that dilemma could be examined and explained within a different domain may bring forth new insights and possible approaches for addressing the dilemma successfully. This approach activates the concept of interdependence to gain new perspectives on old dilemmas. We explain this process below and provide opportunities for practice at the conclusion of the chapter.

Identifying Your Current Dilemma Framing

The first task in **frame shifting** is to identify the primary domain in which you have already framed your dilemma. If you carefully

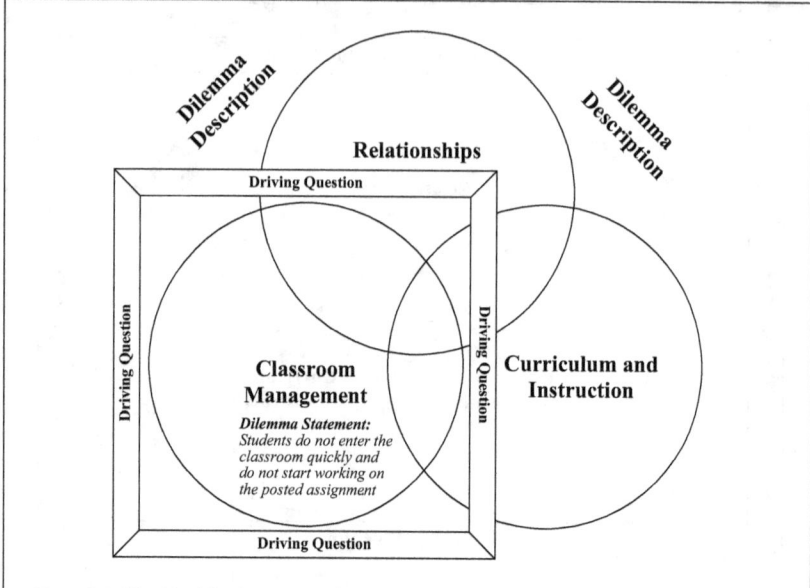

Figure 3.1 Ms. Nash's Current Dilemma Frame Zoomed in on the Domain of Classroom Management.

examine the words and concepts you used in your **dilemma description, driving question,** and **dilemma statement,** you can identify the domain in which you have framed your dilemma. To help you determine your current framing, consider the indicators for each domain that are included in Tables 3.1–3.3.

Let's consider Ms. Nash's dilemma as an example. In her dilemma description, Ms. Nash began by expressing exasperation

TABLE 3.1 *Indicators of the Domain of Relationships*

Does your dilemma involve:

- ☐ Students' perceptions about each other's backgrounds and current lives?
- ☐ Students' perceptions about each other's unique characteristics and abilities?
- ☐ Students' and teachers' responses to each other's limitations?
- ☐ How students treat each other?
- ☐ How students treat the teacher?
- ☐ The quality or nature of the communication between students?
- ☐ The quality or nature of the communication between teachers and students?
- ☐ The quality or nature of teachers' communication with students' families?
- ☐ The behavior of students' families?

TABLE 3.2 *Indicators of the Domain of Classroom Management*

Does your dilemma involve:

- ☐ Students' movements through the classroom?
- ☐ Students' use of materials?
- ☐ Unruly transition periods or transitions that take too long?
- ☐ Students talking out of turn?
- ☐ Students not complying with class rules or norms?
- ☐ Students' off-task behavior?
- ☐ How students interact during group work?

TABLE 3.3 *Indicators of the Domain of Curriculum and Instruction*

Does your dilemma involve:

- ☐ Student misunderstanding of material?
- ☐ Student disengagement?
- ☐ Non-completion of assignments?
- ☐ Student complaints that the class is boring?
- ☐ Student complaints that the class is not relevant?
- ☐ Student underperformance or failure?
- ☐ Unequal participation among students?
- ☐ Challenges related to heterogeneous student (dis)abilities?

at her students' lack of motivation during the transition into class, "I don't know what I'm doing wrong, but the kids come in loud and rowdy. They move from seat to seat, some wandering aimlessly, well past the point when the bell rings, even though I have an assignment on the board waiting for them." In Chapter 2 we described that after engaging the **Habit of Personal Attribution** to ensure the dilemma was proximal and its solution was internally attributed, and then engaging the **Habit of Deliberate Interpretation** to identify the difference between her observations and her interpretations, she revised her driving question and dilemma statement (see Table 3.4).

Categorizing her driving question and dilemma statement within the three **domains of teaching**, we can see that Ms. Nash initially framed her dilemma as a **classroom management** dilemma because she is focused on students' behavior during the classroom transition. Figure 3.1 shows how Ms. Nash's current dilemma frame is actually zoomed in to allow her to primarily see the domain of classroom management, though the other domains are

TABLE 3.4 *Ms. Nash's Driving Question and Dilemma Statement After Applying the Habits of Mind*

Ms. Nash's Driving Question	Ms. Nash's Dilemma Statement
"What will make the students quiet and efficient in finishing the warm-up so we can smoothly transition into the lesson?"	*Students enter the classroom in an unruly manner and are not interested in working on the posted assignment.*

still slightly in view. Now return to the dilemma you described in Chapter 2, and try identifying the domain in which your dilemma is currently placed by completing Exercise 3.1.

Shifting the Frame Among the Domains of Teaching

The first step in **frame shifting** is actually not to shift at all, but rather to explore the initial domain more carefully with the **driving question** in mind in order to gain new insights into why the dilemma might be occurring within that domain. Zooming in on the initial domain may produce additional **dilemma statements** which then result in **focus questions** that help teachers identify relevant teacher moves that they may not yet have tried, a process first described in Chapter 1 and shown in Key Figure 4.

When we asked Ms. Nash to try this by further exploring the initial domain of classroom management, she described how important the **habits of mind** were to helping her be open to this step. She noticed that the **Habit of Personal Attribution** motivated her to consider more useful classroom management

---

Exercise 3.1 *Identifying the Domain of Teaching in Which Your Dilemma is Placed*

1) Review the dilemma description you wrote about in Exercise 1.1 and the revised dilemma statement you wrote in Exercise 2.6.
2) Which domain of teaching have you placed your dilemma in up to this point? Explain why you think so. Use Tables 3.1–3.3 to help you.

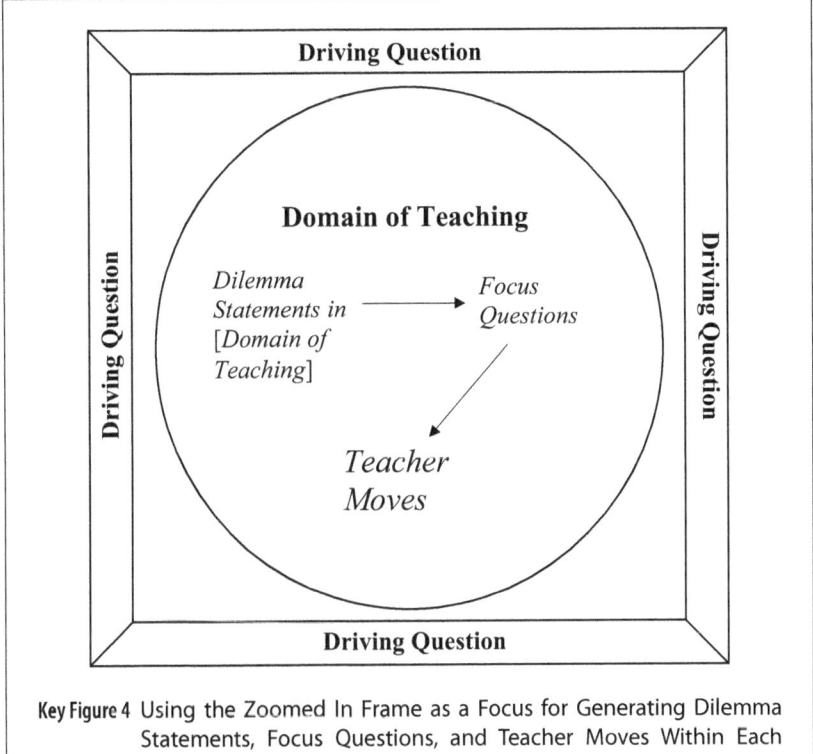

Key Figure 4 Using the Zoomed In Frame as a Focus for Generating Dilemma Statements, Focus Questions, and Teacher Moves Within Each Domain of Teaching.

strategies and different uses of the strategies she currently had. Engaging the **Habit of Deliberate Interpretation** also led her to explore more of the information in her original **dilemma description** to see if there might be additional **dilemma statements** she could generate within this domain.

We gave Ms. Nash a set of guiding questions to help her consider further issues related to her dilemma in the domain of classroom management. Although we had introduced her to the lists of indicators to first identify where she positioned her dilemma (Tables 3.1–3.3), the guiding questions reflected a more generous and robust perspective about what additional issues might be relevant in this domain (see Table 3.5). We asked her to consider her first detailed description of the dilemma with these guiding questions in mind. You can also use this table when you reframe your dilemma to this domain if it is not already framed here.

TABLE 3.5 *Guiding Questions for Reframing Using the Frame of Classroom Management*

Classroom Management
How might the dilemma involve:
☐ Procedures for how and when students should move through the classroom? ☐ Procedures for how and when students should use materials? ☐ Procedures for how and when teachers distribute and collect assignments? ☐ Procedures for how and when students should interact with each other and the teacher? ☐ Procedures for how and when students should demonstrate respect? ☐ Procedures for how and when teachers and students give and receive feedback? ☐ Explicit timing for tasks and behaviors? ☐ Teacher behaviors including nonverbal behavior, movement, and tone of voice? ☐ Clear expectations and consistent (re)enforcement? ☐ The need for teachers to de-escalate conflicts? ☐ Other: _____

The guiding questions prompted Ms. Nash to think about procedures related to seating and how students seemed not to know what they were supposed to do when they entered the classroom. She considered their use of time as well as her own use of time and how she had inconsistent expectations with it. As she pondered the guiding questions and thought back to her dilemma, she generated additional dilemma statements: *Students do not know where to sit* and *Students do not react when I give reminders about what to do*. Although she had strong feelings about the dilemma statements, she was careful to continue to engage all of the habits of mind when writing them. She noticed that these dilemma statements were more specific and precise than her first one because they focused more on the reasons behind the problem. So, we decided to replace her initial dilemma statement with these new dilemma statements that resulted from this first step in frame shifting.

At this point, we reintroduce the creation of focus questions as a way to help us home in on teacher moves that can follow from our new dilemma statements. Each dilemma statement can be reworded as a focus question that can help the teacher see more clearly what to do in order to address the driving question framed within that domain. The answers to focus questions can be found in teacher moves. The focus questions and the resulting teacher moves will all work together to ultimately address the dilemma. Translating dilemma statements within a particular domain to focus questions will allow you to: a) identify teacher moves that you might not have considered relevant in addressing your dilemma; and b) consider how these various teacher moves might be interdependent, meaning that implementing too few of them or implementing them in the wrong order might be why your dilemma persists. To generate a focus question, consider what specific question you would have to answer in order to deal with the dilemma reflected in your new dilemma statement. Table 3.6 shows the focus questions that Ms. Nash generated from her new dilemma statements. Notice how her new focus questions set her up nicely to be able to explore teacher moves, which is what we will do in Part II.

Frame Shifting to the Domain of Classroom Management

Although classroom management is the original domain in which Ms. Nash framed her dilemma, that might not be the case for you. It may be that one of the other domains is where your

TABLE 3.6 *Ms. Nash's Additional Dilemma Statements and Focus Questions in the Domain of Classroom Management*

Additional Dilemma Statements in the Domain of Classroom Management	Focus Questions
Students do not know where to sit.	How can I use and enforce a consistent seating chart?
Students do not react when I give reminders about what to do.	How can I help students remember what to do? How can I get their attention quickly when I need it? How can I project a more serious and consistent demeanor?

dilemma is currently positioned. If that is the case, then as we explain the process of frame shifting below, you will shift the frame of your dilemma to classroom management as a subsequent step. Whether you initially or later framed your dilemma in the domain of classroom management, we want to give you an opportunity to practice developing dilemma statements and focus questions that address your driving question within this frame. So, before we move on, try Exercise 3.2.

To begin frame shifting, we have first stayed within the domain in which the teacher originally positioned the dilemma and explored it further in order to set up our identification of possible teacher moves. In our grounding case, Ms. Nash first positioned her dilemma in classroom management. By using her frame to focus in on the domain more carefully, she was able to identify new focus questions which will sharpen the precision with which she chooses teacher moves in Part II. Figure 3.2 illustrates this process. Notice that even though we have zoomed in to the domain of classroom management and identified additional focus questions within it, all of the teacher moves that answer the focus question will also address her driving question, which has not changed. Ms. Nash was eager to find out what these moves might be. When we apply frame shifting to actual dilemmas, we indeed move straight from generating focus questions to identifying teacher moves, as you will see Ms. Brown and Mr. Lee do in our practice cases in Part III. However, for explanatory purposes, we want to first teach you how to shift frames across all three domains of teaching before identifying teacher moves that answer the focus questions.

Now that we have identified the primary domain in which the dilemma currently resides, we will take the next step to **frame shift** to another **domains of teaching** practice. We want to change the frame to focus on what else is happening in the classroom during the dilemma within the other two domains of teaching because we know that the domains are **interdependent**. Metaphorically, this means we have to move our zoomed in frame over to a different circle in the Venn diagram. Following our example with Ms. Nash, we now explain the frame shifting

Exercise 3.2 *Developing Dilemma Statements and Focus Questions in the Domain of Classroom Management*

1. Review the Guiding Questions in Table 3.5. What classroom management issues are occurring in your classroom during the dilemma that might be relevant for its solution?
2. Fill in the table below with additional dilemma statements and focus questions that address your dilemma just as Ms. Nash did in Table 3.6.

Additional Dilemma Statements in the Domain of Classroom Management	Focus Questions

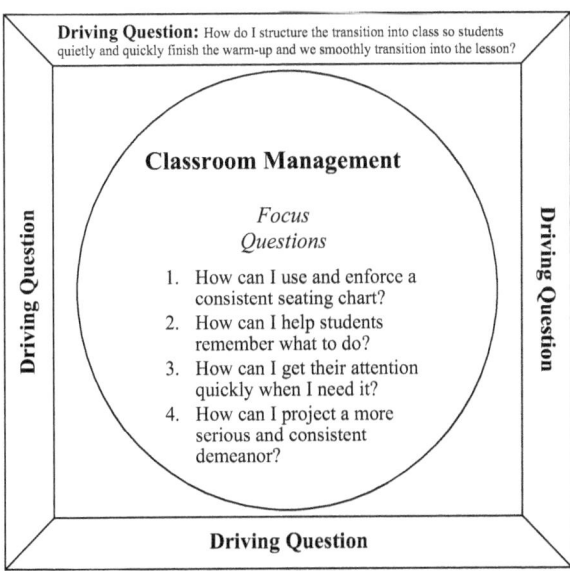

Figure 3.2 Focus Questions Ms. Nash Identified in the Domain of Classroom Management Using the Zoomed In Frame.

approach by shifting from the domain of **classroom management** to the domain of **relationships**.

Developing Dilemma Statements and Focus Questions in the Domain of Relationships

Shifting our dilemma frame from the domain of **classroom management** to the domain of **relationships** will require us to identify what is happening in the classroom during the dilemma with regard to relationships. We zoom our frame back out as in Key Figure 3, and we return to the **dilemma description**, fill in more details, and gather more information as we need it. Then, we zoom the frame back in to contain just the domain of relationships so that the frame is focusing our attention on what is going on in this domain. If your dilemma was originally positioned in the domain of relationships, you can also follow the steps that Ms. Nash will take next.

Just as we had done when focusing on the domain of classroom management, we provided Ms. Nash with a set of guiding questions to help her identify additional issues related to relationships that might be occurring at the time of the dilemma and impacting it (see Table 3.7). Reviewing the guiding questions, Ms. Nash noted that she did not know her students or their

TABLE 3.7 *Guiding Questions for Reframing to the Domain of Relationships*

Relationships

How might the dilemma involve:

- ☐ How much the teacher knows about students' lives outside of school?
- ☐ The teacher's understanding of students' cultural communication?
- ☐ The teacher's appreciation for who the students are as people?
- ☐ The teacher's understanding of, and ability to respond to, each student's social, emotional, and academic needs?
- ☐ The teacher's understanding of how students' developmental phases impact students' lives and learning?
- ☐ Students' knowledge about each other's backgrounds and current lives?
- ☐ Students' appreciations for each other's unique characteristics, abilities, and talents?
- ☐ Students' and teachers' patience with each other's limitations?
- ☐ Teachers' relationships with students' families?
- ☐ Teachers' knowledge about, and involvement in, students' communities?
- ☐ Other: _____

caregivers very well. She had only made caregiver contact to report student misbehavior and usually she did not end up actually speaking to a caregiver when she called home. While she enjoyed her students, she had never interacted with any of them outside of class and did not know much about how they spent their time, what they liked to do, or even what they thought of school. She did know that some of the students did not get along well with each other but she had not been able to focus much on improving that situation during class time.

Shifting our frame to the domain of relationships gives us more information about how to interpret the clues of student behavior in order to improve our **judgments** and **conclusions**. In Ms. Nash's dilemma, we can now recognize that during the transition period at the start of class, students jockeyed for seating positions based on who they wanted to sit next to and who they wanted to avoid. Prior to shifting the frame to focus on the domain of relationships to better understand the dilemma, Ms. Nash had only noticed that the students seemed to make a game out of choosing seats every day. At first, she attributed this behavior to their lack of seriousness about school. However, in developing the habits of mind, she had also learned to use the **Habit of Asset Identification** to see students' attributes instead of deficits. She relied upon the **Habit of Deliberate Interpretation** to withhold her conclusions that students were simply not serious about school and instead learned more about how early adolescents often focus on peer relationships during this stage of their development (Kennedy et al., 2016). She was able to integrate information about early adolescence into the next step of her reframing process. When Ms. Nash considered the quality of teacher–student and student–student relationships in her classroom, she could see how more investment in her own relationships with students and families as well as intentional activities to build a positive classroom climate might have a positive impact on the transition period. These insights resulted from shifting her frame from classroom management to relationships.

Using **frame shifting** to reframe the dilemma within the domain of relationships, she now stated the dilemma as: *Students* *do not feel comfortable sitting next to all of their other classmates and their discomfort affects their seating choices during the transition into class.* She could also state the dilemma as: *The teacher does not have strong enough connections to families and communities to provide sufficient motivation for students to comply with requests or engage in assignments, especially during highly distracting moments such as classroom transitions.* By shifting the frame from the domain of classroom management to the domain of relationships, Ms. Nash can now see how specific areas of relationship building could improve the efficiency of the transition into class. She then used these new dilemma statements to generate focus questions that she would try to answer in selecting teacher moves. You can find her new dilemma statements and focus questions listed in Table 3.8 and you can see the frame shifting process illustrated using the newly identified focus questions in Figure 3.3. Practice this step with your dilemma in Exercise 3.3.

TABLE 3.8 *The Dilemma Statements and Focus Questions Ms. Nash Generated When Frame Shifting to the Domain of Relationships*

Original Framing in Classroom Management	Frame Shifting to Relationships	
Ms. Nash's Original Dilemma Statement	Ms. Nash's Reframed Dilemma Statement	Focus Question
Students do not enter the classroom quickly and do not start working on the posted assignment.	*Students do not feel comfortable sitting next to all of their other classmates and their discomfort affects their seating choices during the transition into class.*	How do I create a positive classroom climate where students feel supported and motivated to work together toward successful completion of the warm-up activity?
	The teacher does not have strong enough connections to families and communities to provide sufficient motivation for students to comply with requests or engage in assignments, especially during highly distracting moments such as classroom transitions.	How can I make positive and meaningful connections with families and communities?

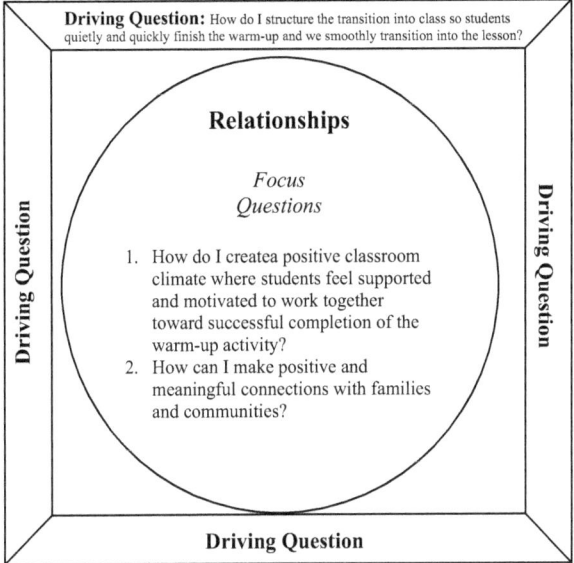

Figure 3.3 Focus Questions Ms. Nash Identified in the Domain of Relationships Using the Zoomed In Frame.

Exercise 3.3 *Developing Dilemma Statements and Focus Questions in the Domain of Relationships*

1. Review the Guiding Questions in Table 3.7. What relationship issues are occurring in your classroom during the dilemma that might be relevant for its solution?
2. Fill in the table below with additional dilemma statements and focus questions that address your dilemma just as Ms. Nash did in Table 3.8.

Additional Dilemma Statements in the Domain of Relationships	Focus Questions

Developing Dilemma Statements and Focus Questions in the Domain of Curriculum and Instruction

So far, we have discussed how further exploration into the domain in which your dilemma is first placed can help you identify new **dilemma statements** and **focus questions** within that domain. We have then shown how frame shifting to another **domain of teaching** provides additional dilemma statements and focus questions to help you answer your **driving question** using a different focus. Now we look at how this process can unfold within the **domain of curriculum and instruction**. We define curriculum and instruction as one domain because curriculum and instruction are enacted together. However, we can sometimes further sharpen our focus if we consider them separately. When we separate them in this book, we will use the phrase, "the focus of [curriculum or instruction] within the domain of curriculum and instruction." So, if we are looking at curriculum for example, we will say "the focus of curriculum within the domain of curriculum and instruction." To further explore whether curriculum and instruction is your original domain, or to make a shift to this domain, consider the guiding questions in Table 3.9. Ms. Nash taught physical science, a subject in which more state standards existed than students could reasonably master in one school year. Like many teachers, she chose which material to focus on. Shifting the focus to curriculum within the domain of curriculum and instruction, we examine how these choices might have affected the dilemma. For this step, we return to the **dilemma description** for further information.

When we met Ms. Nash, she and her students were in the middle of a project in which the students were to build their own solar cars. As a beginning teacher, Ms. Nash explained that her ambition and naivete often resulted in her biting off more than she could chew. She would underestimate the time it took to prepare lessons, spending long hours late into the night working at her school. Ms. Nash did not know how long the unit on solar energy would take to complete and she struggled with organizing

TABLE 3.9 *Guiding Questions for Reframing to the Domain of Curriculum and Instruction*

Curriculum

How might the dilemma involve:

- ☐ Conceptual connections from one part of the lesson to another?
- ☐ Content that interests students?
- ☐ Content that builds upon students' funds of knowledge?
- ☐ Content that taps into students' frames of reference?
- ☐ Hidden curriculum that the teacher has not considered?
- ☐ An appropriate level of difficulty in content knowledge?
- ☐ An appropriate level of difficulty in reading comprehension and writing requirements?
- ☐ Development and maintenance of students' knowledge about their own and other cultures?
- ☐ Opportunities for students to develop critical thinking and social consciousness and take social action?
- ☐ Other: _____

Instruction

How might the dilemma involve:

- ☐ The necessary/appropriate amount of direct instruction?
- ☐ Gradual release for students to receive scaffolded support that leads to successful independent work?
- ☐ Meaningful and equitable participation among students?
- ☐ Interdependent collaboration and/or social learning?
- ☐ A variety of activities and ways for students to demonstrate knowledge and skills?
- ☐ The proper amount of feedback?
- ☐ The accessibility of sufficient assistance?
- ☐ Other: _____

materials and effectively developing students' content knowledge throughout the project. Since her dilemma focused on the transition into the class, we asked Ms. Nash which part of her curriculum she focused on at the start of class. She explained that she always had a warm-up prompt posted as a PowerPoint slide on the screen for students to answer in blank journals upon entering class. The first day we observed Ms. Nash's class to learn more about her dilemma, the prompt on the slide was:

> **Ms. Nash's Warm-up Prompt**
>
> Copy the question and write the answer in a complete sentence. *Yesterday was global Antarctica Day. This continent is still very wild and host to many valuable resources including fish, ice, coal, meteorites, and medicinal plant organisms. In your notebooks, rank these resources from #1 to #5 in terms of value to you, and explain why you chose your #1.*

In thinking through the conceptual connections between the warm-up and the solar car project, Ms. Nash realized that students could not relate the curricular topics in the warm-up either to the rest of the class content or to their everyday lives. Even if students were to follow the classroom **routine** and procedures to quickly take their seats and open their journals, Ms. Nash could not explain why she thought her students might have opinions about whether meteorites were more important than coal. Shifting our focus to curriculum within the domain of curriculum and instruction helped us to see how Ms. Nash's curricular choices might have contributed to students' disengaged behaviors during the transition into class.

Reframing the dilemma as related to curriculum, she could now state the dilemma as: *Students do not understand the content of the warm-up assignments*. She could also state the dilemma as: *Students do not relate to the content of the warm-up assignments*. Both of these reframed **dilemma statements** now point toward the importance of changing the warm-up assignments to make them more accessible, relevant, and engaging. Again, by shifting the frame, this time to curriculum within the domain of curriculum and instruction, she reframed the dilemma in ways that might lead us to new insights about how to address the situation using curricular changes.

We can also shift the focus to instruction within the same domain. When Ms. Nash did so, it helped her think about the role that having students write down the question and answer to the warm-up played in her daily goals for the lesson. Was it important for students to copy the question? Did they need to write complete sentences in their answers? What did they then do with those answers? Was there a legitimate use for their answers in the rest of the class? Did they share their answers or build upon them in some way? How did Ms. Nash provide feedback on the warm-ups? Did the warm-ups provide authentic information as formative assessments?

When she considered these questions, Ms. Nash noticed that the warm-ups played no authentic role in the class and that she was actually using them to fill time while she took attendance. When she articulated that fact, she immediately saw that if she did not care about the content of the warm-up or students' responses, then the students would not care either. It made sense that students lacked motivation to get to work. We could now state the dilemma as: *Students need more assistance to complete the warm-up activities*. We could also state the dilemma as: *The teacher does not use the warm-ups during the rest of the class or give students consistent feedback about their performance on the warm-ups*. Shifting her dilemma frame to the domain of curriculum and instruction, Ms. Nash saw how her instructional decisions came into play in this classroom management dilemma. She then identified new **focus questions** to go along with these new dilemma statements. Using **frame shifting**, she could now consider how changes in her instruction might improve the transition period. You can find her new dilemma statements and focus questions listed in Table 3.10 and you can see the frame shifting process illustrated using the newly identified focus questions in Figure 3.4. Practice this step with your dilemma in Exercise 3.4.

Practicing Frame Shifting With Examples From Different Educational Levels

Ms. Nash originally framed her dilemma in the domain of **classroom management** since it related to students' transitions into the classroom. Using guiding questions from other domains helped her see ways she could shift the frame of her dilemma to the domains of **relationships** or **curriculum and instruction**. Table 3.11 presents a recap of how this reframing process helped Ms. Nash explore other possible sources of her original

TABLE 3.10 *The Dilemma Statements and Focus Questions Ms. Nash Generated When Frame Shifting to the Domain of Curriculum and Instruction*

Original Framing in Classroom Management	Frame Shifting to Curriculum and Instruction	
Ms. Nash's Original Dilemma Statement	Ms. Nash's Reframed Dilemma Statement	Ms. Nash's Reframed Focus Question
Students do not enter the classroom quickly and do not start working on the posted assignment.	*Students do not understand the content of the warm-up assignments.*	How do I create warm-up assignments that are accessible?
	Students do not relate to the content of the warm-up assignments.	How do I create warm-up assignments that are relatable?

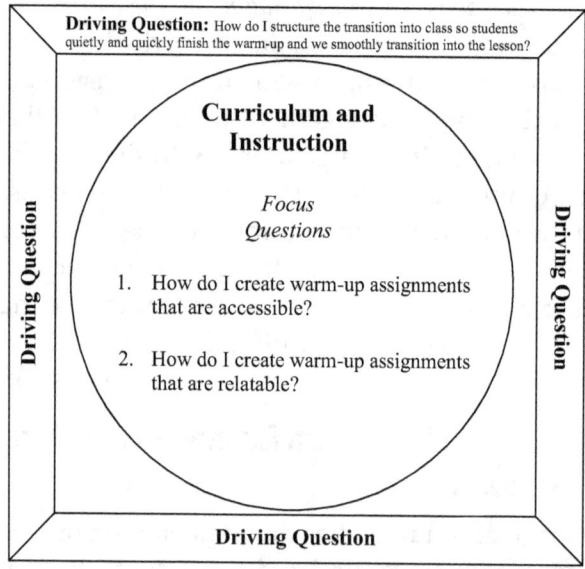

Figure 3.4 Focus Questions Ms. Nash Identified in the Domain of Curriculum and Instruction Using the Zoomed In Frame.

Exercise 3.4 *Developing Dilemma Statements and Focus Questions in the Domain of Curriculum and Instruction*

1. Review the Guiding Questions in Table 3.9. What issues are occurring in your classroom during the dilemma related to curriculum and instruction that might be relevant for its solution?
2. Fill in the table below with additional dilemma statements and focus questions that address your dilemma just as Ms. Nash did in Table 3.10.

Additional Dilemma Statements in the Domain of Curriculum and Instruction	Focus Questions

dilemma. She was able to generate new dilemma statements in these domains which she then used to write additional focus questions. When we first met Ms. Nash, she had focused only on students' unwillingness to sit down and get to work. She had nearly given up on believing that she could address the situation effectively. That meant that her **teacher efficacy** was low and when teachers' self-efficacy is low, teachers are more prone to **deficit thinking** and to concluding that the problem resides with the students and the solution resides with stricter and harsher punishments. However, when she read all of these new focus questions generated using the frame shifting approach (illustrated in Figure 3.5), Ms. Nash experienced a renewed sense of self-efficacy because she saw additional possibilities for solving the dilemma, possibilities that were **proximal** and seemed within reach. She noticed how answering the focus questions by identifying teacher moves would then help her answer her **driving question**. We explore these possible teacher moves in Part II.

TABLE 3.11 *Reframing Ms. Nash's Dilemma*

Dilemma Statement	Domain in Which Dilemma is Currently Framed	Guiding Questions from Other Domains	One Plausible Reframing of the Dilemma Statement	Example Focus Question Generated From New Dilemma Statement
Students do not enter the classroom quickly and start working on the posted assignment.	Classroom Management (Students' movement in the classroom)	*Relationships*: How does the teacher use the transition between classes to build relationships with students by asking about their lives?	*Relationships*: The teacher does not have strong enough connections to students to provide sufficient student motivation.	*Relationships*: How do I create a positive classroom climate where students feel supported and motivated to work together toward successful completion of the warm-up activity?
		Curriculum: What are the conceptual connections between the posted assignment and the rest of the lesson?	*Curriculum*: Students do not understand the content of the warm-up assignments.	*Curriculum*: How do I create warm-up assignments that are accessible?

In Exercises 3.5–3.8 we will use the same process Ms. Nash engaged in as we practice **frame shifting** with new dilemmas. We will provide eight example dilemma statements, two from each of the following educational levels: primary school (Exercises 3.5a and 3.5b), middle school (3.6a and 3.6b), high school (3.7a and 3.7b), and postsecondary education (3.8a and 3.8b). The first example from each educational level (labeled with an 'a') is presented here in the chapter, and its suggested answers, along with an additional example (labeled with a 'b') and suggested answers, are available in the online Study Guide. Each of the **dilemma statements** is initially positioned within one **domain of teaching**.

Frame Shifting ◆ 93

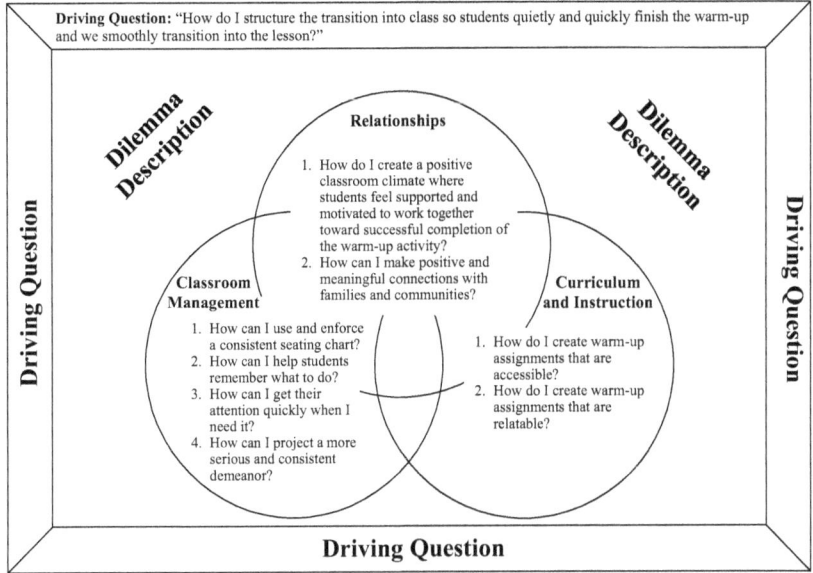

Figure 3.5 Focus Questions Ms. Nash Generated in All Three Domains of Teaching Using the Frame Shifting Approach.

Exercise 3.5a

Reframing a Primary School Dilemma Example #1

Dilemma Statement	Domain in Which Dilemma is Currently Framed	Guiding Questions	Plausible Reframing of the Dilemma Statement	Focus Question
During center time for Language Arts, the group assigned to independent reading spends more time whispering to each other than reading their books.				

Exercise 3.6a

Reframing a Middle School Dilemma Example #1

Dilemma Statement	Domain in Which Dilemma is Currently Framed	Guiding Questions	Plausible Reframing of the Dilemma Statement	Focus Question
Students struggle with Algebra because they do not know fractions or remember their multiplication tables.				

Exercise 3.7a

Reframing a High School Dilemma Example #1

Dilemma Statement	Domain in Which Dilemma is Currently Framed	Guiding Questions	Plausible Reframing of the Dilemma Statement	Focus Question
Many of my students do not complete homework.				

For each dilemma statement, use Tables 3.1–3.3 to identify the domain in which the dilemma is currently framed. Next, identify at least one guiding question from each of the remaining domains that might help the teacher explore the **interdependence** of the domains and alternative framing of the dilemma. You may use the questions from Tables 3.5–3.7 or create your own, as long as they are consistent with all of the **habits of mind** discussed in Chapter 2 (see Table 2.11). Then, create a plausible reframing of

Exercise 3.8a					
Reframing a Postsecondary Dilemma Example #1					
Dilemma Statement	Domain in Which Dilemma is Currently Framed	Guiding Questions	Plausible Reframing of the Dilemma Statement	Focus Question
When students are placed in heterogeneous groups for projects, they do not know how to collaborate effectively. Especially students from nondominant backgrounds complain that their contributions are not accepted and respected.					

the dilemma statement from a different domain. Finally, generate a **focus question** based on this dilemma statement that the teacher could use to identify teacher moves that we will discuss in Part II. For the first dilemma in each education level (labeled 'a'), you see a blank chart that shows which information to discuss and fill in. Blank charts for the second dilemma in each educational level (labeled 'b') as well as suggested answers for all eight dilemmas can be found in the online Study Guide. Refer back to Table 3.11 to see how we modeled this exercise using Ms. Nash's dilemma as an example.

The exercises above helped you practice the process of identifying the **domain of teaching** a dilemma is in, then frame

Exercise 3.9 *Focus Questions: Fill in your* **driving question** *at the top of the frame. Then, list the* **focus questions** *you generated within each of the three domains of teaching.*

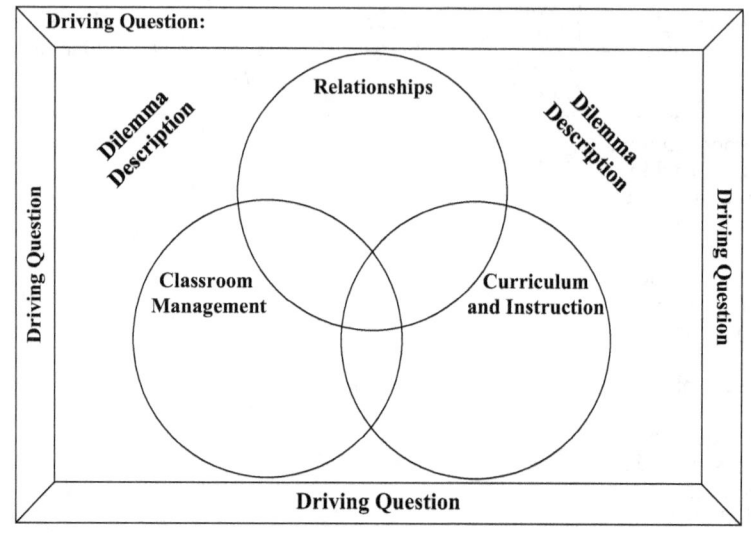

shifting to other domains of teaching and identifying new **dilemma statements** and **focus questions**. Now, to prepare to address your own focus questions as you read Part II, complete Exercise 3.9.

By engaging in **frame shifting**, we can see how the domains of teaching are **interdependent**. Reframing offers us new insights into how a range of teacher moves related to all three domains might help in addressing teaching dilemmas. We hope the process of engaging the habits of mind and shifting the frame to each of the three domains of teaching gives you renewed hope and energy to persist in addressing, and ultimately solving, your **driving question** and other **proximal** teaching dilemmas as they arise.

For Discussion and Practice

Read the following five dilemma descriptions, then proceed by answering the questions below:

A. When I ask questions to the class for discussion, no one wants to answer. If I wait a few seconds, then it's always the same people who chime in.
B. I get so frustrated because we already learned about how to write a paragraph and now that we are focused specifically on thesis statements, the students act like they have never learned about writing structure before. We have made color-coded outlines, played matching games, and even debated various paragraph constructions for clarity. They could all write a basic, logical paragraph. But now they seem so thrown off by the idea of a thesis statement that I'm lucky to get them to write a complete sentence.
C. Some of the students are so mean to each other that I know they must be hurting each other's feelings. But they just trade insults as if their words don't matter at all. When I try to intervene, they brush me off and say that the insults don't matter to them.
D. I tell the students quite explicitly the type of support I will provide, when I will be available, and when I will be unavailable, but quite a few of them are still contacting me for extra help outside of these periods of availability.
E. If I walk by one more laptop and see Snapchat, WhatsApp, Facebook, Instagram, TikTok, or YouTube open during class activities, I think I'm going to scream.

For each of the dilemma descriptions above:

1. Narrow the dilemma description to a dilemma statement. Be sure to apply all three habits of mind.

2. Identify the primary domain of teaching within which it is currently framed and explain which indicators suggest this domain.
3. Speculate about how at least one other domain of teaching could be used to reframe the dilemma in a way that would suggest different areas of focus for addressing the dilemma.
    a. Restate the dilemma in that domain.
    b. Articulate a focus question for your new dilemma statement.
4. Discuss how the concept of interdependence might relate to each dilemma.

References

Kennedy, B. L. (2011). Teaching disaffected middle school students: How classroom dynamics shape students' experiences. *Middle School Journal*, 42(4), 32–42. https://doi.org/10.1080/00940771.2011.11461772

Kennedy, B. L., Brinegar, K., Hurd, E., & Harrison, L. (2016). Synthesizing middle grades research on cultural responsiveness: The importance of a shared conceptual framework. *Middle Grades Review*, 2(3), Article 2 (20 pages). http://scholarworks.uvm.edu/mgreview/vol2/iss3/2

Kennedy-Lewis, B. L. (2012). What happens after students are expelled? Understanding teachers' successes and failures at one alternative middle school. *Teachers College Record*, 114(12), 1–38. https://doi.org/10.1177/016146811211401207

Part II

The Domains of Teaching

In Part I, you learned about **habits of mind** and **frame shifting**, the fundamentals of the frame shifting approach. You developed the skills needed for the approach by completing the exercises along the way, which culminated at the end of Chapter 3 as you listed of all of your **focus questions** for each domain using Key Figure 3.

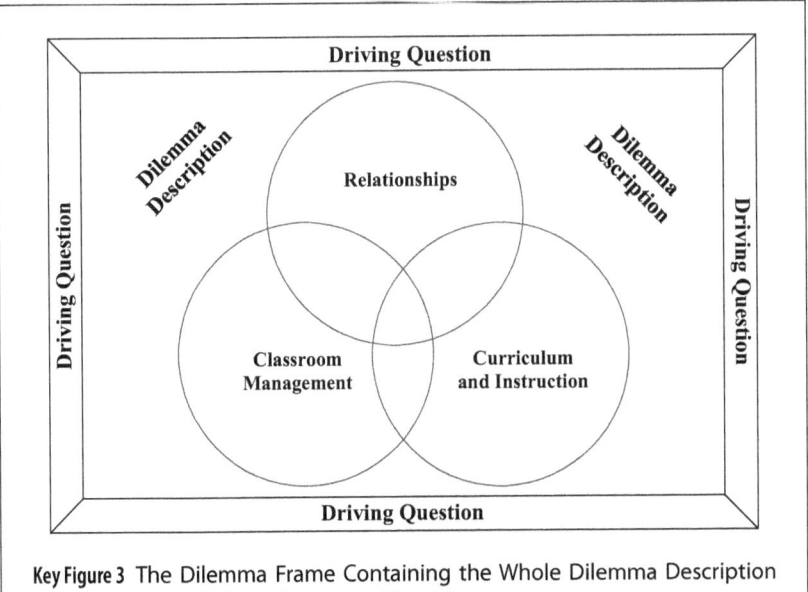

Key Figure 3 The Dilemma Frame Containing the Whole Dilemma Description With All Three Domains of Teaching.

DOI: 10.4324/9781003301806-5

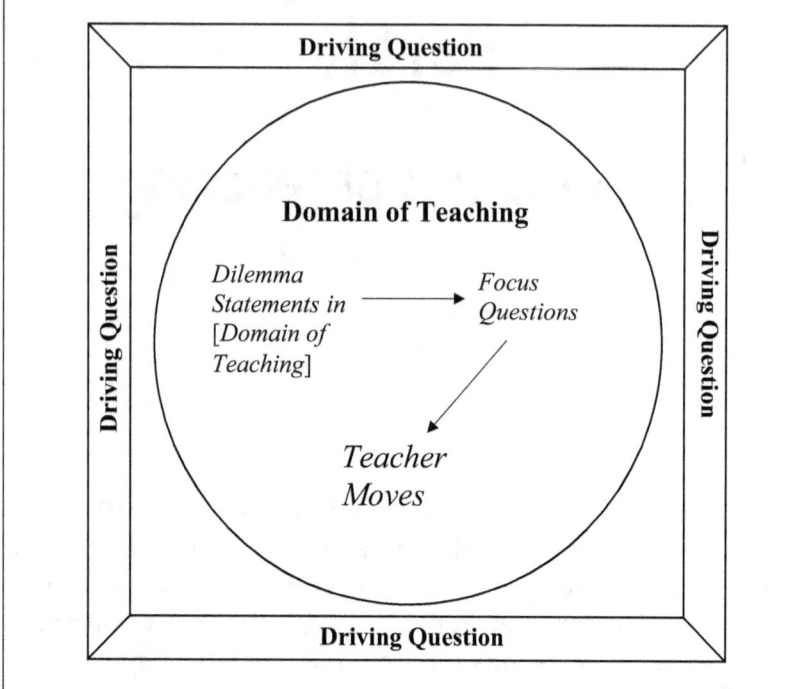

Key Figure 4 Using the Zoomed In Frame as a Focus for Generating Dilemma Statements, Focus Questions, and Teacher Moves Within Each Domain of Teaching.

As shown in Key Figure 4, the next step after identifying **dilemma statements** and focus questions within each domain is to identify teacher moves that answer your focus questions in that domain. In Part II, we look at teacher moves within each domain and explore how shifting frames across the **domains of teaching** can bring new teacher moves to bring to bear on the dilemma and answer your **driving question**.

In Chapter 4, we look at the domain of relationships, exploring how a dilemma might relate to teacher–student, teacher–class, or student–student interactions and what a teacher might do to develop these relationships. In Chapter 5, we name and describe critical components of classroom management and consider how different teacher moves used separately or in combination can have an impact on our dilemmas. Finally, in Chapter 6, we discuss curriculum and instruction, handling each of these two subtopics separately in the chapter, which allows us to consider them independently while acknowledging that they are always occurring in relation to each other. As we first showed in Key Figure 2 in the Part I overview, the three domains of teaching are **interdependent**, meaning that moves suggested in one domain will affect, and be affected by, moves suggested in another. We will point out examples of this interdependence along the way. Each domain of teaching is a vast topic in and of itself, with hundreds of publications dedicated to it. We strategically select topics for discussion in each domain by using Ms. Nash's grounding case along with our previous experience and existing literature as a guide. In this part, we maintain a focus on teachers' success with marginalized student groups. By the end of Part II, you should be able to:

- Name and explain teacher moves in all three domains that may be relevant for answering your driving question.
- Identify and explain particular considerations for dilemmas related to teaching marginalized students.
- Apply the concept of interdependence in the successful selection and implementation of teacher moves across domains.

4
Frame Shifting to the Domain of Relationships

In this chapter, we present evidence-informed ways that teachers can make progress on dilemmas that they have (re)framed in the **domain of relationships**. We are defining this domain as: Sustained patterns of interaction between the teacher and the whole class, the teacher and each individual student, and the students themselves. As all teachers know, relationships affect the social climate of the classroom and provide an important foundation for dealing with other dilemmas, such as those related to **classroom management**. To create optimal learning conditions, the teacher needs to have positive relationships with all students and the students need to trust each other and feel safe in the classroom. Remember that dilemmas **frame shifted** to the domain of relationships have to do with the issues raised by the guiding questions first shared in Chapter 3 and reproduced in Table 4.1.

In Chapter 3, Ms. Nash first framed her dilemma about starting class as a classroom management dilemma but then frame shifted it to the other domains as well. With this reframing, she

TABLE 4.1 *Guiding Questions for Reframing to the Domain of Relationships*

Relationships

How might the dilemma involve:

- ☐ How much the teacher knows about students' lives outside of school?
- ☐ The teacher's understanding of students' cultural communication?
- ☐ The teacher's appreciation for who the students are as people?
- ☐ The teacher's understanding of, and ability to respond to, each student's social, emotional, and academic needs?
- ☐ The teacher's understanding of how students' developmental phases impact students' lives and learning?
- ☐ Students' knowledge about each other's backgrounds and current lives?
- ☐ Students' appreciations for each other's unique characteristics, abilities, and talents?
- ☐ Students' and teachers' patience with each other's limitations?
- ☐ Teachers' relationships with students' families?
- ☐ Teachers' knowledge about, and involvement in, students' communities?
- ☐ Other: _____

TABLE 4.2 *Ms. Nash's Dilemma Statements and Focus Questions in the Domain of Relationships*

Ms. Nash's Driving Question: "How do I structure the transition into class so students quietly and quickly finish the warm-up and we smoothly transition into the lesson?"

Ms. Nash's Dilemma Statements in the Domain of Relationships	Focus Questions
Students do not feel comfortable sitting next to all of their other classmates and their discomfort affects their seating choices during the transition into class.	How do I create a positive classroom climate where students feel supported and motivated to work together toward successful completion of the warm-up activity?
The teacher does not have strong enough connections to families and communities to provide sufficient motivation for students to comply with requests or engage in assignments, especially during highly distracting moments such as classroom transitions.	How can I make positive and meaningful connections with families and communities?

identified new **dilemma statements** and **focus questions** that would lead her search for relevant teacher moves that could answer her **driving question**. Table 4.2 shows the dilemma statements and focus questions she identified in the domain of relationships. The next step is to identify the teacher moves that will answer her focus questions. You will do the same with the focus questions you listed in the domain of relationships in Exercises 3.3 and 3.9.

If the original framing of your dilemma was in the domain of relationships, then perhaps you have one student or a small group of students that continually pose a challenge. As Eric Toshalis (2015) stated when writing to teachers about students' challenging behaviors, "You've got to connect to correct" (p. 255). The **Habit of Asset Identification** can be especially helpful in making connections with hard-to-reach students. We encourage you to engage this habit by considering students' strengths as you read about the topics discussed in this chapter, which we think apply to dilemmas that are both initially framed as well as re-framed in the domain of relationships.

Improving Teacher–Student Relationships

Students are affected by high-quality **relationships** with their teachers even up through the university level. Therefore, addressing this domain can potentially bring important results to many dilemmas. Students who report having positive interactions with teachers believe that they can succeed in school (Hargrave et al., 2016), and this affirmation is especially important among marginalized students who may have a history of struggles both inside and outside the classroom (Kennedy-Lewis, 2013, 2015; Milner, 2013; Toshalis, 2015). Positive teacher–student relationships impact student engagement and student achievement (Roorda et al., 2011). We know that some students adjust their level of engagement depending on their relationships with their teacher. They work for teachers they like and who make them feel cared for (Cothran & Ennis, 2000; Cushman, 2003; Kennedy et al., 2016; Murphy et al., 2013). When specifically discussing students from nondominant racial groups, Delpit (2012) stated, "It is the quality of the relationship that allows a teacher's push for excellence...[M]any of our children of color don't learn from a teacher as much as for a teacher" (p. 86). Students may not be willing to put in extra effort to comply with the teacher's requests if they do not value their relationship with the teacher. For some students, having trust in a teacher is a prerequisite for academic engagement and learning (Gregory & Ripski, 2008).

With students who seem especially hard to reach, we encourage a generous application of the **Habit of Deliberate Interpretation**. We discussed the importance of moving from **judgment** to **observation** in developing the Habit of Deliberate Interpretation and in stating the dilemma neutrally. Separating out observable behaviors from the teacher's **interpretations** of students' intents or potential causes and refraining from judgment can create the space necessary to give these strategies the best opportunity for success. That means that when students behave in ways that offend or annoy the teacher, or somehow violate the teacher's boundaries, the first step the teacher can take is to pause and ask, "What do I observe here?" That pause provides the possibility for the teacher to develop relationships using the tools we discuss next.

What can a teacher do to improve relationships? Showing care is both a strategy and a disposition that can have a big impact. Research tells us that a good balance of warmth, having instructional agency in the classroom, having high academic expectations, providing enough academic support, and developing and maintaining connection and communication with families lead to positive teacher–student relationships (Alder, 2002; Ross et al., 2008; Wubbels et al., 2016). We will look at each of these attributes separately in order to create a clear picture of what each one means, and we will discuss the balance that is required among them to lead to the good relationships that teachers and students both desire. Throughout this section, we will also hear from the US middle and high school students who participated in Kathleen Cushman's (2003; Cushman & Rogers, 2008) studies about how teachers can develop these relationships. So far, we have distinguished between the teacher's relationship with a whole class and the teacher's relationships with individual students. These overlap, of course. We begin by discussing what research tells us about relationships with individual students and we connect our discussion to whole-class relationships within each subsection below and in a dedicated section called "Teacher–Class Relationships" later in the chapter.

Warmth and Friendliness

Teachers show warmth and friendliness through positive contact moments when they may ask students' opinions, explore their ideas, use their names with positive tones, ask about a topic of importance to the student, or appropriately use nonverbal behaviors such as eye contact and touch (Korthagen et al., 2014). There are endless ways that teachers can show warmth to students depending on what suits both student and teacher. It could be a simple smile and high five, kneeling down next to a student's desk while checking an assignment, or giving authentic praise during class. Teachers can consider their own skill sets, preferences, and capacities in choosing strategies to develop and use. An important consideration is how authentic these behaviors are to who the teacher is as a person. Students report seeing through teachers' efforts if they are not authentic. As one student stated, "It doesn't work when a teacher tries to force the connection or tries too hard to relate to us. When they say, 'I understand what you're going through,' we know they don't" (Cushman, 2003, p. 1). The key is to use authentic approaches to make connections with students and to do that before any potential **loaded moments** may arise (Kennedy & Junker, 2023).

> **Focus on Culture 5: Culturally Based Communication and Teacher–Student Relationships**
>
> Teachers and students may have different cultural communication styles, which can make **relationship** development even more challenging. Nieto and Bode (2017) remind us that culture is not a static or monolithic set of traits that can be easily generalized. Instead, cultural practices can be enacted at certain times and places and may change depending on

circumstances. It is useful for teachers to be able to recognize situations where there may be a conflict between students' cultural practices, norms, and values and those of the teacher or school. Ideally, you will be able to identify these potential conflicts without stereotyping students or making false assumptions about them. Honoring and bridging cultural divides can help students feel seen, understood, and respected. But stereotyping incorrectly can have the opposite effect.

Here are some examples of how culturally based communication may impact teacher–student relationships. Roland Tharp (1989) described possible mismatches in wait time, with students from more reflection-oriented cultural backgrounds requiring more wait time before answering the teacher's questions. A teacher's inadequate wait time may lead to such students being repeatedly left out of whole-class instruction, which could cause alienation. John D'Amato (1988) found that teachers of Native Hawaiian students needed to know that some of their students who came from collectivist cultures did not want to compete with peers, be singled out from the group, or be expected to report on a peer's misbehaviors because this would be viewed as betrayal. Students resisted teachers who did not have this knowledge or these competencies. Sonia Nieto and Patty Bode (2017) gave an example of a new teacher of Puerto Rican students who did not know that these students used nonverbal nose wrinkling to express confusion, which this teacher missed until they learned about this cultural communication. Conversely, Michele Foster (1997) described teachers' appropriate uses of African American preaching styles in certain parts of a lesson, which created resonance between culturally similar students and teachers.

When confronted with cultural differences, it is easy to interpret the differences as a personal slight or a sign of intentional disrespect (Marcucci & Elmesky, 2023). Consequently, these sorts of mismatches between teachers' and students' cultural styles and expectations can cause real rifts in classroom relationships. Such rifts may ultimately culminate in student resistance and defiance if teachers impose their perspectives rather than being culturally responsive (Nieto & Bode, 2017;

Toshalis, 2015). It is not necessary for you to have the same cultural background as your students in order to support alignment in communication, but just as we first discussed in Chapter 2 in relation to developing the **Habit of Deliberate Interpretation**, it is necessary to know enough about your students' cultural communication styles to be able to detect, **interpret**, and build on them appropriately.

Teachers can get to know more about students' styles by spending time in locations or at events that are important to them, such as a Black church or ethnically-focused place of worship in the students' community, and then discussing their **observations** with students. During such conversations, it is important that teachers convey a sense of nonjudgmental curiosity, position students as experts, and create space for negotiating a shared set of classroom expectations based on mutual understanding and respect for difference. This does not mean that the teacher has to adopt a communication style similar to that of an African American pastor if students are most familiar with that style—your efforts should reflect who you are at your core and what you are able to authentically do with your students—it means that the teacher communicates directly, knowledgably, and respectfully with students about differences so that each party can participate in negotiating shared classroom norms. Having knowledge about cultural communication is a first step in developing a style that works for you and your students. Misalignments in cultural communication can break down trust, whereas agreements about cultural communication can build a sense of mutual understanding in teacher–student relationships.

Some teachers choose to greet students individually and by name when they enter the classroom, which sets the tone of connection and also gives the teacher information about how each student is doing and what sort of support or accommodation each student might need that day. For example, when Ms. Nash was working on her dilemma, she decided to try this approach as part of building stronger relationships that could motivate students to successfully navigate the transition into class. As she greeted each student by the door, we witnessed her learn which students were not feeling well, who had not slept well, or who had just had a test. She also paid more attention to physical changes that might be important to students, like who had done their hair differently, and she listened to students share about important events in their lives.

Teachers using this strategy can also take this opportunity to follow up with students about things the teacher knows are important to the student, such as sharing a resource that the student might be interested in, remembering to comment about a task the teacher promised to accomplish, or asking students about recent extracurricular events. In these small connections, the teacher builds a positive climate that supports learning and motivates students to engage and respond. For some students, this may be the only time during the day that a teacher individually connects with them. You may notice that this strategy does not directly address Ms. Nash's reframed dilemma, which is about students' relationships with each other or Ms. Nash's relationships with families, but Ms. Nash's contribution to building a positive climate does set the scene for improved peer relationships. Ms. Nash was connecting before she was correcting.

Getting to Know Students Well

It is easier to be warm and friendly when teachers know their students well, when they really understand what makes them tick as people. Later we will discuss knowing about students' lives outside of school and how that can help teachers build relationships with students, but here we mean just really knowing *them*. What are their strengths and how can you build on those? What are the things they need help with, both academically as well as socially, personally, and interpersonally? We know that teachers are tasked with supporting students' cognitive development and academic mastery and that teachers cannot be all things to all students. But having insight into who students are as humans can help students feel seen and known, which not only supports positive teacher–student **relationships** but are also pillars of motivation (Deci & Ryan, 2008). When teachers know their students well, they will be more in tune when things are "off" and better able to **interpret** students' intentions rather than just their behaviors. This is particularly important with students who are hard for you to reach. Those students may behave in ways that seem unpleasant or that cause you to withdraw or disengage. But persisting in really getting to know these students who seem hardest to know can reap particular benefits.

Part of getting to know students well is also understanding where they are developmentally. Students have individual experiences, skills, and cognitive and emotional needs. At the same time, human development follows general trends that affect all students in some way even if their individual developmental trajectories vary by age. For example, knowing that early adolescents might be acting out because they want to impress their peers might help teachers "leave their egos at the door" (Beaty-O'Ferrall et al., 2010, p. 7) and not take things personally. The high school students in Cushman's (2003) study explained that they wanted to be understood without teachers being overly personal or invasive. One student stated, "Don't be afraid to talk to us one on one, but don't try too hard to be our friend" (Cushman, 2003, p. 4). Elementary students may seek out hugs and physical affection whereas high school students may look for evidence of being respected and taken seriously. As we mentioned before, teachers should avoid presuming or generalizing and ask students and families what would feel warm and supportive.

One reliable way to demonstrate warmth and friendliness to students is to accommodate these developmental needs. That means that teachers not only need to know what those needs are, but also need to be able to adjust accordingly. For example, for a teacher with a sarcastic sense of humor, that may mean reigning in that sarcasm if they are teaching young children or early adolescents who may be hurt by sarcasm or may not understand it. It also means providing appropriately challenging intellectual tasks and supporting engaging instructional activities, which shows again how the domains of relationships and **curriculum and instruction** are **interdependent**. In Ms. Nash's reframed dilemma, students struggled with open seating arrangements. We will discuss student to student relationships later in this chapter, but it is useful to note here that Ms. Nash's students were early adolescents. In this developmental phase, students tend to be oriented toward their peer relationships and peer opinions while still needing adult assistance to navigate challenges. Understanding this aspect of student development helped Ms. Nash to better support peer relationship building and to structure classroom seating and grouping.

Instructional Agency and Warm Demanding

Being warm and getting to know students well needs to be coupled with high academic expectations in order for teachers to fully demonstrate care. This coupling requires teachers' competent use of instructional agency. Agency can have multiple, important meanings, and we do not want to confuse them. Here we distinguish between **human agency**, **personal agency**, and **instructional agency**.

> **Key Terms**
>
> *Human Agency* **(from sociology, related to social change):** The resources and power necessary to fulfill one's purpose or potential (Toshalis, 2015).
>
> *Personal Agency* **(from psychology, related to a sense of autonomy and self-efficacy):** The ability to act on an object or situation and see an impact of one's actions (Bandura, 2001; Gallagher, 2000).
>
> *Instructional Agency* **(from educational sciences):** Active leadership in directing class activities (Wubbels et al., 2016).

Here we will focus on **instructional agency**, the active leadership that members of the classroom community take in directing class activities. Both teachers and students can have this type of agency during each class session. Kleinfeld (1975) and Wubbels et al. (2016) argued that teachers develop good relationships with students as well as good **classroom management** by balancing warmth and agency. Kleinfeld (1975) first named this teacher behavior **"warm demanding."** Ross and colleagues (2003) explained that "warm demanding" (p. 142) means that teachers maintain positive classroom climates while insisting that students reach academic mastery. The work of both Kleinfeld and Wubbels et al. (2016) give us further insight into how warm demanding might work in class.

> **Key Terms**
>
> *Warm Demanding*: Maintaining a positive classroom climate and good relationships with students while insisting that students reach academic mastery.

Kleinfeld (1975) used a two-dimensional Cartesian plane to illustrate warm demanding, which Wubbels et al. (2006) later developed in their research. In the plane, the x-axis measures a scale of professional distance to warmth and the y-axis measures a scale of passive to active agency. Teacher behavior may be charted throughout the entire plane during any particular class session by pinpointing how much warmth and how much agency a teacher is demonstrating in a particular moment. Teachers who have good relationships with their students tend to have more stable profiles and spend most of their class sessions high in both warmth and agency. Kleinfeld (1975) named these teachers "warm demanders" and found that teachers with this profile tended to be successful with indigenous students regardless of the teacher's own ethnic background because these students expected personal warmth as a prerequisite for granting teachers respect and choosing to participate in class.

Wubbels et al. (2006) further developed this typology and argued that teachers need to be able to move throughout the plane in order to manage relationships with students and maintain positive classroom dynamics. According to Wubbels et al. (2016), there is a principle behind each axis, a way that it works when teachers interact with students. When teachers demonstrate warmth, it evokes friendliness in students' behavior (and vice versa). When teachers demonstrate agency, students become more passive. That means that if a teacher wants to promote friendlier student behavior, the teacher should display more warmth. Warmth attracts warmth in the other. If the teacher wants to guide the lesson activities more directly, the teacher should demonstrate more agency. If the teacher wants the students to be more involved in the lesson, the teacher should reduce their active agency, at which point students will take instructional agency. Agency attracts passivity in the other. However, teachers should not enact agency in a way that completely shuts students down. In Kleinfeld's (1975) study, students remained resistantly silent when teachers displayed active agency that was coupled with professional distance or emotional disengagement. Students report better relationships with teachers and higher levels of engagement in classrooms where teachers are mostly high in both warmth and agency. Agency has to be coupled with warmth in order to contribute to positive relationships and an overall positive climate. Teacher agency is a vehicle for organizing and implementing highly engaging instructional activities. Here we again see the **interdependence** of the **domains of relationships** and **curriculum and instruction**. When Ms. Nash reflected on her use of warm demanding, she identified warmth as a strength that came naturally, but instructional agency as more challenging. One teacher move that she ultimately selected was increasing her instructional agency so that students would perceive her warmth more positively.

Focus on Culture 6: Demonstrating Authentic Care with Students

It's possible to interpret Wubbels et al.' (2006) interpersonal theory as a strategy. A teacher can strategically decrease their agency in order to get students to increase theirs. This may be true. However, research also tells us that students have less respect for teachers who they consider to be more strategic than genuine. Angela Valenzuela (1999) focused on the distinction between aesthetic care and authentic care in the educational trajectories of the Mexican American high school students in her study. *Aesthetic care* is knowledge and interest about things and ideas whereas *authentic care* is a relational exchange between people that both people experience as caring (Noddings, 2005). That means that even if a teacher thinks they are demonstrating warmth, students may not consider it as warmth if it is not authentic and relational.

For example, a teacher may say that they care for students by grading assignments strictly so that students will have more of a sense of how they will need to perform as they progress through higher levels of education. This is aesthetic care. Students may not experience this approach as warm or caring because the teacher is not caring for them as *people*, but rather as students. In another example, the teacher may use slang words that the students often use in order to connect and display warmth, but the students may perceive it as disingenuous and inauthentic. Valenzuela (1999) found that participants respected and performed for teachers who demonstrated authentic care rather than aesthetic care. One student said of a teacher that demonstrated authentic care, "The way she laughs at us makes us happy…like she *really* likes us. I learn easier that way" (p. 101). When relating to students with diverse cultural backgrounds, teacher authenticity is key to conveying warmth and being a **warm demander**.

High Academic Expectations Coupled With Academic Support

In our work with teachers, we sometimes hear how teachers do not want to overburden students by asking them to complete too much work or tackle tasks that are complex or challenging. Remember in Chapter 2 when we discussed the **Habit of Asset Identification** that we described this perspective as the "'You-Poor-Dear' Syndrome" (Ladson-Billings, 2007, p. 319). Teachers with this perspective often work with students living in poverty and want to show care and respect to students by not increasing students' anxiety or stress. But students don't interpret teachers' low expectations or lax classroom management as warmth or care. When asked in research studies which types of teachers they have the best relationships with or like the most, students repeatedly express the importance of teachers' high academic and behavioral expectations coupled with adequate academic support (Delpit, 2012; Kennedy et al., 2019; Kennedy-Lewis, 2013; Milner, 2013; Murphy et al., 2013).

What do high expectations look like? **Warm demanders** combine warmth with the act of pressing students toward academic excellence. As we first discussed in Chapter 2, they engage the **Habit of Personal Attribution** by taking an "It's My Job" approach (Corbett et al., 2002, p. 131) to making sure that all students succeed. This approach means that teachers take it upon themselves to continue to address barriers to students' success in the classroom without blaming students and giving up on them. That does not mean that students are not held accountable. In fact, it's just the opposite. Students are not allowed to fail because teachers keep pressing them to succeed.

At Granite Junior High, where Corbett and colleagues conducted their study, this looked like teachers rating students' work as either "quality" or "not there yet." Students who received the latter mark on an assignment continued to work on it, with additional teacher and peer support, until they reached the "quality" rating. Teachers collaborated on creating support structures to provide extra help when needed. At the beginning, some students resisted the requirement to persist with assignments rated as "not there yet" because it could be easier to accept a failing mark. But they came to see the policy as warm demanding. One student explained, "I think it's good. At the beginning of the year, I was against it. But I've noticed how it helps me. And your grade average is always way higher than it was" (Corbett et al., 2002, p. 85). Maintaining high expectations and providing support were strategies through which these teachers invested in their relationships with students, which in turn supported student learning and academic achievement.

> **Focus on Culture 7: Rightful Presence as a Classroom Pillar to Support Equity and Justice**
>
> Calls for culturally responsive pedagogy (CRP) have long included discussions about the need for high expectations and the ensuring of students' academic success (Ladson-Billings, 1995). You will read more about the relevance of CRP for curriculum and instruction in Chapter 6. Here, we discuss how CRP scholars have made a distinction between equality and equity. Equality means the provision of similar investments and resources for all students and equity means the provision of different investments and resources according to what a particular group needs. Equitable investment ensures similar access for all students to valued goods, services, or experiences by leveling the playing field for everyone.
>
> Calabrese Barton and Tan (2020) have recently argued that this focus on equity has led to a discussion mainly about inclusion, making sure that all students get what they need in order to obtain valued educational goods by being fully included in the current system. These scholars argue that equity conversations have not led to substantial system change because they focus on including all students in existing academic structures that are inherently exclusionary—including curriculum, instruction, and assessment. That means that these structures systematically exclude students who belong to certain groups. For example, we might promote equity by providing extra tutoring for learners whose home language differs from the

language of instruction so that they can achieve better in their history classes. However, the content they learn about in those classes may not include them or reflect their experiences or the histories of the communities where they live. In this example, we might achieve equity, but not justice, because we are requiring students to accept their own erasure from the content of their lessons in order to succeed in class. These types of system-level inequities continue to play out daily in classrooms even if teachers strive for justice. Leveling the playing field does not change the rules of the game, and many students from groups that are disadvantaged by the current system already know this (Toshalis, 2015).

Calabrese Barton and Tan (2020) explain the concept of *rightful presence* (p. 434) as an antidote to promoting equity without justice. Rightful presence asserts that students from nondominant and/or minoritized or historically underrepresented backgrounds have the right to be fully present in the school context without having to make accommodations or modifications that conflict with, or erase, their cultural backgrounds, histories, or values. When children are rightfully present in classrooms, the political struggles of their communities for full social inclusion are also taken up within the three **domains of teaching**.

That means that **warm demanding** is a necessary but not sufficient teacher move. Teachers should also explore ways to make changes in all three domains of teaching that reflect, respect, and incorporate students' backgrounds and current situations. In order to do this, teachers will draw upon caregiver communication and teachers' knowledge of community life. Embedding rightful presence as a classroom pillar helps students from nondominant backgrounds to feel seen, which supports a positive teacher–student relationship. However, teachers are often positioned within unjust systems upon which they have limited influence. We do not suggest that teachers jeopardize the positions they do have but rather that they use the **Habit of Personal Attribution** to take a critical look at what (additional) elements of these systems they can influence in the classroom.

Caregiver Communication and Community Life
So far in this chapter, we have discussed warmth and friendliness, getting to know students well, **instructional agency**, and high academic expectations and support as ways that teachers can further invest in and improve their relationships with students. These are all behaviors that occur in the classroom and during instruction. Forming positive connections with students might also involve deepening connections with caregivers, families, and communities outside of class time. When teachers and caregivers collaborate to provide structure, care, and support, students experience this connectedness and further engage in class and school (Corbett et al., 2002; Milner et al., 2019).

Although Ms. Nash's original dilemma may seem far removed from her relationships with families, she noticed when she **frame shifted** to the **domain of relationships** that the need for stronger ties with students' families and communities may have been contributing to the situation. There was a gap in Ms. Nash's communication with caregivers and understanding of students' lives outside of school, so she incorporated a systematic approach to increasing positive communication with caregivers as part of her solution. Each day, she called the caregivers of five different students to share one positive remark about that student's recent participation in class. Caregivers were often surprised to receive positive news since most teachers only contacted them if something negative had happened. Students commented on these calls, proudly describing how their caregivers had reacted. Then, if Ms. Nash needed to contact a caregiver due to a problem at a later time, she already had these positive connections to pave the way for a productive and collaborative conversation.

> **Focus on Culture 8: Developing Authentic Teacher Solidarity With Families**
>
> It is particularly important for teachers to focus on building connections with families and communities if there are cultural or socioeconomic differences between teachers and

students. When teachers are connected to students' lives outside of school, the teacher can also help students navigate across the boundary that sometimes exists between home and school. Students from nondominant racial backgrounds particularly highlight the importance of teachers' relational approaches and knowledge of students' cultures, values, and community experiences (Alder, 2002; Kennedy & Melfor, 2021; Nelson, 2016). For teachers, that means exploring and getting to know communities, attending activities that students and families participate in outside of school, and learning the most effective and most highly valued way that teachers can communicate with families.

Above we discussed how teachers need to engage in authentic rather than aesthetic care, or genuinely care about students as people rather than having only an instrumental focus on improving student achievement in an unjust system. We also described *rightful presence*, the ability for students to be fully engaged in the classroom without having to change fundamental aspects of their cultural backgrounds, as critical to successful culturally responsive teaching. Here we can consider how these same principles apply to teachers' relationships with parents and how the **Habit of Asset Identification** and the **Habit of Deliberate Interpretation** might again be engaged. Hong et al. (2022) described how authentic teacher solidarity with families involves teachers challenging their own **deficit views** of families by learning about the systemic barriers that families often face as well as valuing caregivers' own understandings of how they support their children.

It may require a particularly challenging engagement of all three **habits of mind** in order for teachers to succeed in building lasting bonds with families. In Chapter 2, we explored the example of caregivers not attending Back to School Night when applying the **Habit of Deliberate Interpretation**. In that exercise, we asked you to separate out the **observation** that caregivers did not attend from the **interpretation** that they find other things more important. Then we asked you to separate both the observation and the interpretation from the **judgment** that caregivers do not care about their children's education. Making creative and committed attempts to build connections with families, such as doing home visits, or asking knowledgeable and respected community leaders such as church pastors, imams, community center staff, or caregiver advocates for insights, can help teachers imagine alternative ways to interpret their observations related to caregiver behavior. You will engage the **Habit of Personal Attribution** when committing time and effort to these activities.

It is also important to keep the other skills and ideas in mind that we have discussed, such as getting to know students well. For example, in their interviews with middle and high school students, Cushman and colleagues (2003; 2008) noted that middle school students were supportive or neutral about teachers doing home visits whereas high school students found them intrusive. Teachers need to tailor any particular approach to their own students and communities, which means you have to prioritize getting to know students well as a preliminary and ongoing effort. The habits of mind will provide the essential framework for supporting you through these efforts.

In one example that we ourselves experienced as teachers, we particularly needed to meet with a student's caregivers in order to review the supports that student was receiving related to a learning disability. The meeting could only be scheduled at a time when the school psychologist could attend and since the psychologist oversaw cases at multiple schools, the appointment possibilities were limited. The caregiver did not attend and the educators at the meeting jumped directly to the judgment that the caregiver did not care about the child. When we later asked the student why their caregiver was not there, they told us that their family did not own a car and that to get to the school during the school day required three bus transfers. The caregiver took care of four children, three of whom were younger than this student. The youngest rode in a stroller and the second youngest was a toddler. This student's 8-year-old brother, the third child in the family, had to be picked up from the local elementary school because it was too dangerous for him to walk home alone. The caregiver could not accomplish the three bus transfers with the two youngest children and make it back in time to pick up the student's brother. When we heard this story, we immediately saw how we had superimposed particular assumptions about the family's circumstances based on middle-class norms, such as having ready access to childcare and transportation. Learning more about this family helped us create alternative interpretations when using the Habit of Deliberate Interpretation and see the caregiver's commitment to caring for all of the children when using the **Habit of Asset Identification**.

Understanding caregiver realities can help teachers find ways to establish and build connections of communication with caregivers. It may be particularly important to keep in mind that caregivers may have had numerous negative encounters with educators both as students and as caregivers in the past and that you will need to build trust in order to restore open communication. Creating **routines** that allow caregivers to hear from teachers frequently and more often for positive celebrations than for negative chastisements can help build these relationships. When teachers have open communication with caregivers and there exist trusting bonds between teachers and families, students experience a network of care that can support and guide them. Here are some questions that can guide your efforts to build caregiver communication and get to know about communities that might be different from yours:

- With whom does each of your students live?
- Where does each of your students live?
  - Have you visited them at home?
- What are each of your student's hobbies or activities outside of class?
  - How could you become involved in these activities in some way?
- Which community organizations and community leaders are important in the place where students live?
  - What can you learn from these resources?

- What would caregivers like you to know about their child?
  - What would they like you to know about their expectations of teachers and schools?
- What are caregivers' preferred mode and frequency of communication?

Teacher–Class Relationships

In the previous section, we described and discussed how teachers can develop and maintain positive teacher–student relationships. We have not made a clear distinction between teachers' relationships with individual students and teachers' relationships with their whole group of students. The approaches of **warm demanding**, maintaining high academic expectations, getting to know students well, and developing positive connections with families and communities can improve teachers' relationships with both individuals and the group. As a teacher, you already know that you will not have relationships equal in depth or scope with every individual student. This is normal. It is also not necessary to have deep connections with every student in order to have a positive classroom culture that supports thinking, learning, and growth. What is necessary is that each student feels liked by the teacher and each student's relational needs that have to do with the teacher are met.

In Kleinfeld's (1975) model of warm demanding and Wubbels et al.'s (2006) development of interpersonal theory, we learned about the connection between the **domains of relationships** and **classroom management**. Teachers' ability to enact positive **instructional agency** both supports and is supported by effective classroom management. Relationships with the group facilitate the management within the group. For many students, the teacher's interpersonal style will be enough to help them feel connected (although we recommend investing time in getting to know each student since it will also facilitate your ability to develop relevant instruction). For marginalized students, more robust relationships with teachers might be necessary to meet students' relational needs. You can determine which students respond best to the teacher's class-wide approach and which ones need a personalized one as you get to know them. A student who frequently challenges you may be using those challenges as a way to request an individualized teacher–student relationship, whereas a silent student may be using silence to do this as well.

Throughout the previous sections, we have described the principles and research supporting teachers' development of relationships with both individual students and the whole class. Here, we focus on approaches that address teacher–class relationships. Specific ways that teachers can convey warmth to the entire class include:

- *Using appropriate humor.* When a teacher uses appropriate humor, all students understand the joke; they understand that the joke is a joke; and the joke does not target anyone inside or outside of the class.
- *Following up on promises or commitments.* Even just mentioning things that the teacher committed to previously and linking the current situation to that commitment can strengthen relationships. That might sound like, "Yesterday, I said _____, so now we will _____," or "I promised you I would____, but I have to change that to _____ because____."
- *Sharing about one's life outside of school.* Students like to know if you have children, pets, or hobbies, and they enjoy updates about these things. We don't recommend sharing personal information related to adult relationships. A teacher may want to create a bond with students by sharing such personal information, but we recommend maintaining a boundary around topics that specifically pertain to adult life since students expect the teacher to be the adult. One student stated, "[Teachers] should be friendly, but not too friendly or else they'll lose their authority" (Cushman & Rogers, 2008, p. 44).

Keep in mind that what is considered appropriate to share may vary by student developmental level and cultural context.

- *Admitting when one is wrong.* This is a useful strategy both with individual students as well as with the whole class. When a teacher has made an error that affects the entire class or was done in front of the class, the teacher can address this publicly, whereas if the commission happened individually or involves a personal situation with an individual student, the teacher can do this privately.
- *Adjusting deadlines or assignment requirements if there are shared difficulties among the students.* In general, consistency is key to maintaining high expectations, but there may be times when flexibility is called for and when students will appreciate this flexibility. For example, a research participant recently shared with one of us that a high school teacher had changed a test date because it happened to fall on the first day of Ramadan, when the students were not yet used to fasting. These Muslim students considered this date change as an act of consideration.

Improving Student–Student Relationships by Creating Classroom Communities

In the first half of this chapter, we discussed how teachers could improve relationships with individual students and with the class as a whole. As teachers build their relationships with the whole class, they can reinforce those efforts by supporting positive student–student relationships as well. Ms. Nash's original dilemma was about students' transition into class and one way that she reframed it to the **domain of relationships** was: *Students do not feel comfortable sitting next to all of their other classmates and their discomfort affects their seating choices during the transition into class.* With this reframing, she could explore how her support of positive peer relationships might be a way to improve her dilemma. Here we will focus on how teachers can address dilemmas that may be related to relationships between students. Classrooms contain arbitrary collections of individuals who are forced to be together, get along, and accomplish communal tasks without ever opting in to the group. That is a strange situation and means that teachers will not necessarily like all students and students will not necessarily all like each other. Nevertheless, the teacher has to prioritize care for every student and support the development of a functional classroom community (Cushman, 2003). Although class building and team building activities can take some time on the front end, they pay off in dividends later when teachers ask students to work together and take academic risks.

In order for all students to thrive, they must feel emotionally safe and secure within the classroom. That means that students encounter a sense of belonging and know that their peers will protect each other from verbal and physical harm (Midgett et al., 2017). In safe classrooms, students know that teachers will intervene in substantive, meaningful, and relational ways if someone is being harmed, and that the teacher will always seek to preserve the classroom community and all of its members. This sense of social and emotional safety provides a foundation for students to take academic risks, to know that they can have a bad day, and to trust and rely upon teacher and peer feedback. This is another example of how we see the **interdependence** of the three **domains of teaching**: As teachers support peer relationships, students are more likely to engage in instruction and scaffold each other's mastery of academic content. Since we know that not all students will become genuine friends with all other students and that the teacher is not responsible for micromanaging these relationships, we suggest a couple of practical questions to help teachers gauge the quality of their classroom community. Try these out in Exercise 4.1 while keeping your own classroom in mind.

In many classrooms, especially in middle and high school, the answers to these questions would be "no." If that

> **Exercise 4.1** *Evaluating the Quality of Student–Student Relationships*
>
> **Directions**
>
> Consider the following questions to help you evaluate how well your students know each other and how comfortable they are working together.
>
> 1. Does every student know the first name of every other student?
> 2. Can every student identify at least one positive and personal attribute, interest, or experience of every other student?
> 3. Is every student willing and able to work successfully with every other student (which does not mean that all groupings are equally desirable from the teacher's perspective)?

is also true for your classroom, we will discuss some possible approaches to improvement.

Helping Students Get to Know Each Other

In many school contexts, the emphasis is on performance and achievement, which means that aesthetic care, or the value placed on things and ideas, is prioritized over authentic care, or the mutually beneficial relational approach to schooling (Valenzuela, 1999). In such contexts, teachers may think that they have prioritized caring while students still do not know each other at all. As both students and teachers, we can remember our participation in contexts where teachers definitely cared, but students could not name everyone else in the room. If you have a persistent dilemma related to the **domain of relationships** and this description fits your classroom, this could be a place to start. We recognize that it is important to be able to develop student relationships and team building as you also maintain a quick curricular pace, differentiate according to students' academic needs, and meet all of the other demands that make up classroom life.

The particular approach that teachers can use to support students getting to know each other will depend on students' ages and developmental phase as well as the subject and context of the class. We argue that short activities can be included regardless of these circumstances by including personal or personalized activities embedded in classroom transitions. Many elementary classrooms start with a morning meeting, which is a time at the start of the day for students to share with one another and for the teacher to engage students as a group. To support the ultimate goal of students treating each other well during instructional activities, teachers can help students practice showing their appreciation for each other during morning. In an elementary classroom, it may be useful to provide sentence stems for students as you model what it sounds like to appreciate a peer. For example, you might help students show active listening and respect by starting a response to a peer as, "I agree with [student name] because…" or "I have a different idea than [student name] because I think…"

One of us currently starts every university seminar class with students seated in a circle where each person answers a short, fill-in the blank check-in question that is either related to life outside of class or to class content itself. This activity can be built directly onto a homework activity so it also provides a type of warm demanding that students have completed previous work (although it should also be accessible to students who may not have been able to do so). See Table 4.3 for some examples, which can be modified to suit your specific situation (see also Michael et al., 2023, for more ideas that connect beginning-of-class **routines** with relationship development).

To make sure this activity meets your goals of community building and concept development while being efficient and tapping in to the experiences of all students, we suggest: a) giving students a few options to choose from, and making sure that everyone can answer at least one of the choices; b) giving students "think time," time spent in silence for everyone to come up with their own answer before sharing; c) being comfortable with "wait time," meaning that each student has their own time to share and must share during that time, without prodding or

TABLE 4.3 *Example "Check-In" Questions by Subject*

Languages, Humanities, and Social Sciences	My favorite [story/chapter/scene] is ___ because ___. The [fictional/historical] character I admire most is ___ because ___. The character I am most similar to is ___ because ___.
Mathematics, Natural Sciences, Technology, Electives, Other Skill Development	What I find [easiest/most challenging/most useful] about [the skill we are studying now] is ___ because ___. I know I got better at [this skill] during this unit because ___. One place I have seen [class content/skill] in my life outside of class is ___. One way I want to apply [class content/skill] in the future is ___.

help from others; d) enforcing a "no feedback" rule so that each student can share without immediate judgment; and e) asking students to fill in the blanks without elaborating, which ensures an efficient use of time. An additional step teachers can take in order to maximize the potential of this activity for class building is to ask students to recall what five of their peers said. If teachers do this on a regular basis, it will normalize students carefully listening to each other. The "no feedback" approach at the postsecondary level differs from the positive feedback approach at the elementary level. This is an example of how a teacher can adjust a specific strategy depending on students' developmental needs as well as instructional considerations.

Another method we have seen teachers use effectively at all levels is Quiz-Quiz-Trade (Kagan & Kagan, 2009), a community-building **structure** which can also be used to build students' content knowledge in the **domain of curriculum and instruction**. In this structure, the teacher provides students with index cards that each have a different question on them such as, "Do you have any pets? If so, what kind and what are their names," or "If you had a superpower, what would it be?" The questions should be something each student can answer, and the teacher should be mindful to avoid questions that highlight socioeconomic differences (such as, "Where did you go on your last vacation?" since some students' families may not be able to afford to travel). Each student receives a card. When the teacher says "go!" students find someone they do not already sit next to and they high-five each other. They ask each other the questions on their cards and then they trade cards. They then find another partner and repeat the process until time is called. This can be a fun activity to use as a brain break and can last as short as three minutes just to get students moving around and learning about one another. Having effective **routines** in place in the **domain of classroom management** is a necessary prerequisite for making activities such as Quiz-Quiz-Trade run smoothly. We will discuss these in more detail in Chapter 5.

Building a Class Culture to Support Collaborative Teams

Whole-class check-ins are one way for teachers to promote and support students getting to know each other and getting comfortable working together. Students' openness to working together and supporting each other builds a positive classroom culture that will later support effective instructional teaming of students. We will explore more about the mechanics of team configurations in Chapter 6 when we discuss instruction. Here, we will home in on the relational aspect of classroom culture and relate it to student teams. To build classroom relationships, we suggest mixing students as often as possible in strategic ways and with specific goals. At the beginning of activities or when new groups or teams are formed, teachers can embed an exercise that helps to increase students':

- knowledge of each other's lives;
- appreciation for each other's unique characteristics, abilities, and talents; or
- patience with each other.

One first task might be to ask students if they know each other's full names, or something else about each other. Creating an environment where each individual's success leads to the success of the entire class is particularly important to maintain a supportive atmosphere. We suggest limiting competition between students, teams, or classes so that there is minimal cost associated with taking risks (Kagan & Kagan, 2009).

Teachers should not assume that students will have the skills, confidence, or emotional safety to engage in these team-building activities without explicit instruction (Michael et al., 2023). Depending on the teacher's context, it can be useful to provide specific prompts for students to ask each other, and to engage the classroom management strategy of **precorrection** to tell students beforehand what types of comments or actions might be considered hurtful and are therefore off-limits (Haydon & Kroeger, 2016). When beginning to build classroom community, each step can be scaffolded, just as each new cognitive skill is scaffolded. The teacher can again engage the **Habit of Personal Attribution** in making sure that each social skill is taught step by step even if "the students should already know this." Helping students think through and practice how to handle challenging emotional situations before they occur can yield big benefits. For example, in the field of bullying prevention, bystander training gives bystanders specific verbal and nonverbal body language to use before they are in a situation when they need it (e.g., Midgett et al., 2017). Helping students learn to participate in a collaborative team or classroom community can be approached similarly.

Continuing to Provide Appropriate Structure and Boundaries

Investing in teacher–student and student–student relationships works. Study after study has established the importance of these relationships for learning. But let's face it, kids are kids (and young adults are young adults). No matter how much time and effort you spend investing in a positive classroom culture, you may still find that students are not always kind and considerate toward each other or that some students continue to feel hesitant about their peer connections. To provide additional safety, the teacher can consider ongoing necessary structures for reducing social anxiety and preventing bullying. For example, to address her dilemma, Ms. Nash decided to begin using and enforcing a seating chart. Remember that her dilemma had to do with students coming in to class smoothly and getting to work quickly and after reading some teacher-friendly literature, Ms. Nash realized that a seating chart might help create emotional safety (Toshalis, 2015).

Seating charts are also part of the **routines** that support teaching and learning, which means they belong to the **domain of classroom management**. We will discuss them again in Chapter 5. We name them here as tools that not only support classroom management but also student–student relationships, which shows again how the three **domains of teaching** are **interdependent**. By creating and consistently maintaining intentional assigned seats, the teacher assumes the decision-making about who will sit where so that students do not need to negotiate possibly complicated peer dynamics during the transition into class, which may decrease student anxiety (Toshalis, 2015). Additionally, by having students consistently seated near the same peers, the teacher can scaffold peer relationship development through repeated interactions among these groupings. Seating charts are one example of a strategy that can provide structure while also supporting relationship development. In Ms. Nash's case, we noticed over time that as students got used to assigned seating, Ms. Nash spent less time transitioning students to different activities and students were more open to working together.

Key Takeaways: Teacher Moves to Address Dilemmas Related to Relationships

Remember that this is not a book about "tips and tricks" but rather about developing a mindset that supports the persistent exploration of approaches that can improve each teaching dilemma you face. We also realize that to maintain the **Habit of Personal Attribution**, your **teacher efficacy** needs to remain high, which means you might need support from literature, peers, or other professional resources to come up with relevant and evidence-supported ideas to address each new dilemma. In each of the chapters in Part II of this book, we offer some specific strategies to try. The examples we give are not intended to be exhaustive and we know that not all strategies will work for all teachers depending on your own context, personality, values, and style. Nevertheless, we do think it's important to be specific and concrete about some example strategies in order to inspire your motivation and sense of possibility. Here are a selection of teacher moves drawn from this chapter that we suggest for addressing dilemmas related to the **domain of relationships**. This first list addresses teacher-student relationships:

- Have an open mindset by starting fresh each day with each student;
- Greet students;
- Ask them about their lives;
- Show care by asking the student in a sincere way what is going on with them;
- Be attentive to students' emotions;
- Meet caregivers;
- Attend extracurricular activities;
- Understand students' developmental phases and interact accordingly;
- Be mindful of tone and avoid sarcasm.

Here are some additional specific teacher moves we mentioned to improve student–student relationships:

- Explicitly teach students how to speak to each other;
- Incorporate class-building activities;
- Help students learn about each other's backgrounds and current lives;
- Develop students' appreciation for each other's unique characteristics, abilities, and talents.

In this chapter, we have discussed the importance of positive teacher–student and student–student relationships and given concrete examples of how teachers might work on the domain of relationships to improve their dilemmas. We began the chapter with Ms. Nash's **dilemma statement** frame shifted to: *Students do not feel comfortable sitting next to all of their other classmates and their discomfort affects their seating choices during the transition into class,* or *The teacher does not have strong enough connections to families and communities to provide sufficient motivation for students to comply with requests or engage in assignments, especially during highly* *distracting moments such as classroom transitions.* Her **focus questions** homed in on the creation of a positive classroom climate (listed in Table 4.1). Considering the first reframing, we encouraged Ms. Nash to try some of the class-building strategies we just discussed, including the check-in or 'get-to-know-you' questions to promote a sense of class community and to ensure that all students could effectively work with all others.

To address the second reframing, Ms. Nash began to call caregivers systematically and to build positive connections by sharing student successes. These teacher moves helped to answer her reframed focus question: "How do I create a positive classroom climate where students feel supported and motivated to work together toward successful completion of the warm-up activity?" In Figure 4.1, we illustrate Ms. Nash's process of moving from articulating dilemma statements to generating focus questions to deciding upon teacher moves that she would try in order

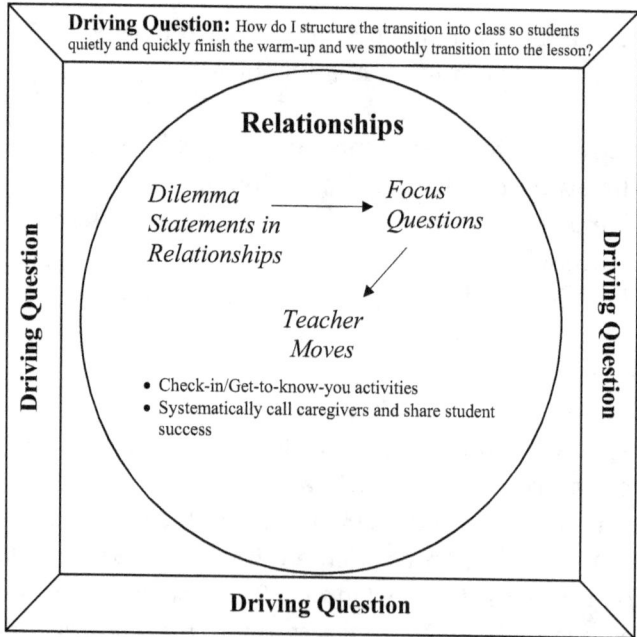

Figure 4.1 Teacher Moves Ms. Nash Identified in the Domain of Relationships Using the Zoomed in Frame.

> **Exercise 4.2** *Identifying Teacher Moves in the Domain of Relationships*
> 1. Jot down the focus questions you listed in the domain of relationships in Exercise 3.3 in the left-hand column below.
> 2. Using the information presented in this chapter, use the right-hand column to identify one or more teacher moves that answer each focus question and that you have not tried before.
>
> | Focus Questions in the Domain of Relationships | Teacher Moves to Try |
> | --- | --- |
> | | |
> | | |

to answer her focus questions. These strategies were not the first ideas on Ms. Nash's mind when she identified her **driving question**, which had an initial framing in the classroom management domain: "How do I structure the transition into class so students quietly and quickly finish the warm-up and we smoothly transition into the lesson?" **Frame shifting** the dilemma from the **domain of classroom management** to the domain of relationships allowed Ms. Nash to see the relevance of strategies from the domain of relationships that might ultimately improve the quality and efficiency of students' transition into class, thereby answering her driving question. Using check-in activities and calling caregivers to develop her relationships with students and families could indeed make the transition into class go more smoothly. Now return to your own focus questions as you complete Exercise 4.2.

For Discussion and Practice

1. Describe the most successful demonstration you have ever seen of warm demanding in a classroom context.

2. Which of the following questions can you answer about your students? (How) has this information been important? And/or what challenges have you faced in trying to address these topics and how have you handled them?
   - With whom does each of your students live?
   - Where does each of your students live?
     - Have you visited them at home?
   - What are each of your student's hobbies or activities outside of class?
     - How could you become involved in these activities in some way?
   - Which community organizations and community leaders are important in the place where students live?
     - What can you learn from these resources?
   - What would caregivers like you to know about their child?
     - What would they like you to know about their expectations of teachers and schools?
   - What are caregivers' preferred mode and frequency of communication?
3. In your classroom:
   - Does every student know the first name of every other student?
   - Can every student identify at least one positive and personal attribute, interest, or experience of every other student?
   - Is every student willing and able to work successfully with every other student (which does not mean that all groupings are equally desirable from the teacher's perspective)? If so, how did you accomplish this? If not, what could you do to support this?
4. Which of the *Focus on Culture* sections in this chapter is most relevant to your own teaching and why?
5. Which habit of mind do you think will be the most important one for your success at implementing strategies related to the domain of relationships? Explain.
6. Below are three of the additional sample dilemmas for different education levels that you saw in the online Study Guide materials for Chapter 3. All three of the dilemmas

were originally framed in a domain other than relationships and have been frame shifted to the domain of relationships. Choose at least one of the dilemmas and discuss which teacher moves related to relationships as presented in this chapter could address the focus questions in the right-hand column that were generated from the reframed dilemma.

Dilemma Statement	Domain in Which Dilemma is Currently Framed	Guiding Questions	Plausible Reframing of the Dilemma Statement	Focus Question
Middle School Dilemma Example #2				
No matter what I do, the students simply will not stop touching each other.	Classroom Management (Non-compliance with class rules)	Relationships: Do the students completely understand why the teacher does not want them to touch each other?	Relationships: *The students do not understand why they should not touch each other.*	Relationships: How can I foster an understanding of each other's needs among the students?
High School Dilemma Example #2				
After some students come into class, they immediately put their heads on their desks and do nothing.	Classroom Management (Transition periods)	Relationships: Do the students feel motivated by a close relationship with the teacher?	Relationships: *The students are not willing to put in extra effort to comply with the teacher's requests because they do not value their relationship with the teacher.*	Relationships: How can I develop trusting relationships with my students?
Post-Secondary Dilemma Example #2				
During each lecture a number of students come late and many others leave early. I find it very disruptive and a bit demoralizing.	Classroom Management (Non-compliance with class norms)	Relationships: Does the instructor know the students personally?	Relationships: *The instructor cannot ask the students about their attendance because they do not have a trusting individual relationship.*	Relationships: How do I develop better individual relationships with my students?

7. Explain how the teacher moves you identified in Exercise 4.2 can help you answer your driving question.

References

Alder, N. (2002). Interpretations of the meaning of care: creating caring relationships in urban middle school classrooms. *Urban Education, 37*(2), 241–266. https://doi.org/10.1177/0042085902372005

Bandura, A. (2001). Social cognitive theory: An agentic perspective. *Annual Review of Psychology, 52*(1), 1–26. https://doi.org/10.1146/annurev.psych.52.1.1

Beaty-O'Ferrall, M. E., Green, A., & Hanna, F. (2010). Classroom management strategies for difficult students: Promoting change through relationships. *The Middle School Journal, 41*(4), 4–11. https://doi.org/10.1080/00940771.2010.11461726

Calabrese Barton, A., & Tan, E. (2020). Beyond equity as inclusion: A framework of "rightful presence" for guiding justice-oriented studies in teaching and learning. *Educational Researcher, 49*(6), 433–440. https://doi.org/10.3102/0013189X20927363

Corbett, D., Wilson, B., & Williams, B. (2002). *Effort and excellence in urban classrooms: Expecting—and getting—success with all students*. Teachers College Press.

Cothran, D. J., & Ennis, C. D. (2000). Building bridges to student engagement: Communicating respect and care for students in urban high schools. *Journal of Research and Development in Education, 33*(2), 106–117. https://eric.ed.gov/?id=EJ604260

Crenshaw, K. W. (2015). *Black girls matter: Pushed out, overpoliced, and underprotected* [Report]. Center for Intersectionality and Social Policy Studies. https://static1.squarespace.com/static/53f20d90e4b0b80451158d8c/t/54dcc1ece4b001c03e323448/1423753708557/AAPF_BlackGirlsMatterReport.pdf

Cushman, K. (2003). *Fires in the bathroom*. The New Press.

Cushman, K., & Rogers, L. (2008). *Fires in the middle school bathroom*. The New Press.

D'Amato, J. (1988). "Acting": Hawaiian children's resistance to teachers. *The Elementary School Journal, 88*(5), 529–544. https://doi.org/10.1086/461555

Deci, E. L., & Ryan, R. M. (2008). Self-determination theory: A macrotheory of human motivation, development, and health.

Canadian Psychology/Psychologie canadienne, 49(3), 182–185. https://doi.org/10.1037/a0012801

Delpit, L. (2012). *Multiplication is for White people*. The New Press.

Foster, M. (1997). *Black teachers on teaching*. The New Press.

Gallagher, S. (2000). Philosophical conceptions of the self: Implications for cognitive science. *Trends in Cognitive Science*, 4(1), 14–21. https://doi.org/10.1016/S1364-6613(99)01417-5

Gregory, A., & Ripski, M. B. (2008). Adolescent trust in teachers: Implications for behavior in the high school classroom. *School Psychology Review*, 37(3), 337–353. https://doi.org/10.1080/02796015.2008.12087881

Hargrave, L. D., Tyler, K. M., Thompson, F., & Danner, F. (2016). An examination of the association between student–teacher interactions and academic self-concept among African male high school students. *Journal of African American Males in Education*, 7(2), 33–49.

Haydon, T., & Kroeger, S. D. (2016). Active supervision, precorrection, and explicit timing: A high school case study on classroom behavior. *Preventing School Failure*, 60(1), 70–78. https://doi.org/10.1080/1045988X.2014.977213

Hong, S., Baloch, M. H., Conklin, K. H., & Warren, H. W. (2022). Teacher–family solidarity as culturally sustaining pedagogy and practice. *Urban Education*. [Advance online publication] https://doi.org/10.1177/00420859221131809

Kagan, S., & Kagan, M. (2009). *Kagan cooperative learning*. Kagan.

Kennedy, B. L., Acosta, M. M., & Soutullo, O. (2019). Counter narratives of students' experiences returning to comprehensive schools from an involuntary disciplinary alternative school. *Race Ethnicity and Education*, 22, 130–149. https://doi.org/10.1080/13613324.2017.1376634

Kennedy, B. L., Brinegar, K., Hurd, E., & Harrison, L. (2016). Synthesizing middle grades research on cultural responsiveness: The importance of a shared conceptual framework. *Middle Grades Review*, 2(3), Article 2. (20 pages). Retrieved from http://scholarworks.uvm.edu/mgreview/vol2/iss3/2

Kennedy, B. L., & Junker, R. (2023). The evolution of "loaded moments" toward escalation or de-escalation in student-teacher interactions. *Review of Educational Research.* [Accepted Manuscript] https://doi.org/10.3102/00346543231202509

Kennedy, B. L., & Melfor, S. N. (2021). Experiences of (not) belonging among higher education students from nondominant ethnic backgrounds. *Education and Society, 39*(2), 69–91. https://doi.org/10.7459/es/39.2.05

Kennedy-Lewis, B. L. (2013). Persistently disciplined urban students' experiences of the middle school transition and "getting in trouble." *Middle Grades Research Journal, 8*(3), 99–116. http://www.infoagepub.com/middle-grades-research-journal.html

Kennedy-Lewis, B. L. (2015). Second chance or no chance? A case study of one urban alternative middle school. *Journal of Educational Change, 16*(2), 145–169. https://doi.org/10.1007/s10833-014-9242-0

Kleinfeld, J. (1975). Effective teachers of Eskimo and Indian students. *The School Review, 83*(2), 301–344. http://www.jstor.org/stable/1084645

Korthagen, F. A. J., Attema-Noordewier, S., & Zwart, R. C. (2014). Teacher-student contact: Exploring a basic but complicated concept. *Teaching and Teacher Education, 40,* 22–32. https://doi.org/10.1016/j.tate.2014.01.006

Ladson-Billings, G. (1995). But that's just good teaching! The case for culturally relevant pedagogy. *Theory Into Practice, 34*(3), 159–165. https://doi.org/10.1080/00405849509543675

Ladson-Billings, G. (2007). Pushing past the achievement gap: An essay on the language of deficit. *The Journal of Negro Education, 76*(3), 316–323. Retrieved from http://www.jstor.org/stable/40034574

Marcucci, O., & Elmesky, R. (2023). Advancing culturally relevant discipline: An ethnographic microanalysis of disciplinary interactions with Black students. *Urban Education, 58*(6), 1118–1150. https://doi.org/10.1177/0042085920909165

Michael, E., Bailey, P., Benner, G. J., & Sanders, S. (2023). Welcome to our class! Building classroom rapport to support the development of social and emotional learning skills. *Beyond Behavior. 32*(1). https://doi.org/10.1177/10742956221145951

Midgett, A., Doumas, D., Trull, R., & Johnston, A. D. (2017). A randomized controlled study evaluating a brief, bystander bullying intervention with junior high school students. *Journal of School Counseling, 15*(9). http://www.jsc.montana.edu/articles/v15n9.pdf

Milner, H. R. (2013). Analyzing poverty, learning, and teaching through a critical race theory lens. *Review of Research in Education, 37*(1), 1–53. https://doi.org/10.3102/0091732X12459720

Milner, H. R., Cunningham, H. B., Delale-O'Connor, L., & Kestenberg, E. G. (2019). *"These kids are out of control": Why we must reimagine "classroom management" for equity.* Corwin.

Murphy, A. S., Acosta, M. M., & Kennedy-Lewis, B. L. (2013). "I'm not running around with my pants sagging, so how am I not acting like a lady?": Intersections of race and gender in the experiences of female middle school troublemakers. *The Urban Review 45*(5), 586–610. https://doi.org/10.1007/s11256-013-0236-7

Nelson, J. D. (2016). Relational teaching with Black boys: Strategies for learning at a single-sex middle school for boys of color. *Teachers College Record, 118*(6), 1–38. https://doi.org/10.1177/016146811611800608

Nieto, S., & Bode, P. (2017). *Affirming diversity: The sociopolitical context of multicultural education* (7th ed.). Pearson.

Noddings, N. (2005). *The challenge to care in schools: An alternative approach to education* (2nd ed.). Teachers College Press. https://eric.ed.gov/?id=ED377590

Roorda, D. L., Koomen, H. M. Y., Spilt, J. L., & Oort, F. J. (2011). The influence of affective teacher–student relationships on students' school engagement and achievement: A meta-analytic approach. *Review of Educational Research, 81*(4), 493–529. https://doi.org/10.3102/0034654311421793

Ross, D. D., Bondy, E., & Hambacher, E. (2008). Promoting academic engagement through insistence: Being a warm demander. *Childhood Education, 84*(3), 142–146. https://doi.org/10.1080/00094056.2008.10522992

Tharp, R. G. (1989). Psychocultural variables and constants: Effects on teaching and learning in schools. *American Psychologist, 44*(2), 349–359. https://doi.org/10.1037/0003-066X.44.2.349

Toshalis, E. (2015). *Make me! Understanding and engaging student resistance in school*. Harvard Education Press.

Valenzuela, A. (1999). *Subtractive schooling: U.S.–Mexican youth and the politics of caring*. State University of New York Press.

Wubbels, T., Brekelmans, M., den Brok, P., & van Tartwijk, J. (2006). An interpersonal perspective on classroom management in secondary classrooms in the Netherlands. In C. M. Evertson & C. S. Weinstein (Eds.), *Handbook of classroom management: Research, practice, and contemporary issues* (pp. 1161–1191). Lawrence Erlbaum Associates Publishers. https://doi.org/10.4324/9780203874783

Wubbels, T., Brekelmans, M., Mainhard, T., den Brok, P., & van Tartwijk, J. (2016). Teacher-student relationships and student achievement. In K. R. Wentzel & G. B. Ramani (Eds.), *Handbook of social influences in school contexts* (pp. 127–142). Routledge.

5
Frame Shifting to the Domain of Classroom Management

Many teachers say that the skills they have (or lack) related to classroom management have the most impact on their ability to teach well (Evertson & Weinstein, 2006). We define the **domain of classroom management** as the **rules, routines**, and teacher behaviors that structure teaching and learning (Weinstein & Novodvorsky, 2015). Classroom management dilemmas may include students' movements, talk, interaction with materials and each other, or (lack of) responsiveness to teacher requests. Teachers may particularly struggle with transitions between activities which are the phases during a lesson when all of these student behaviors are activated. Research shows that classroom management is necessary but not sufficient for high-quality teaching (Kennedy-Lewis, 2012), meaning that teachers have to be able to do this domain relatively well in order to be effective in the other domains. In this chapter, we further explore how to address classroom management dilemmas and how **frame shifting** dilemmas to the domain of classroom management may result in unexpected and positive results. As we discussed in Chapter 3, a dilemma originally framed as a relationship or curriculum and instruction dilemma can also have something to do with classroom management because the domains of teaching are **interdependent**.

The reason that so much hinges on successful classroom management is because classroom management sets guidelines and expectations that create predictability and organization and allow relationships to flourish. Without at least minimally effective classroom management, the teacher does not have the opportunity to engage the skills related to the other domains. For example, if a teacher cannot efficiently get students' attention, then instruction is at risk. Managing a classroom can be complex because it requires employing a number of skills and strategies simultaneously. The teacher is always multitasking just to keep this domain running smoothly, while also engaging the **domains of relationships** and **curriculum and instruction** at the same time. The good news is that classroom management skills are often concrete and discrete. In contrast to the sometimes intangible processes required to build and maintain good relationships with students, classroom management skills are observable, have clear beginnings and endings, and can be built upon one at a time.

Remember that Ms. Nash's **dilemma statement** after she applied the habits of mind was: *Students do not enter the classroom quickly and do not start working on the posted assignment.* While we shift her dilemma's frame to the other domains in other chapters, in this chapter we will further explore Ms. Nash's dilemma in its original framing in the domain of classroom management so that you can see the relevance and interdependence of all three domains, using this consistent example. Ms. Nash was perplexed by her students' behaviors and had nearly given up on her own ability to manage the class. She noticed that she was increasingly blaming students for being unruly and disrespectful as she grew more desperate for an effective approach.

In Chapter 2, we discussed how the blaming of students is a natural response to a situation in which the teacher feels that they are out of options for solving the problem. Of course, it is reasonable to conclude that students should take charge of behaving differently, and in this chapter we will discuss strategies teachers can use to effect that change. In order to use these strategies well when addressing your own dilemmas, you first have to engage the **Habit of Personal Attribution**. That means that you need a renewed sense of self-efficacy in order to attribute the power of solving the dilemma as within your control. This is a delicate situation because the dilemma itself may have eroded your sense of **teacher efficacy** and now we are asking you to have enough self-efficacy to try something new. We believe this is possible and recognize that it may not be easy. It means giving both the students and yourself the benefit of the doubt as you identify and try new classroom management moves.

Ms. Nash had first used the indicators in Tables 3.1–3.3 to position her dilemma statement in the domain of classroom management. Some of these indicators reflect an **external attribution** or **deficit thinking**. The guiding questions that we first introduced in Chapter 3 may deepen your own exploration of this domain as they reflect a more generous and curious probing, thereby helping you engage the habits of mind by giving you new aspects of the dilemma to consider. Table 5.1 shows the

TABLE 5.1 *Guiding Questions for Reframing Using the Frame of Classroom Management*

Classroom Management
How might the dilemma involve:
☐ Procedures for how and when students should move through the classroom?
☐ Procedures for how and when students should use materials?
☐ Procedures for how and when teachers distribute and collect assignments?
☐ Procedures for how and when students should interact with each other and the teacher?
☐ Procedures for how and when students should demonstrate respect?
☐ Procedures for how and when teachers and students give and receive feedback?
☐ Explicit timing for tasks and behaviors?
☐ Teacher behaviors including nonverbal behavior, movement, and tone of voice?
☐ Clear expectations and consistent (re)enforcement?
☐ The need for teachers to de-escalate conflicts?
☐ Other: _____

TABLE 5.2 *Ms. Nash's Dilemma Statements and Focus Questions in the Domain of Classroom Management*

Ms. Nash's Driving Question: "How do I structure the transition into class so students quietly and quickly finish the warm-up and we smoothly transition into the lesson?"

Dilemma Statements in the Domain of Classroom Management	Focus Questions
Students do not know where to sit.	How can I use and enforce a consistent seating chart?
Students do not react when I give reminders about what to do.	How can I help students remember what to do? How can I get their attention quickly when I need it? How can I project a more serious and consistent demeanor?

guiding questions for the domain of classroom management. As we described in Chapter 3, when we asked Ms. Nash to use these guiding questions when further exploring the connection between her dilemma and this domain of teaching, she ended up writing more specific dilemma statements that she then used to generate new **focus questions** (Table 5.2). These focus questions ultimately would help guide her toward teacher moves to address her **driving question**, "How do I structure the transition into class so students quietly and quickly finish the warm-up and we smoothly transition into the lesson?" You also wrote focus questions within this domain in Exercise 3.2. Review those now in order to focus your reading of this chapter.

As with all of the domains of teaching, there are many resources published about classroom management. In this chapter, we will focus on the things teachers can do to structure their classrooms to maximize learning, drawing upon Ms. Nash's focus questions to both ground and narrow our discussion. As is true for each of the domains, different teacher behaviors and classroom management strategies apply across contexts and student groups (Milner et al., 2019; Murphy & Kennedy, 2019). Therefore, we will be discussing the role of context and culture throughout the chapter as we have done in previous chapters.

Rules

First, we will start by defining what we mean by rules and routines. We draw upon Weinstein and Novodvorsky's (2015) distinction between "expectations for general conduct (*rules*) and the procedures that students will follow in specific situations (*routines*)" (p. 97). They explain that good rules meet the following criteria (p. 98):

- Reasonable
- Necessary
- Clear
- Understandable
- Consistent with instructional goals and how people learn
- Consistent with school rules.

Alfie Kohn (2006) encourages consideration of the additional following questions when deciding if a rule is reasonable:

- Who benefits from the rule? How?
- Is it truly necessary?
- What would happen if the rule were not in place?
  - How bad would it really be if that happened?
- Is the rule fair to all learners?

In addition to these considerations, we would also encourage teachers to consider whether the rules that focus on control interfere with their **relationships** with students. If that's the case, perhaps rules can be framed in ways that focus on what the students should do rather than what they should not do (i.e., do's rather than don'ts).

> **Key Terms**
> *Rules*: General expectations for behavior.
> *Routines*: Procedures used to guide student behaviors in particular situations.

In defining reasonable rules that are consistent with how people learn, we might also consider whether each rule is developmentally appropriate, such as whether it leaves room for the movement needs or social needs of students at different developmental phases. Furthermore, as Kohn (2006) points out, we should make a distinction between rules and routines that mostly reinforce adult control and student compliance versus rules and routines that are in service of student learning. We underscore that **classroom management** should always be in the service of learning rather than obtaining student compliance just for the sake of compliance or because the teacher has certain pet peeves. If you are a new teacher, these guidelines can help you formulate or revise your current rules.

If you are a more experienced teacher, chances are you've finely honed your classroom rules over the years and have settled on the most crucial ones that help your classroom run smoothly. But if you have a classroom management dilemma, it is worth revisiting these rules to see if there might be ways to make them better fit these criteria. Weinstein and Novodvorsky (2015) give the example of a rule that students may not talk during independent work time. They point out that this rule actually contradicts what we know about how people learn in interaction with each other. It might be an appropriate rule to apply at particular times, but there may be other times when applying this rule actually hinders learning. Table 5.3 offers some clarifying questions that might help you evaluate if your current rules are the most effective possible options.

Note that revisiting your classroom rules to look for ways that they might actually hinder your classroom management will benefit from the **Habit of Deliberate Interpretation** as you search for different possible **interpretations** of your current rules and how you currently apply them. What that means is that when you separate out the actual language used in the rule from how you yourself interpret it, you might find words like "respect," "polite," or even "objects" (as in the age-old rule in elementary school: "Keep your hands, feet, and objects to yourself") refer to particular behaviors that students might interpret differently.

As we will see in the sections below, how the teacher implements the rules is arguably more important than the rules themselves. However, if your dilemma is related to students not following classroom rules, then revisiting the rules might be a helpful step. Try Exercise 5.1.

Considering the role students play in setting and maintaining rules in the classroom can also lead to insights about classroom management dilemmas. Students may react to teacher authority if they do not trust the teacher based on past experiences, or they may yearn for more autonomy and decision-making power in

TABLE 5.3 *Evaluating Classroom Rules*

Example Current Rule	Criteria to Test	Possible Considerations
1. Do not talk when the teacher is talking.	Is it consistent with instructional goals and how people learn?	Students may need clarification of the rule, such as whether it is permissible for students to ask each other questions about directions or materials in a whisper if they misunderstood the teacher.
2. Be polite.	Is it clear?	Students may interpret politeness differently from the teacher and each other. To be clearer, the rule could describe examples of what being polite looks or sounds like.
3. When you enter the classroom, go immediately to your assigned seat and sit quietly.	Is it reasonable? Is it developmentally appropriate?	Students may need to retrieve supplies or interact regarding unfinished business or ask clarifying questions so that they can focus on class. Also, humans are inherently social and it is to be expected that students would interact with each other upon coming into class.
4. Raise your hand for permission to leave your seat for materials.	Who benefits from this rule? Is it truly necessary?	If students need materials, it may be more disruptive to instruction for teachers to stop what they are doing to grant permission to students to get materials they need. Requiring students to wait to be called on if they need learning materials can also result in lost work time.

> **Exercise 5.1** *Evaluating Your Classroom Rules*
> 1. List the rules that students are expected to comply with when your dilemma is occurring.
> 2. Test your rules using the criteria listed above. (How) Do your rules meet the criteria? What do you notice?
> 3. What possible considerations does this process raise when you consider your dilemma (see the third column of Table 5.2 for examples)?

the classroom and disengage from situations that do not offer them the autonomy they seek (Toshalis, 2015). Engaging students' needs for autonomy and helping them learn to think critically about rules and to use freedom responsibly can become part of the rule-setting process (Charney, 2002; Kohn, 2006). Depending on your context, students' developmental levels, and your own perspectives about rules, you may find that positioning students as partners and collaborators in rule setting yields great benefits.

Teachers interested in creating rules with students might approach the process by first discussing the type of learning environment that children would like to co-create together and then moving from that conversation to a deliberation about what types of norms and rules would be needed to create this environment (Charney, 2002). All members of the classroom community can then periodically check in to evaluate whether the desired learning environment is being achieved and whether adjustments in the rules might be called for. These conversations might take place, for instance, in morning meetings or dialogue circles (Charney, 2002; Toshalis, 2015). Authentic conversations about the learning environment that are conducted safely and respectfully also serve to build relationships between the teacher and the class as well as between the students themselves, again showing the interdependence of the domains of relationships and classroom management.

Routines

Routines and consistency support a sense of safety and help with providing a space conducive to learning. To manage specific situations that frequently occur in class, the teacher can rely upon what Weinstein and Novodvorsky (2015) characterize as **class-running routines, lesson-running routines,** and **interaction routines**. Class-running routines apply to procedures that students will need to use throughout the class period during each lesson. Some examples might be when to sharpen your pencil, what to do if you need to use the restroom, or what to do with your cell phone. Lesson-running routines are specific to each lesson and help the lesson run smoothly, such as specific transitions between lesson activities, or what to do when you're finished. Interaction routines specifically inform students about how, when, and with whom to interact, such as routines for group discussions or talking to a partner.

Key Terms

Class-Running Routines: Procedures that students will need to use throughout the class period during each lesson.
Lesson-Running Routines: Procedures specific to each lesson that help the lesson run smoothly.
Interaction Routines: Procedures for how, when, and with whom to interact; used across lessons as indicated by the teacher.

Learning the distinctions between the different types of routines is less important than knowing that establishing a variety of routines to structure your class in specific ways and implementing them consistently could be key in addressing your dilemma. For example, in Ms. Nash's **dilemma description**, she explained that she had a routine for getting students' attention, but that her "attention getters" did not work. As we explored Ms. Nash's use of attention getters, we learned that she had started trying a variety of attention getters because the original one she was using had stopped working. As we observed Ms. Nash using attention getters, we began to suspect that issues related to nonverbal communication and inconsistency were more relevant to addressing the dilemma than the attention getter itself. We discuss these issues next.

Focus on Culture 9: Considerations for Rules and Routines When There are Cultural Differences Between Teacher and Students

When evaluating the appropriateness of **rules** and **routines**, teachers should pay particular attention to cultural differences between different groups of students and between students and the teacher. Rules and routines teachers establish in their classroom reflect particular norms and values that might conflict with the norms and values that different students bring from home or from their communities. Plenty of debates occur regarding the role of education in socializing students into one shared set of norms and values based on dominant culture (Apple, 2014; Biesta, 2009, 2014). We propose a pragmatic approach to solving classroom dilemmas that requires teachers to create space for diversity and differentiation. Since consistency is also critical in classroom management, the balance between consistency and flexibility can be challenging to achieve, as we will further discuss below. We will give one specific example here of ways that students' and teachers' norms and values may conflict and how the teacher might negotiate that potential clash. However each teacher decides to address such clashes, we propose that teachers' responses should maximize student learning while continuing to nurture and maintain positive relationships.

In one example we have seen, African American students talk at different moments during **direct instruction** while White teachers expect silence. From the teacher's perspective, silence is the most conducive environment for clear communication that promotes learning, and silence also communicates respect and deference for the person speaking. From the students' perspective, responding during direct instruction is a cultural style that they have learned at church. Their African American pastors expect vibrant verbal articulations of assent during sermons. It is simply considered negligent not to offer an exuberant "Amen!" when the pastor makes relevant points. The pastor himself communicates these points using a carefully curated combination of volume, pitch, cadence, hand and arm gesticulations, and other body movements. For these students, a sermon is the equivalent of direct instruction at church and is most effective when there is a back-and-forth interaction between speaker and listener. In school, these students may verbalize their engagement in instruction in the precise way that the teacher interprets as distracting and disrespectful (Nieto & Bode, 2017).

As this example shows, students may also be used to learning in environments that are considerably noisier than what the teacher expects. Because it can be difficult to recognize one's own cultural style as cultural rather than just as "normal" or given, we recommend that teachers who are unfamiliar with how culture is reflected in schooling engage with materials on this topic. We list recommended resources that we use in coursework with pre-service and practicing teachers in the Resources section. These resources might be helpful in laying a foundational understanding that can help you make sense of your experiences when you further explore students' cultural styles in the contexts of their communities.

Deciding which classroom routines require which degree of detail and specification will depend on the level and context within which you teach. It is possible for a teacher to over-plan routines in ways that feel stifling to students, but it is far more common for teachers to assume that certain routines are self-evident to students when they are actually not. For example, in one of her own teaching dilemmas, Brianna was noticing that her early adolescent students often did not have a pencil or pen, which students needed throughout every class period in order to complete assignments. At first, she applied punitive consequences when this occurred since coming prepared was one of the classroom rules. However, this approach was not solving the problem. Even with a punitive consequence, the student still needed a pencil and if she lent the student a pencil, it was likely not to be returned. So, she found herself in a situation where students were regularly punished for not being prepared and she was going through a lot of pencils!

She then applied the **Habit of Personal Attribution** and the **Habit of Deliberate Interpretation** and reflected on the source of her dilemma. Previously she was approaching the dilemma through an **interpretation** that students were not following rules. However, she considered other plausible interpretations and realized that up to that point there was no explicit routine in her classroom for what to do to solve the problem if students did not have a pencil. She recognized that the implied expectation was that students would just borrow one from another student, but this approach did not work well because many students did not have extra materials. She had not created an alternative option because she felt that students needed to learn how to be responsible and did not think she should have to organize this for them. However, she realized that sticking to this belief was not helping to solve the persistent problem. This new interpretation that the source of the dilemma was the need for more a more explicit routine resulted in the following procedure, which was much more effective:

1. You can borrow a pencil any day you do not have one, but it must be done silently and during the first two minutes of class.
2. Bring something of yours to my desk for collateral. It has to be something you will not forget (e.g., your house keys, phone).
3. Wait until I acknowledge you and hand me your item. I will hand you a sharpened pencil. Silently return to your seat and get started.

4. During our clean-up routine in the last two minutes of class, silently approach me and wait until I acknowledge you.
5. Return your pencil to me and I will hand you your item.

On the one hand, she felt that creating the option for students to borrow a pencil without penalty was enabling students' irresponsible behavior. But on the other hand, the previous version of the routine was also not actually increasing student responsibility. Instead, it was resulting in time wasted on punishing students, which negatively impacted her relationships with them, and did not end with them being more prepared for class. This new approach maintained positive relationships, maximized learning time, and empowered students to effectively handle the situation before it became a problem.

In addition to organizing materials, another specific class-running routine that teachers must negotiate is student seating. We saw in Ms. Nash's description of her dilemma that part of her challenge with starting class had to do with students not being seated in a timely way or in a position that would facilitate the lesson. We suggest that intentional seating is a productive strategy at all levels of education. Teachers can adjust how they organize and communicate this seating based on student age and level. Ms. Nash taught early adolescents and needed to balance students' intensive needs for peer interaction with her need to gain and keep their attention when she needed it. She also needed to consider students' emotional safety in a context where bullying could quickly occur if a supportive classroom culture was not built and maintained (Toshalis, 2015). During our professional development work with Ms. Nash, she learned that seating charts were the best tool for addressing these different priorities. She considered how the physical layout of her classroom space and furniture could best support her goals. Because she had a front section of the room with individual student desks and a back section of the room with long laboratory tables and equipment, she decided to position the individual student desks in the front in rows and use the laboratory for interactive and group activities. In assigning students to seats, she considered which students would benefit from being closest to the front as well as how to position students next to each other who could quickly work together in mutually beneficial ways if she wanted to pair or group students for a task. She changed these seats every six weeks but during the time between these transitions, she worked on continually reinforcing her expectations that students would quickly take their place in their assigned seat at the beginning of class.

Establishing and Maintaining Rules and Routines

One commonality we see when considering Brianna's and Ms. Nash's dilemmas is that students needed explicit instruction about **rules** and **routines**. Students may also need to practice rules and routines before they become habit (Charney, 2002; Weinstein & Novodvorsky, 2015) which is true of both procedural and instructional routines (Kagan & Kagan, 2009), as we will further discuss in the next chapter. As a teacher, you undoubtedly go over rules and routines with students when you first start working with them. In most contexts, this occurs during the first days of the semester or school year. Time spent on practicing a new routine with students will return dividends in saved time later on when the learned routine facilitates the smooth running of lessons.

In describing the explicit teaching of rules and routines, Charney (2002) advises that teachers engage in five steps:

1. Demonstrate how the rule or routine should look if practiced effectively.
2. Help students notice what it is about the demonstration that makes the behavior effective.
3. Summarize the observations and remind students about what they noticed.
4. Have students demonstrate the rule or routine while peers repeat what makes their behaviors effective.
5. Have everyone practice the rule or routine.

The developmental levels and specific classroom dynamics of a group may require a teacher to engage with some of these steps more or less frequently. An early elementary teacher might engage students in more discussion about the reasoning behind rules whereas a high school teacher might do this step more quickly or be able to skip it altogether, depending on which rule is being presented. Regardless of students' developmental levels, a teacher may be able to improve a dilemma positioned in the **domain of classroom management** by working through this collection of practices.

Weinstein and Novodvorsky (2015) also recommend adding demonstrations of what not to do along with explanations or discussions about why these counterexamples are undesirable. Demonstrating counterexamples to rules and routines can be done with humor, which can be particularly enjoyable for elementary and early adolescent students, while effectively preventing these undesirable behaviors from occurring. For example, during a coaching trajectory with an elementary teacher, we were modeling how to teach students to do an interactive activity. We did an exaggerated and humorous role play with us playing the roles of students and displaying behavior we wanted students to avoid. Because we were playing the roles, we could insert humor, ensure that the students themselves would not have their feelings hurt during the demonstration, and show precisely what we meant as we described how to do and not do the activity.

Specific articulation of teacher expectations is necessary for effective classroom management, but it is far from sufficient for maintaining a smooth, well-run classroom. Teachers do this through repeated verbal and nonverbal behaviors that are consistent with what they first say about the rules and routines in the class. In this section, we will discuss those verbal and nonverbal behaviors. When further exploring discrete strategies related to voice, body positioning, and the other moves discussed below, teachers should also keep in mind the material from the previous chapter about building positive relationships with students because these positive relationships provide the foundation upon which effective classroom management is built. In the previous chapter, we presented Toshalis' (2015) point that teachers first have to "connect to correct" (p. 255). The nature of teachers' rapport and quality of ongoing interactions with students plays a key role in how well the strategies discussed below will work. Accordingly, it's important to try each of these approaches with an eye toward building upon and maintaining positive connections with students.

Teacher Verbal Behaviors

It's obvious that teacher communication plays a vital role in the **domain of classroom management**. In this section, we will explore some verbal behaviors that can have a big impact on how your classroom runs. We have selected the behaviors to focus on by considering research literature, personal experience, and those most relevant to Ms. Nash's dilemma, but by no means are these the only verbal behaviors teachers can employ when communicating with students about classroom management. These behaviors include **precorrection**, **explicit timing**, and **redirection** (Haydon & Kroeger, 2016; Weinstein & Novodvorsky, 2015).

Precorrection

Precorrection is when the teacher anticipates ways that a transition or activity could descend into students' inattention, unruliness, or other behaviors that distract from the teacher's instructional priorities, and the teacher uses that anticipation to prevent those behaviors from occurring (Haydon & Kroeger, 2016). For example, when Ms. Nash was building solar cars with her students, there were many times when they needed to transition from sitting at the front of the classroom to moving to the back of the room to gather materials and begin the hands-on part of the lesson. In one instance, they needed to get a ruler to measure and mark where they would place the axles on the car's frame. Ms. Nash knew from past experience that students might be tempted to take the rulers and hit each other with them as they walked from the materials box to their lab tables. In this situation, Ms. Nash could engage the strategy of precorrection before releasing the students to get rulers by playfully saying something like, "Now, some of my more mischievous students in the past might have seen this as an opportunity to hit each other with the rulers before arriving at their tables. But you guys are nothing like this." In this example, Ms. Nash's positive rapport with students facilitated her specific classroom management moves.

> **Key Terms**
>
> *Precorrection*: When the teacher anticipates ways that a transition or activity could descend into students' inattention, unruliness, or other behaviors that distract from the teacher's instructional priorities, and the teacher uses that anticipation to prevent those behaviors from occurring.

Next, she could ask a student who would most likely to do this type of hitting—let's call that student Julian for this example—to model the routine by saying something like, "Julian, show us how an excellent group of students like you all will walk from the materials box to the lab table" and then hand Julian a ruler to demonstrate to the class how they should walk with it. This is a precorrection because Ms. Nash has prepared Julian for the behavior she desires by having him do an example for the class, which will make him and his classmates less likely to hit others with the ruler. She has corrected the potential misbehavior in advance, or "precorrected" it.

To succeed at precorrection, the teacher has to accurately anticipate what students might do that the teacher would consider disruptive or off-task, when that behavior might occur, and what part of the activity might propel that behavior forward. In our example, Ms. Nash had to know that students might hit each other, and that it would occur during the transition in which they were individually gathering rulers. Then the teacher has to take action before that sequence of activities begins. When using precorrection, the teacher should always stay positive and be mindful of the tone they use. For example, there is a wide difference in saying, "It seems like every time we do this, you all want to get out the rulers and hit each other like fifth graders, so this time we are going to try a different routine and see if you can follow it," and simply explaining the behavior the teacher wishes to see with a positive expectation that the students will follow through. This approach preserves the teacher–student **relationship** because the teacher does not have to correct the student. This strategy also saves a lot of instructional time that might otherwise be spent on redirection or discipline.

It can be challenging for teachers to anticipate what and when to precorrect. Engaging the **Habit of Deliberate Interpretation** before you start can be useful in separating out the undesirable behavior from your automatic emotional response and examining the behavior with more neutral eyes. It can also help you pinpoint the precise moments that are important for your precorrection by **observing** the behavior separately from **interpreting** it as distracting or disrespectful. The questions in Exercise 5.2 will help you in this process.

Exercise 5.2   *Anticipating What and When to Precorrect*

Directions

Consider the following questions to help you determine what behaviors may need to have precorrections and when they occur.

1. During a recent lesson, what behavior would I like to have prevented my student(s) from doing?
2. What was happening in the lesson when that behavior occurred? What was I saying or doing? What were students supposed to be doing?
3. Which students were involved and what specifically did they do? Describe this objectively without judgment.
4. What materials were involved in the lesson? What were the conditions in which the materials were being used?
5. What activities were being transitioned? What was expected of students at this time? How was the time managed?

Now let's use the questions from Exercise 5.2 to walk through the example of Julian and the rulers. When Ms. Nash considered which behavior she wanted to prevent, she identified that it was the students hitting each other with the rulers that was undesirable because it riled them up and derailed the activity. She noted that this behavior was happening during a transition in which students had to move to a new location in the class. During that transition, each student also had to obtain materials. Although students were dismissed from their seats in groups to get the materials, they could not begin the next activity until the teacher helped them, so those students who got their rulers first needed to sit idly with their rulers and wait.

Certain students, like Julian, tended to be very active during class and they seemed to be the ones who hit their peers with rulers during the transition. The shape and size of the rulers seemed to particularly lend themselves to hitting others, as Ms. Nash noted that she did not have this problem with other types of materials. The conditions surrounding this event were that students had a discrete task to do that might not have held enough cognitive challenge. They had to measure and attach axles, but they were not all ready to take that step and Ms. Nash also had the impression that many of them did not understand what they needed to measure and why, which is why they needed to wait for her help after they got their rulers.

Ms. Nash could use this information to start to form patterns about times when she would need to make a precorrection in the future: (1) when transitions were occurring, (2) when particularly enticing materials were being used, (3) when her most active students needed to move around the class and engage with those materials, and (4) when students were transitioning in groups but were not able to begin the next activity independently. If Ms. Nash could recognize when this pattern was coming up in the lesson, she could choose a precorrection strategy such as the one we described. She could choose other ways to precorrect as well, such as by having a **routine** established about which students would collect and return supplies, or how students would move from the front or back of the room. She might say something like, "Group 3, it's your turn to get your rulers and car frames and then to wait quietly. Show us how an excellent and calm group of students would do that."

Explicit Timing

Explicit timing means telling students exactly how much time they have to complete a certain task and then providing reminders throughout the task of how much time is left (Haydon & Kroeger, 2016). The reminder could be in the form of a digital timer visibly displayed in the room largely enough for all students to see it, or it could be the teacher verbally announcing the amount of time left. This simple and straightforward strategy can increase the efficiency and motivation with which students work toward completion, which can help with dilemmas in which students take too long to complete a task. There are two things that can make or break the effectiveness of this strategy. First, the amount of time needs to be realistic and just enough to push students a bit without causing a paralyzing amount of anxiety. Second, the teacher has to be consistent about the timeframe, keeping good track of it, and then holding students to being finished or to moving on once the allotted time is up.

> **Key Terms**
>
> *Explicit Timing*: Letting students know exactly how much time they have to complete a certain task and providing reminders throughout the task of how much time is left.

For example, one of Ms. Nash's instructional routines was to start each class with a warm-up activity. She used a timer and always set it at five minutes, regardless of the prompt. This meant that sometimes students answered a prompt that required little effort very quickly, and inevitably some students spent the rest of the time talking with each other or getting up out of their seats to play with the cars in the back of the class. Other times, the timer would go off and students would complain that they needed more time. If they had been diligently working during the three minutes, it would have been reasonable for Ms. Nash to have added more time for the warm-up. However, we frequently observed that many students did not get started on the warm-up until the time was almost up and then they would ask for more time. If teachers acquiesce in this situation, they are reinforcing students' off-task behaviors and are inadvertently expressing to students that the timer does not matter. As Ms. Nash worked on the timing of her warm-ups, she became intentional when determining the amount of time it took to complete each warm-up. She also began making announcements about the time throughout the warm-up period such as, "Okay, everyone, I have set the timer. You have five minutes to complete today's warm-up," and "We have one minute left. Wrap up what you are writing." These verbal cues helped students stay focused on the task. Ms. Nash also gave more attention to the complexity of the tasks required during each warm-up. Since the amount of time allotted was always the same, she learned to create a consistent level of difficulty in the warm-up activities as well.

Redirection By Focusing on the Instructional Task

Another verbal behavior that you can draw upon in getting your classroom to run smoothly is redirection. The most frequent type of redirection that we see in classrooms is disciplinary, which means it is focused on students' lack of compliance with rules or routines. This type of redirection might sound like this: "It's getting very loud in here. Let's quiet down," or "Please turn around and face the front." There is nothing inherently wrong with this type of redirection unless a large percentage of a teacher's time, and therefore a large percentage of the messages students receive, is focused on discipline-related redirections. Even in the best-case scenario though, where the teacher uses disciplinary redirection sparingly and in a way that preserves positive relationships, these types of redirection create disruption to a smooth instructional flow. These disruptions can add up and result in much lost time and instructional focus, so we want to present another type of redirection that can serve the same purpose of facilitating the activity at hand while reducing the distractions created through the focus on discipline. We think this is an important strategy to discuss for teaching dilemmas that could be related to time on task or **lesson-running routines**.

Redirection by focusing on the instructional task differs from redirection by focusing on discipline because the teacher never refers to student misbehavior or inattention. The teacher does notice student misbehavior or inattention, but instead of mentioning those behaviors, the teacher addresses them by drawing attention to the instructional task instead. In this way, redirection occurs, but the redirection is always in service of learning as opposed to redirection focused on misbehavior where the redirection is in service of compliance. In Table 5.4, we compare the two different types of redirection by using an example.

Key Terms

Redirection by focusing on the instructional task: Shifting students' attention away from a distraction and back to the task at hand by referring to or emphasizing instructional activities, goals, or learning benefits.

In this example, you can see how both approaches to redirection may get Jonah back to his seat and working on the puzzle. However, these approaches have different potential impacts. When Mr. McBride redirects Jonah with a focus on behavior, the redirection has a nagging quality to it that may slowly erode Mr. McBride's relationship with Jonah and cause Jonah to lose motivation to participate in these after-lunch activities. But when Mr. McBride redirects Jonah by focusing on the task, he can also convey how he has tailored the task to Jonah's interests, thereby strengthening his relational connection to Jonah and also making Jonah excited about the activity itself. In this second example, the purpose of the redirection is clearly on the learning, whereas in the first example, the purpose of the redirection is on Jonah's

TABLE 5.4 *Comparing the Two Types of Redirection*

Scenario
Thomas McBride teaches third grade. During the first hour after lunch, his students have center time where small groups rotate through a set of four different types of puzzles that each support their knowledge and skill development related to the current topics they are learning across subject areas. He has noticed that during center time, sometimes Jonah and Maria begin talking to each other instead of focusing on their puzzles. He has struggled with addressing the situation and has named it as his teaching dilemma. We suspect that the dilemma might need to be reframed within the domain of instruction, but we first encourage Thomas to shift from redirecting with a focus on behavior to redirecting with a focus on instruction. Here are the examples of how he changed from one approach to the other. In this scene, Jonah has walked across the room to Maria's desk and started to tell her a story about something that happened at lunch. He furtively looks across the room at Mr. McBride to see whether he is being observed.

Redirection with a Focus on Behavior	Redirection with a Focus on Instruction
Mr. McBride: Jonah, where should you be right now? **Jonah**: At my desk. **Mr. McBride**: And why aren't you at your desk? We have this conversation almost every day. I don't want to keep having to remind you. **Jonah**: I just want to tell Maria something really quick. **Mr. McBride**: You know that this is center time. Please go back to your seat now and get started.	**Mr. McBride**: Jonah, be sure to pick up your puzzle on the way back to your seat because we are starting now. I think you will really enjoy the yellow puzzle. It's about how to make tacos. I know you love tacos! **Jonah**: Ooh, yummy! I do love tacos! **Mr. McBride**: Well, I just started the timer, so you should head there now so that you have enough time to work on it. You will get to explore how the tacos will taste different if you use different proportions of ingredients.

compliance. By keeping the focus on instruction in this moment, Mr. McBride is also more likely to keep Jonah engaged at other times as well. This situation provides a good example of the connection between all three **domains of teaching**. Mr. McBride's relationship with Jonah is affected by the way that Mr. McBride addresses this classroom management challenge, and, ultimately, the success of Mr. McBride's instruction is supported by both of these other domains. At the same time, Mr. McBride refers to an instructional topic here in order to maintain the smooth running of the class, which relates to his classroom management.

Focus on Culture 10: Cultural Differences in Verbal and Nonverbal Behaviors

As we discuss verbal and nonverbal behaviors, it may seem that we presume that these behaviors will be enacted by teachers and perceived by students in similar ways regardless of background and context. However, we encourage readers to review the *Focus on Culture* sections in Chapters 2 and 4 where we discuss how different behaviors may lead to different **interpretations** and **judgments** across cultures and contexts. We know that students and teachers from different cultural backgrounds may have different needs and views related to classroom management approaches in general, and verbal and nonverbal behaviors in particular (Nieto & Bode, 2017). These differences especially become important when teachers hold students from nondominant racial and ethnic groups responsible for behaving and communicating in ways that reflect dominant culture (Milner et al., 2019).

Culturally responsive classroom management describes teacher behaviors for effectively managing diverse classrooms (Murphy & Kennedy, 2019). Culturally responsive classroom managers maintain high academic expectations while keeping all students in class and focused on learning (Gaias et al., 2019). In the early research that would come to have the name "culturally responsive classroom management," we see how positive relationships and effective management are intertwined and are particularly important for, and affected by, culturally competent communication. In one early study, researchers found that teachers of students from indigenous backgrounds who were able to effectively manage their classes understood the values and communication styles of students and their communities (Kleinfeld, 1975). For example, teachers needed to understand that nonverbal behaviors like eye contact had a different meaning for students from some groups, who learned that looking at adults in the eye was a sign of disrespect even though some teachers expected students to look directly at them as a sign of respect and attentiveness.

Communication styles also played an important role, with Black working-class parents using direct commands and

White teachers using questions to give directives with their own children (Heath, 1983). In the classroom, this difference meant that teachers would ask questions such as "What should you do with those scissors," which they meant as an indirect command for the students to put scissors away, but which students interpreted as a question, and a rather inane one at that. When the students did not respond by putting the scissors away, they would be sanctioned by the teacher for disrespect.

Contemporary research on culturally responsive classroom management has continued to build on these foundational studies, particularly in the US context where the predominant minoritized social groups are Black and Latinx. Students belonging to these groups are often **judged** by teachers to be disrespectful due to cultural differences and are sent out of class more often than their White peers even if they are behaving similarly to those peers (Skiba et al., 2011). Teachers who do not know their students well may misinterpret student communication as disrespectful when no disrespect is intended. For example, in one study we conducted with Black middle school girls in the US, we found that teachers often critiqued the girls as being too "loud and unladylike" (Murphy et al., 2013, p. 590) when the girls were simply interacting in ways that were appropriate in their home culture. Teachers punished them for being too loud, too confrontational, and too active. Such punishments occur six times more frequently with Black girls than White girls even when the types of disruptions displayed are the same (Crenshaw, 2015; Morris, 2015). Teachers must continually employ all three **habits of mind** when determining appropriate classroom management strategies and evaluating their results.

Teacher Nonverbal Behaviors

In the previous section, we described **precorrection, explicit timing,** and **redirection with a focus on instruction** as verbal behaviors teachers can use to implement and maintain the **rules** and **routines** that structure teaching and learning in their classrooms. In this section, we will describe nonverbal behaviors. Research has established the importance of nonverbal messages in teaching (Woolfolk & Brooks, 1985). The tricky thing about nonverbal behavior is that most of it occurs unconsciously (Babad, 2005). That means that nonverbal behaviors may be playing a big role in your teaching dilemmas without you realizing it, but it also means that by becoming conscious of your nonverbal behaviors and choosing them more intentionally, you may have access to strategies that you have not yet considered. The nonverbal behaviors we will discuss are **withitness, active supervision, planned ignoring, prosody, kinesics, proximity, haptics,** eye contact, and facial expression.

Withitness

Jacob Kounin (1970) coined the term "withitness" to describe the behaviors of teachers who had demonstrated the ability to manage their classes. Withitness means conveying a sense that you know what is happening in all areas of the classroom at all times and incorporates the intentional use of all of the behaviors we describe in this section. Students describe teachers who have withitness as having "eyes in the back of their heads." Students know that they cannot get away with things in the classroom of a teacher who has this quality, not because they fear the teacher but because the teacher is able to send a continuous message that they know what is going on. If your dilemma has to do with entire classes of students continually not listening to you, then developing withitness might be a good place to start. One first step is to project confidence simply by standing up straight, giving the class your full attention, and using a strong, steady, and determined voice. These simple tips combine verbal and nonverbal behaviors in a way that projects the teacher's awareness and high expectations. Careful attention to combining and implementing the other nonverbal behaviors we describe next will also contribute to your withitness.

> **Key Terms**
>
> *Withitness*: Conveying a sense that the teacher knows what is happening in all areas of the classroom at all times ("having eyes in the back of your head").

Active Supervision

When a teacher walks around the room to check on students' progress and support their learning, the teacher is actively supervising the group (Haydon & Kroeger, 2016). **Active supervision** involves a continuous scanning of the room, interaction with a range of students in one lesson—and all students over the course of several lessons—and praise for desirable behavior (De Pry & Sugai, 2002). When the teacher is actively supervising, they can skillfully select when and how to address student behavior that is not focused on instruction. One response might be planned ignoring.

> **Key Terms**
>
> *Active Supervision*: Continuously checking on students' progress by walking around the classroom, scanning the room, or interacting with students.

Planned Ignoring

In planned ignoring, the teacher is aware of a student's disruptive behavior but intentionally ignores it in order to keep the focus on the learning. You may notice in these strategies that we keep coming back to prioritizing a focus on learning over a focus on compliance. Planned ignoring is a strategy that many teachers use when they decide that keeping the focus on the instructional activity is more important than disrupting the activity in order to gain compliance from a student. We recommend that teachers use planned ignoring as often as possible in order to maintain high expectations for academic performance, which requires a continual focus on learning. Note that planned ignoring is different than not noticing student behavior or allowing students to derail instruction with no recourse. Planned ignoring is only effective if the teacher can successfully keep the instruction moving forward and convey a sense of withitness. The planned ignoring of students' misbehavior requires that students know that the teacher knows that the behavior is occurring. Students can tell the difference between a teacher who knows what's happening and is prioritizing instruction versus a teacher who is oblivious and has low expectations of students. They cooperate more readily with the first than with the second.

> **Key Terms**
>
> *Planned Ignoring*: When the teacher is aware of a student's disruptive behavior but intentionally ignores it in order to keep the focus on the learning.

Prosody

Prosody describes the tone, rhythm, and volume of your voice. It has to do with the words and phrases you stress in your speech and how you do that. Although prosody relates to sound, it is considered a nonverbal behavior because it communicates information that is separate from the content of the verbal message you are saying. Use the questions in Exercise 5.3 to become conscious of how you use prosody and the effects of your choices. You might even want to experiment in your classroom as you consider these.

> **Key Terms**
>
> *Prosody*: The tone, rhythm, and volume of one's voice; how one stresses words and phrases.

When Brianna was a new teacher, she found that as her students did interactive activities and began to speak loudly, she began to speak even louder so that she could talk over them. However, she noticed that the volume in the class just continued to rise when she did this and she had no voice left at the end of the day. So, she tried a different approach. Instead of speaking louder when students got loud, she tried speaking more quietly. She wondered if such an approach could ever work, but indeed she

> **Exercise 5.3** *Using Prosody*
> **Directions**
> Consider the following questions to help you identify when and how you use prosody and what effects that has in your classroom.
>
> - When do I speak loudly and when do I speak softly? Why? What happens when I change the volume of my voice in different moments?
> - When do I speak quickly and when do I speak slowly? Why? What happens when I change the speed of my speaking?
> - When do I change the pitch of my voice? Why? What happens when I change my pitch?
> - When do I change the rhythm of my voice? Why? What happens when I change my rhythm?

noticed that as she spoke more quietly, students would stop speaking in order to hear her. It was like magic, which many of these nonverbal strategies can seem to be when the teacher consciously and effectively uses them. Brianna also noticed, though, that lowering the volume and cadence of her voice only garnered students' attention when she combined it with intentional uses of withitness and kinesics.

Kinesics

Kinesics is the intentional use of body positioning and gestures to help to manage a class. Walking around the classroom while lecturing or during discussion can particularly hold students' attention. Standing in the middle of the room when giving directions can also be useful. Moving away from students who are speaking in order to put as many of the students who are listening as possible between the speaker and the teacher can motivate the speaking student to elevate the volume of their voice. This teacher positioning physically includes the listening students in the conversation because those students are sitting between the teacher and the speaker. This approach is much more effective than remaining at the front of the room and engaging in question-and-answer sessions with students sitting near you because when this situation occurs, students sitting in other places in the room can lose attention. If your dilemma relates to keeping the attention of students who are often passive in class, this strategy might be helpful.

> **Key Terms**
>
> *Kinesics*: The intentional use of body positioning and gestures to help manage a class.

Proximity

Proximity is a form of kinesics that involves teachers moving close to a particular student or students. You can use proximity to great effect by standing next to students whose attention you want to hold. This movement can serve as a redirection without you having to even say anything to the student. If your dilemma relates to a student who you often correct because they talk during instruction, intentional use of proximity might be worth trying. For example, instead of giving directions at the front of the class, you might stand near this student when explaining an activity, which will likely have the effect of the student not speaking to their friends when you are standing near them, and ultimately them paying attention.

> **Key Terms**
>
> *Proximity*: Moving close to a particular student or students in order to redirect behavior.

Haptics

Haptics in classroom management is the strategic use of touch to focus attention or connect with students. The use of physical touch can be important and meaningful depending on the age and preference of the student and the comfort level of the teacher. In early elementary school, some students love to hug their teacher, which can be great for building bonds. In late elementary school and middle school, many teachers like to greet students with a hand shake or a high five. During class, these teachers might also touch a student on the arm or shoulder to make a connection or express care. These same strategies can be used with some high school students as well.

> **Key Terms**
>
> *Haptics*: The strategic use of touch to focus attention or connect with students.

In some cultural contexts, teachers and students are uncomfortable with teachers physically touching students. But haptics not only describes touching students themselves, it also describes any strategic use of touch. One way we have seen haptics used to great effect is when a teacher gets a student's attention by touching that student's desk. A teacher can be talking to the whole class and looking around, while simultaneously walking over to a distracted student and touching that student's desk. The student then tends to immediately pay attention without the teacher having made a verbal redirection. In this example, the teacher is making a connection with the student using nonverbal behavior without drawing any attention to the student or distracting from the instructional flow. Also note that in this example, the teacher combines proximity and haptics to conduct a nonverbal redirection.

Eye Contact

Eye contact is a self-explanatory strategy that has also been mentioned in combination with other strategies. Eye contact can be an important way to build connections with hard-to-reach students and to hold the attention of all students during instruction. As with all of the verbal and nonverbal strategies we are describing, eye contact addresses both the **domains of classroom management** and **relationships** while supporting the **domain of instruction**. A withit teacher might combine this strategy with kinesics and active supervision by physically walking to all areas of the room during the lesson and making eye contact with all students (Marzano et al., 2011).

Facial Expression

This is the final nonverbal behavior we will discuss that can promote strong classroom management. It may seem unimportant but in our experience, it can have a big impact on how students respond to the teacher. One teacher we worked with conducted a teacher inquiry related to projecting more warmth and one way she pursued that goal was by working on unfurling her brow. Students mentioned this trait as a reflection of an unfriendly demeanor, saying, "Why do you always look so serious?" Even though this teacher cared deeply about her students and wanted to be sure that they left her class with fundamental skills they would need for life, many of her students did not respect her simply because they did not think that she liked them. They misread her concerned looking facial expression as meanness. This teacher's monotone voice, lack of eye contact, and infrequent praise of students only served to reinforce their negative impressions of her, which prevented her genuine concern for them from coming across. During her inquiry she made an intentional effort to soften her facial expressions while still expressing concern for her students' learning and well-being. She also needed to focus on her use of prosody and eye contact to accomplish this goal. In this section, we have examined the role that teachers' verbal and nonverbal behaviors play in classroom management. Use Exercise 5.4 to help you evaluate your own uses of verbal and nonverbal behavior.

> **Focus on Culture 11: Culturally Responsive Classroom Management**
>
> Teachers need to adjust their expectations and behaviors to accommodate cultural differences if they want to create positive learning experiences for students (Brinegar et al., 2016; Marcucci & Elmesky, 2023; Milner et al., 2019). This process

will require the **Habit of Deliberate Interpretation** as teachers separate their **interpretations** about student "misbehavior" from the **observation** of what students are actually doing and a consideration of why that might be the case. By making this distinction, teachers may be able to reinterpret student behaviors as culturally appropriate. To be able to do this, teachers need to have the following dispositions or competencies:

a) Recognition of how they center their own cultural background and the biases that creates in them;
b) Knowledge of students' cultural backgrounds;
c) Understanding of how schools exist within social, economic, and political systems that structure advantages and disadvantages for different groups;
d) Ability and willingness to use culturally appropriate teaching strategies and approaches;
e) Commitment to care for students and build classrooms of caring (Siwatu et al., 2017; Weinstein & Novodvorsky, 2015).

In the previous chapter, we discussed **warm demanding**, which connects teachers' high expectations with their care for students. Warm demanders rely on their positive relationships with students to implement consistent, strong classroom management in service of rigorous academic instruction. Culturally responsive warm demanders understand that their authority with students comes through an ongoing exchange of respect (Ford & Sassi, 2014). That means that these teachers do not rely on their titles or positions as teacher to instill respect in students but rather engage students through care and academic support in order to continually earn respect. Culturally responsive classroom management hinges upon teachers' abilities to view students' respect as something that must be earned rather than automatically given. In a dominant culture that views respect for authority indeed as a given, this position requires intentional questioning. You will need to engage the **Habit of Personal Attribution** if you find yourself wondering why students from marginalized backgrounds do not respect you and consider how you could better earn their respect.

As we have mentioned before, this step requires a foundation of **teacher efficacy**, or the belief that you have or can learn the skills to successfully solve your dilemma (Siwatu, 2007; Siwatu et al., 2017). Siwatu et al. (2017) have developed a tool for measuring teachers' self-efficacy in implementing culturally responsive classroom management. A few of their indicators, listed here verbatim, might be helpful as you consider your own level of self-efficacy and moves you could make in your own classroom to be more culturally responsive in your classroom management. Ask yourself, "How well do I:

- Assess students' behaviors with the knowledge that acceptable school behaviors may not match those that are acceptable within a student's home culture?
- Create a learning environment that conveys respect for the cultures of all students in my classroom?
- Establish high behavioral expectations that encourage students to produce high-quality work?
- Use what I know about my students' cultural background to develop an effective learning environment?
- Address inappropriate behavior without relying on traditional methods of discipline such as office referrals?
- Critically analyze students' classroom behavior from a cross-cultural perspective?
- Personalize the classroom so that it is reflective of the cultural background of my students?
- Critically assess whether a particular behavior constitutes misbehavior?
- Develop a partnership with parents from diverse cultural and linguistic backgrounds?
- Implement an intervention that minimizes a conflict that occurs when a student's culturally based behavior is not consistent with school norms?" (Siwatu et al., 2017, pp. 873–874).

Exercise 5.4 *Evaluating Your Uses of Verbal and Nonverbal Behaviors*

Directions: In the table below, you will find a list of the verbal and nonverbal behaviors that teachers can use to manage their classes more effectively. For each behavior, rate how conscious you are about using this strategy in your classroom. Then, rate how well your use of this strategy works in your classroom. At the conclusion of your ratings, determine if any of these strategies might help you improve your dilemma.

(Non)Verbal Behavior	I consciously use this strategy... Never ←————————→ Continuously throughout every class	My use of this strategy (positively OR negatively) affects my students... Not at all ←————————→ A whole lot
Precorrection		
Explicit Timing		
Redirection by Focusing on the Instructional Task		
Withitness		
Active Supervision		
Planned Ignoring		
Prosody		
Kinesics		
Proximity		
Haptics		
Eye Contact		
Facial Expression		

Navigating Classroom Management Tensions

Even when teachers are stellar classroom managers, there are times when they have to navigate tensions in the classroom. Those tensions may be related to students not focusing on assignments, directly challenging the teacher, or bullying peers. In such moments, teachers may balance consistency with flexibility in order to keep the class running smoothly. While consistency is crucial for successfully implementing **rules** and **routines**, flexibility is also sometimes necessary. Striking a good balance between these two, such as is required in **planned ignoring**, can be a challenge. Having an authoritative stance while implementing **warm demanding** allows the teacher to make exceptions to rules when necessary while still maintaining student respect. If such exceptions are based on the teacher's authentic care for students, students are likely to know this and follow the teacher's lead when they set and maintain boundaries.

For example, when Amy was teaching a ninth-grade class, students sometimes came to school with aches and pains and wanted to sit at the back of the room and rest. In some cases, Amy knew that these students did not have access to immediate medical care. She used her knowledge of students' personal situations to gauge when to deviate from the seating chart and make these exceptions. If this started to happen too frequently with a particular student, Amy took further action by following up with caregivers and the school nurse so that the student did not fall behind. She balanced warmth and care with high expectations for student learning. Due to her positive relationships with the rest of the students and her otherwise consistent implementation of rules and routines, they accepted these occasional deviations and further respected her for the flexibility she showed in her care for her individual students (Cushman & Rogers, 2008). For some teachers, taking this caring and authoritative stance will feel uncomfortable. In the previous chapter, we encouraged teachers to enact relationships in ways that were authentic to them, whereas here teachers need to be able to learn behaviors even if those behaviors do not feel authentic. The most important one is having an authoritative stance, which requires consistent demonstrations of **withitness**.

Even with skilled teachers, explicit conflicts sometimes erupt in class. In these situations, teachers must choose which reactions are most appropriate. Sometimes teachers choose to send misbehaving students out of class. We understand that when teachers make this choice, they may have different motivations. One motivation may be the belief that a main purpose of education is socialization and a big part of teachers' job descriptions is to socialize students into a certain way of behaving that reflects dominant norms and values (Biesta, 2009). In this book, we argue that teachers' core business is maximizing the learning of all students and equalizing opportunities for all students to learn. Pursuing this goal will sometimes require teachers to question which behaviors are really most important to reinforce in a classroom focused on learning. We find that many student behaviors that teachers identify as disruptive can have more to do with the teacher's pet peeves than with a major disruption to the learning environment. If this is the case, keeping students in class will require a shifting of what the teacher considers as behaviors worthy of being sent out of class. All three **habits of mind** may be necessary to engage in this process.

Another motivation for sending misbehaving students out of class may be the belief that it is necessary so that the rest of the students can learn. But recent research tells us that it can have the opposite effect (Del Toro & Wang, 2023). One thing that the non-disciplined students learn when the teacher sends their peer out of class is that some students do not belong in class and that they, too, might be sent out under certain circumstances. According to this research, the consequence of non-disciplined students fearing that they too could be disciplined may actually increase their disruptive behavior. Non-disciplined students may also perceive that the disciplined student is "bad" and deserves to be ostracized, which can further damage the classroom community. When these disciplined students are from minoritized racial or ethnic backgrounds, the teacher may be inadvertently sending the additional message that students from this group are inherently bad, which is one way that institutional racism may be perpetuated. Both teachers and students are better off if all students can be supported to stay in class and focus on learning.

A third motivation may be that teachers are simply at the end of their ropes and do not know what else to do or try. This situation leads to a lack of **teacher efficacy** that can make it impossible to continue to engage the **Habit of Personal Attribution**, which is necessary for effectively managing a classroom where students also feel cared about. Although we don't focus exclusively on classroom management in this book, we will offer a few ideas here for addressing teaching dilemmas related to handling conflict and disruption.

De-Escalation

Classroom conflicts are inevitable even for the most confident and competent teachers. In the face of conflict, or when **loaded moments** occur that could lead to conflict, teachers have an opportunity to prevent the situation from spiraling to the point of excluding students from class (Kennedy & Junker, 2023). This prevention requires **de-escalation**. When working with educators on de-escalation, we teach the **"SIMMER down" method**. As you may have guessed, "SIMMER" is an acronym, with each letter explained in Table 5.5. Here is an example of a scenario in which a teacher uses the SIMMER down method:

TABLE 5.5 *The SIMMER Down Method for De-Escalating Conflicts*

Step #	Acronym	Description
1	S=Slow	Slow down enough to make a different choice in your response.
2	I=Ignore	Ignore the manner in which the other person is communicating.
3	M=Message	Instead, focus on the **M**essage being sent.
4	M=Meaning	Respond to the **M**eaning behind the message, not the manner. Try: "It sounds like you feel _____. Is that right? Tell me more about that."
5	E=Examine	Examine whether your response changes the other person's manner.
6	R=Repeat or Resolve	If steps 1–4 did not successfully de-escalate, **R**epeat them. If they did, **R**esolve the conflict and then debrief it later when you and the student(s) are calm again.

> **Key Terms**
>
> *Loaded Moment*: The moment of friction when the teacher and student(s) have conflicting needs and must negotiate their different needs before the friction becomes a full-fledged conflict.
> *De-escalation*: Preventing a loaded moment from becoming a conflict or preventing a current conflict from getting worse.
> *SIMMER Down Method*: A method for de-escalating a situation that encompasses the slowing down of a heated interaction to notice and respond to the meaning of the message the other is trying to send. The acronym stands for: Slow down, Ignore the manner, focus on the Message, respond to the Meaning, Examine the outcome, Repeat or Resolve.

Context:
Mr. Van Dyke has been teaching for three years in a community that is very different than where he grew up. As in many geographical regions, the neighborhood is racially and socioeconomically segregated, with most of his students being ethnic minorities living in subsidized housing close to the school. Mr. Van Dyke cares deeply for his students, but he finds himself torn between his care for them and his frustration at what he interprets as their disrespect and defiance. He often does not understand why they don't care as much about their own education as he does. Lately he has been having challenges with Ahmed. Mr. Van Dyke knows Ahmed well and has attended some of Ahmed's baseball games after school. Mr. Van Dyke has greeted Ahmed's parents at school events, but has not had extended conversations with them due to language barriers. Despite Mr. Van Dyke's investment in his relationship with Ahmed, they sometimes have a strained connection, with Ahmed lashing out and Mr. Van Dyke not understanding why. Ahmed has even more strained relationships with other teachers and is often sent to the office for counseling or punishment.

Scene:
Ahmed arrives late to Mr. Van Dyke's class. All of the other students have settled in and are working quietly on the warm-up assignment posted on the screen. Ahmed is agitated. He stands at the door before entering the room, looks at the warm-up, and announces loudly, "I ain't doin' that" as he points at the screen. At this point, all of the other students have stopped working. They first look at Ahmed and then at Mr. Van Dyke to see what he will do.

In our recent research, we have called this moment a "loaded moment" (Kennedy & Junker, 2023, p. 2), the moment when teacher and student have obviously different needs and must negotiate that difference. The reason we characterize the moment as "loaded" and not yet as full-fledged conflict is because such conflict is not yet inevitable. Teacher and student can still cooperate to dissolve the tension and avoid eruption. The loaded moment is the moment to employ the SIMMER down method. Here's how Mr. Van Dyke does that:

The SIMMER Down Method in Action:
Mr. Van Dyke feels his heart start to beat faster and his face begin to flush. He knows these are physiological changes that indicate anger and he recognizes them as the messages that tell him he needs to "simmer down." He takes step 1 by slowing down his reaction. He first wants to yell at Ahmed and punish him, but he stops himself from doing that so that he can take the rest of the steps. He then takes step 2 by ignoring Ahmed's loud voice, disrespectful tone, and blatant defiance of the task at hand. He knows he can come back to Ahmed's style of communication once the core issue is resolved. He also remembers that Ahmed's manner of communication is different than the message Ahmed is trying to communicate. He really has to engage the **Habit of Deliberate Interpretation** in order to separate out his **observation** of Ahmed's message from his **interpretation** of the message as defiant. Mr. Van Dyke takes step 3 by focusing

on that message. He has to ask himself, "What does Ahmed really want and need here? What is he really trying to tell me?"

Mr. Van Dyke tells the rest of the students to keep working and walks over to Ahmed to speak to him privately. Mr. Van Dyke is careful to engage **kinesics** here by positioning his body toward the rest of the students which nudges Ahmed to position his back toward the class. This move ensures that Mr. Van Dyke can continue to display **withitness** by facing the room and it also removes Ahmed's peers as an audience for the interaction because he is no longer facing them. Mr. Van Dyke could also have accomplished this by asking Ahmed to stand just outside the door while Mr. Van Dyke positioned himself with one foot inside the room and one foot outside the room with his chest facing the class and Ahmed simultaneously. A proper use of kinesics is crucial in this situation because Mr. Van Dyke must diffuse the loaded moment with Ahmed while also keeping the other students focused on the instructional task. Kinesics can accomplish this goal efficiently and nonverbally.

Once Mr. Van Dyke has positioned himself closer to Ahmed, he continues his focus on Ahmed's message by trying to clarify what might be happening. He says, "Ahmed, I'm not sure what's happening right now. Did something happen before you came to class, or are you maybe confused about the warm-up assignment?" Ahmed responds, "I don't know. I just think it's stupid!" Mr. Van Dyke moves to step 4 by guessing at what the meaning behind Ahmed's message might be and testing out his interpretation by asking Ahmed. He asks, "It sounds like you might be feeling frustrated or tired. Is that true?" Ahmed has lowered the volume of his voice slightly but continues to use **prosody** and body language indicating annoyance when he responds, "It's just dumb! I don't know!" Mr. Van Dyke takes step 5 and examines whether his approach has worked. Clearly it has not, so he moves on to step 6 by repeating steps 1 to 4.

He maintains a calm demeanor and even tone and continues to ignore Ahmed's disrespectful tone and posture. In repeating step 3, he notices that he now has more information. Ahmed used the key words, "I don't know." Mr. Van Dyke suspects that this is the real message that Ahmed is trying to communicate, that Ahmed either does not know how to do the assignment or does not know why he is acting the way that he is. So, Mr. Van Dyke focuses on that message and takes step 4 again. He responds to the meaning behind Ahmed's message, saying, "In the past, sometimes students have said something is stupid when they think it's irrelevant to them. Other times, students have said that because they think the assignment is hard but they don't want to feel bad about not being able to do it. Do you think either of those might be true for you now?" Ahmed finally softens and admits, "I don't know what the question is asking and I always get a bad grade on this." Mr. Van Dyke moves to step 5 and sees that his approach is working to de-escalate the moment. Ahmed's body posture is softening and he is lowering the volume of his voice. Mr. Van Dyke then moves to step 6 in an attempt to resolve the situation. He first affirms Ahmed's feelings so that Ahmed knows his message was heard, and he redirects Ahmed to the instructional task. He says, "I know that can feel very frustrating. How about if you quietly take a seat and get your materials ready and I can come help you?" Ahmed agrees and then Mr. Van Dyke rounds out step 6 by telling Ahmed how he would prefer that Ahmed would communicate his feelings in the future and why that change his important. Before Ahmed walks away, Mr. Van Dyke adds, "Ahmed, I always want to help you, but I feel frustrated when you ask for help in a way that disrupts the class like you just did. I would prefer that you come in quietly and ask me privately next time." Ahmed agrees and heads to his seat.

As with much of teaching, the SIMMER down method requires a lot of emotional labor because the teacher has to contain an immediate reaction and diffuse their own difficult emotions in order to be able to help the students with theirs. We don't want to ignore the intensity of the demands of this task. We do think that the investment the teacher makes in this process will lead to the best immediate outcome of preserving teacher–student and student–student relationships while also keeping everyone focused on the instructional goals.

Time-Outs

It could be that in attempting to **de-escalate**, the student or the teacher just becomes too dysregulated to be able to proceed and cannot control their emotions. In our example above, perhaps Mr. Van Dyke had a fight with his own child before coming to school and is already angry and distracted, or Ahmed did not have breakfast and remains irritable and inconsolable during their interaction. In these moments of dysregulation, teacher or student may need a **time-out**. Most of the time, the teacher cannot leave the room, so the teacher's time-out has to occur within the classroom context. The teacher can create a time-out for themselves or for the student by first having agreements with colleagues in place for time-outs to occur. Colleagues can create shared procedures for monitoring each other's individual students in their own classrooms during an agreed-upon amount of time. Teachers can teach all students the **routines** for time-outs at the beginning of the school year so that everyone knows what to do and will also interpret a time-out, whether for themselves or for others, as a much-needed break rather than as a disciplinary sanction.

> **Key Terms**
>
> *Time-out*: A non-punitive break during which a student and teacher disengage from interaction for an agreed-upon amount of time in order to compose themselves.

Restorative Practices

Sometimes students behave in ways that severely and negatively affect their peers or the school community. As we mentioned previously, we are not focusing on rules and consequences as a primary topic in this book, but we do want to encourage you to choose responses to these situations with the three **domains of teaching** in mind. That means, your responses to classroom management dilemmas should serve the goal of building and maintaining positive relationships while maximizing instructional time and student learning. **Restorative practices** can help you do just that. Restorative practices aim to restore any damage that a student causes to the classroom community through their behavior and then to maintain that community by also supporting the student (Smith et al., 2015). They build upon other relationship-focused efforts that teachers make, such as those discussed in Chapter 4. For example, the restorative justice circle can be used when a community norm is broken, and students may recognize such a circle format if teachers already use it during the class check-in. In the restorative justice circle, all members of the community affected by the event being discussed sit together to identify the impact of the event and how any damage its perpetrators caused can be restored.

> **Key Terms**
>
> *Restorative Practices*: Practices aimed to restore any damage a student causes to the classroom community through their behavior and then to maintain that community by also supporting the student.

Another strategy that Dominique Smith et al. (2015) propose as a restorative practice is the use of **affective statements**. Affective statements focus on the social and emotional impacts of different behaviors in order to support self-regulation and create collaboration and community. We witnessed Mr. Van Dyke use an affective statement with Ahmed when he told Ahmed that his confrontational style of communicating frustrated Mr. Van Dyke because it disrupted the class. When you engage the **Habit of Asset Identification**, you can also more easily affirm what students are doing in a given situation that contributes to the community. One school leader who we work with designed a sheet for his staff comparing traditional statements with affective statements. We are sharing an adaptation of it with you here in Table 5.6 with his permission. He has also created a practice activity and we have included it as a discussion activity at the end of the chapter. Remember that not all strategies will work well for

TABLE 5.6 *Affective Statements*

Affective Statements

Affective statements are an informal restorative practice that share the impact of an action or behavior on the community in an effort to build emotional intelligence and to encourage empathy. They provide an opportunity for students and adults to express their feelings, both positive and negative. Affective statements allow teachers and students to converse about behavioral situations *without assigning blame. They should not be used with the intent to harm or embarrass and should ideally be used one-on-one with students.*

Traditional Statement	Affective Statement
Start/Stop _____ activity.	I feel _____ when you _____ because of _____. OR Your behavior may damage our community/hurt other students' feelings by _____.
Stop running in the hall!	It makes me nervous when you run in the hall because I am afraid you are going to hurt yourself or others.
You are disrupting the class!	I feel frustrated when you interrupt the class because your classmates do not have an opportunity to learn.
You are late, that is a demerit!	I am concerned that you are late because our starter introduces the topic of the lesson and you won't know what is going on.
Keep your hands to yourself.	I want everyone to feel safe, and I am worried that some students might get nervous when you are rough-housing.
Stop calling people names.	That hurts our community because some people might not feel safe in class and then they won't be able to learn.
Good job on your homework!	I am excited to see your homework, because I know you have been working very hard this week.

all teachers. You have to choose an approach that will work for you. For example, if you read the list of affective statements and think, "Yeah, right, I could never pull that off," then maybe that is not the right approach for you to try. The most important thing is to be able to maintain a positive classroom community that supports high academic expectations and learning.

> **Key Terms**
>
> *Affective Statements*: Comments that focus on the social and emotional impacts of different behaviors in order to support students' self-regulation and create collaboration and community.

Key Takeaways: Teacher Moves to Address Dilemmas Related to Classroom Management

We began this chapter by reviewing Ms. Nash's **dilemma statements**: *Students do not know where to sit* and *Students do not react when I give reminders about what to do* and **focus questions**:

- How can I use and enforce a consistent seating chart?
- How can I help students remember what to do?
- How can I get their attention quickly when I need it?
- How can I project a more serious and consistent demeanor?

Remember that while we argue throughout the rest of the book that Ms. Nash could expand her understanding of the dilemma by reframing it within the **domains of relationships** and **curriculum and instruction**, in this chapter we reviewed **classroom management** moves that might also address her dilemma. Using the **Habit of Personal Attribution**, Ms. Nash focused on structures and behaviors that supported students' attention and ways of interacting during instruction. Here are a selection of teacher moves drawn from this chapter that we worked with Ms. Nash to implement (also shown in Figure 5.1):

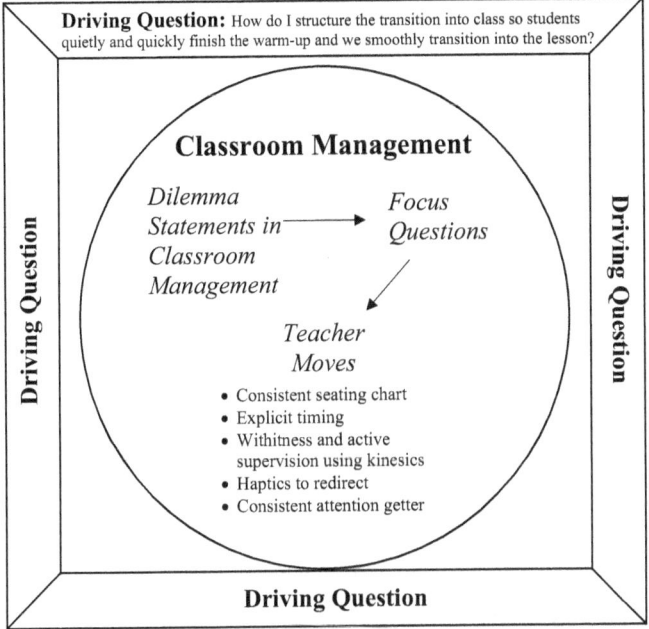

Figure 5.1 Teacher Moves Ms. Nash Identified in the Domain of Classroom Management Using the Zoomed In Frame.

- Create and reinforce a consistent seating chart;
- Use **explicit timing** by posting the time allotted for the warm-up assignment. Be sure that the time allotted matches the level of difficulty of the task;
- Demonstrate **withitness** and **active supervision** using **kinesics** during students' silent work by moving among them;
- Use **haptics** to redirect off-task students by touching their desks;
- Use a consistent attention getter when necessary; use nonverbal strategies to reinforce the attention getter rather than changing the strategy itself.

When Ms. Nash first started to make these adjustments, she felt like it was a lot to remember and manage. So, we focused on each strategy separately, introducing a new one only after she had started to become a bit more comfortable with the previous one. The difficulty with this was that it was the combination of strategies that ultimately led to the improvement, meaning that no one single change seemed to have any effect. Ms. Nash sometimes concluded that the strategies were not working when she did not see an immediate change. In these moments, we coached her to just keep going by continuing to practice all of the strategies she had tried while also adding to them. Once Ms. Nash was able to use enough of the strategies at the same time to convey withitness to her students, she began to see a real improvement. This improvement also came because she was working on developing relationships, selecting relevant curriculum, and scaffolding engaging instruction. Her classroom management was still in service of the other **domains of teaching**, which ultimately supported rigorous learning. This new way of thinking about the interdependence of the domains helped her in answering her **driving question**: "How do I structure the transition into class so students quietly and quickly finish the warm-up and we smoothly transition into the lesson?" Now return to your own focus questions and complete Exercise 5.5.

Exercise 5.5 *Identifying Teacher Moves in the Domain of Classroom Management*

1. Jot down the focus questions you listed in the domain of classroom management in Exercise 3.2 in the left-hand column below.
2. Using the information presented in this chapter, use the right-hand column to identify one or more teacher moves that answer each focus question and that you have not tried before.

Focus Questions in the Domain of Classroom Management	Teacher Moves to Try

In this chapter, we have discussed many approaches that teachers can use to address dilemmas related to management throughout the class period. As in Ms. Nash's example, an important takeaway is the need for teachers to be able to use more than one strategy at a time in order to make certain strategies work. For example, we stated above that we would recommend that Ms. Nash use explicit timing, but that explicit timing may not work if Ms. Nash does not also demonstrate withitness. When you (re) frame your dilemma within the domain of classroom management, consider how you could experiment with different combinations of strategies in order to ultimately effect the change you would like to see. If you are reading this book with colleagues, consider observing each other with these specific questions in mind.

For Discussion and Practice

1. In the discussion activities in Chapter 4, we asked you to describe the most successful demonstration you have ever seen of warm demanding in a classroom context. Using the new information you have learned in this chapter about warm demanding as a classroom management approach, explain how your example is important for both teacher-student relationships and for classroom management.
2. How can a teacher maintain an authoritative stance while using restorative practices that prioritize teacher-student relationships?
3. Use the following questions to reflect on class running, lesson running, and interaction routines in your classroom.
    a. How would you describe the routines in your classroom?
    b. Which ones are most important?
    c. How did you teach students to do them?
    d. Which ones go smoothly and which do not? Why do you think that is?
4. How do you handle conflicts in your classroom? Compare and contrast your approach to the SIMMER down method.

5. How do you think your cultural background and personal experiences shape your approach to classroom management?
6. Discuss possible approaches to handling the dilemmas listed in the table below. These scenarios were adapted from a document first created by school leader Christopher Pendley for practicing affective statements. They relate to other approaches described in the chapter as well. As you discuss the scenarios, name and explain how you could use the strategies described throughout this chapter to effectively prevent, address, or de-escalate the situation.

TABLE FOR DISCUSSION ACTIVITY #6

1. A student receives a failing grade on a test. She protests her grade and is adamant about your changing the grade or allowing her to re-take the exam. You stand firm and say that is the grade she got and you will not change it. She becomes very angry, says an expletive, and refuses to calm down. Her tone becomes increasingly rude and somewhat aggressive. What do you do?
2. Christopher constantly makes snide, snarky, or hurtful comments to other students in your class. Because he is a little taller than other students, the rest of the class defers to him and does not typically respond. He frequently will make jokes or interrupt other students, especially if he disagrees with their opinion, and his disrespectful behavior impacts class discussion frequently. Today in class, as you were discussing an Advisory topic, he made comments that were disrespectful and shut down the conversation.
3. Two students are playing in your class, stealing things from each other's desks, calling each other names, and just being disruptive. You have corrected them several times, but they are not stopping. Finally, both students get really angry and start to shove each other, refusing to stop when you approach them.
4. Due to students not paying attention, you decide to use a new seating chart. As students enter the class, you begin to shift them to their new seats. One student screams out that she is not sitting where you assigned her because she does not like to sit near "that boy."
5. A student in your class is not following directions. Instead, he is sitting on the floor, moving around the room, and being generally disruptive. You redirect him several times and he does not respond. You ask him to go to the door and say that you will come and talk with him. At first he refuses, but he relents and walks outside. In a minute, you go to the door and he is not there. He has walked down to the restroom.

Sources: Adapted from a document created by Christopher Pendley, Clarke County School District, Georgia, United States.

References

Apple, M. W. (2014). *Official knowledge: Democratic education in a conservative age* (3rd ed.). Routledge.

Babad, E. (2005). Nonverbal behavior in education. In J. Harrigan, R. Rosenthal, & K. Scherer (Eds.), *New handbook of methods in nonverbal behavior research* (pp. 283–311). Oxford University Press. https://doi.org/10.1093/acprof:oso/9780198529620.001.0001

Biesta, G. (2009). Good education in an age of measurement: On the need to reconnect with the question of purpose in education. *Educational Assessment, Evaluation and Accountability*, 21(1), 33–46. https://doi.org/10.1007/s11092-008-9064-9

Biesta, G. (2014). Evidence based practice in education: Between science and democracy. In A. Reid, E. Hart, & M. Peters (Eds.), *A companion to research in education* (pp. 391–400). Springer. https://doi.org/10.1007/978-94-007-6809-3_52

Brinegar, K., Kennedy-Lewis, B., Harrison, L., & Hurd, E. (2016). Cultural responsiveness. In S. B. Mertens, M. M. Caskey, P. Bishop, N. Flowers, D. Strahan, G. Andrews, & L. Daniel (Eds.), *The MLER SIG research agenda* (pp. 4–6). http://mlersig.net/research/mler-sig-research-agenda/

Charney, R. S. (2002). *Teaching children to care* (Revised edition). Northeast Foundation for Children, Inc.

Crenshaw, K. W. (2015). *Black girls matter: Pushed out, overpoliced, and underprotected* [Report]. Center for Intersectionality and Social Policy Studies. https://static1.squarespace.com/static/53f20d90e4b0b80451158d8c/t/54dcc1ece4b001c03e323448/1423753708557/AAPF_BlackGirlsMatterReport.pdf

Cushman, K., & Rogers, L. (2008). *Fires in the middle school bathroom*. The New Press.

Del Toro, J., & Wang, M. (2023). Vicarious severe school discipline predicts racial disparities among non-disciplined Black and White American adolescents. *Child Development*. 94(6), 1762–1778. https://doi.org/10.1111/cdev.13958

De Pry, R. L., & Sugai, G. (2002). The effect of active supervision and pre-correction on minor behavioral incidents in a sixth-grade general education classroom. *Journal of Behavioral Education, 11*, 255–267. https://doi.org/10.1023/A:1021162906622

Evertson, C. M., & Weinstein, C. S. (2006). Classroom management as a field of inquiry. In C. M. Evertson & C. S. Weinstein (Eds.), *Handbook of classroom management: Research, practice, and contemporary issues* (pp. 16–30). Taylor & Francis. https://doi.org/10.4324/9780203874783

Ford, A. C., & Sassi, K. (2014). Authority in cross-racial teaching and learning (re)considering the transferability of warm demander approaches. *Urban Education, 49*(1), 39–74. https://doi.org/10.1177/0042085912464790

Gaias, L. M., Johnson, S. L., Bottiani, J. H., Debnam, K. J., & Bradshaw, C. P. (2019). Examining teachers' classroom management profiles: Incorporating a focus on culturally responsive practice. *Journal of School Psychology, 76*, 124–139. https://doi.org/10.1016/j.jsp.2019.07.017

Haydon, T., & Kroeger, S. D. (2016). Active supervision, precorrection, and explicit timing: A high school case study on classroom behavior. *Preventing School Failure, 60*(1), 70–78. https://doi.org/10.1080/1045988X.2014.977213

Heath, S. B. (1983). *Ways with words: Language, life, and work in communities and classrooms.* Cambridge University Press. https://doi.org/10.1017/CBO9780511841057

Kagan, S., & Kagan, M. (2009). *Kagan cooperative learning.* Kagan.

Kennedy, B. L., & Junker, R. (2023). The evolution of "loaded moments" toward escalation or de-escalation in student-teacher interactions. *Review of Educational Research.* [Accepted Manuscript] https://doi.org/10.3102/00346543231202509

Kennedy-Lewis, B. L. (2012). What happens after students are expelled? Understanding teachers' successes and failures at one alternative middle school. *Teachers College Record, 114*(12), 1–38. https://doi.org/10.1177/016146811211401207

Kleinfeld, J. (1975). Effective teachers of Eskimo and Indian students. *The School Review, 83*(2), 301–344. http://www.jstor.org/stable/1084645

Kohn, A. (2006). *Beyond discipline* (10th Anniversary ed.). ASCD.

Kounin, J. S. (1970). *Discipline and group management in classrooms.* Holt, Rinehart & Winston.

Marcucci, O., & Elmesky, R. (2023). Advancing culturally relevant discipline: An ethnographic microanalysis of disciplinary interactions with Black students. *Urban Education, 58*(6), 1118–1150. https://doi.org/10.1177/0042085920909165

Marzano, R. J., Frontier, T., & Livingston, D. (2011). *Effective supervision: Supporting the art and science of teaching*. ASCD.

Milner, H. R., Cunningham, H. B., Delale-O'Connor, L., & Kestenberg, E. G. (2019). *"These kids are out of control": Why we must reimagine "classroom management" for equity*. Corwin.

Morris, M. (2015). *Pushout: The criminalization of Black girls in school*. The New Press.

Murphy, A. S., Acosta, M. M., & Kennedy-Lewis, B. L. (2013). "I'm not running around with my pants sagging, so how am I not acting like a lady?": Intersections of race and gender in the experiences of female middle school troublemakers. *The Urban Review 45*(5), 586–610. https://doi.org/10.1007/s11256-013-0236-7

Murphy, A. S., & Kennedy, B. L. (2019). Preparing teachers to prevent classroom management challenges using culturally responsive classroom practices. In K. Brinegar, L. Harrison, & E. Hurd (Eds.), *Equity and cultural responsiveness in the middle grades* (pp. 311–334). Information Age Publishing.

Nieto, S. & Bode, P. (2017). *Affirming diversity: The sociopolitical context of multicultural education* (7th ed.). Pearson.

Siwatu, K. O. (2007). Preservice teachers' culturally responsive teaching self-efficacy and outcome expectancy beliefs. *Teaching and Teacher Education, 23*(7), 1086–1101. https://doi.org/10.1016/j.tate.2006.07.011

Siwatu, K. O., Putnam, S. M., Starker-Glass, T. V., & Lewis, C. W. (2017). The Culturally Responsive Classroom Management Self-Efficacy Scale: Development and initial validation. *Urban Education, 52*(7), 862–888. https://doi.org/10.1177/0042085915602534

Skiba, R. J., Horner, R. H., Chung, C., Rausch, M. K., May, S. L., & Tobin, T. (2011). Race is not neutral: A national investigation of African American and Latino disproportionality in school discipline. *School Psychology Review, 40*(1), 85–107. https://doi.org/10.1080/02796015.2011.12087730

Smith, D., Fisher, D., & Frey, N. (2015). *Better than carrots or sticks: Restorative practices for positive classroom management.* ASCD.

Toshalis, E. (2015). *Make me! Understanding and engaging student resistance in school.* Harvard Education Press.

Weinstein, C. S., & Novodvorsky, I. (2015). *Middle and secondary classroom management* (5th ed.). McGraw Hill Education.

Woolfolk, A. E., & Brooks, D. M. (1985). Nonverbal communication and the study of teaching. *Theory into Practice, 24*(1), 513–528. https://www.jstor.org/stable/1001153

6
Frame Shifting to the Domain of Curriculum and Instruction

Curriculum and instruction is likely to be the domain that a more experienced teacher focuses on once they have a sense of mastery in the **domains of relationships** and **classroom management**. If that is you, perhaps you have already framed your dilemma here. For other teachers, even a dilemma originally framed in the domains of relationships and classroom management can be fruitfully reframed in the domain of curriculum and instruction. We define **curriculum** as the content taught in the classroom both explicitly and implicitly through physical materials, verbal exchanges, and classroom activities. **Instruction** describes the formats, activities, and teacher moves designed and used to support the students' learning of specific curricular content. Remember that dilemmas frame shifted to the domain of curriculum and instruction have to do with the issues raised by the guiding questions first shared in Chapter 3 and reproduced in Table 6.1.

TABLE 6.1 *Guiding Questions for Reframing to the Domain of Curriculum and Instruction*

Curriculum

How might the dilemma involve:

- ☐ Conceptual connections from one part of the lesson to another?
- ☐ Content that interests students?
- ☐ Content that builds upon students' funds of knowledge?
- ☐ Content that taps into students' frames of reference?
- ☐ Hidden curriculum that the teacher has not considered?
- ☐ An appropriate level of difficulty in content knowledge?
- ☐ An appropriate level of difficulty in reading comprehension and writing requirements?
- ☐ Development and maintenance of students' knowledge about their own and other cultures?
- ☐ Opportunities for students to develop critical thinking and social consciousness and take social action?
- ☐ Other: _____

Instruction

How might the dilemma involve:

- ☐ The necessary/appropriate amount of direct instruction?
- ☐ Gradual release for students to receive scaffolded support that leads to successful independent work?
- ☐ Meaningful and equitable participation among students?
- ☐ Interdependent collaboration and/or social learning?
- ☐ A variety of activities and ways for students to demonstrate knowledge and skills?
- ☐ The proper amount of feedback?
- ☐ The accessibility of sufficient assistance?
- ☐ Other: _____

> **Key Terms**
>
> *Curriculum*: Content taught both explicitly and implicitly in the classroom through physical materials, verbal exchanges, and classroom activities.
>
> *Instruction*: Formats, activities, and teacher moves designed and used to support the students' learning of the curriculum.

Curriculum and instruction are intertwined with each other because the content contained in the formal curricular materials gains meaning and becomes comprehensible to students during instruction. We artificially separate curriculum and instruction in this chapter so that we can provide a thorough examination of each, but they usually occur together in the classroom. The teacher makes instructional decisions related to curriculum, thereby "enacting" curriculum, so teacher moves involve both curriculum and instruction at the same time. This is why we begin the chapter by treating the topics separately, but often discuss them together when exploring teacher moves in relation to a particular dilemma. When we discuss curriculum and instruction separately, we use the phrase "the focus of [curriculum or instruction] within the domain of curriculum and instruction" to show that although we are narrowing our focus, this remains one **domain of teaching**.

As we have discussed throughout the book, the domain of curriculum and instruction is **interdependent** with the other domains. As the maxim goes, "Kids don't care what you know until they know that you care," which demonstrates the connection between motivation, relationships, and learning. Especially for students from marginalized backgrounds, trust and mutual connection pave the way for successful engagement with curriculum and instruction (Kennedy-Lewis, 2012). Nel Noddings, an educational scholar on the ethics of care, stated, "…subject matter cannot carry itself. Relation, except in very rare cases, precedes any engagement with subject matter. Caring relations can prepare children for an initial receptivity to all sorts of experiences and subject matters" (Noddings, 2005, p. 36). Creating and selecting curriculum and designing instruction that is relevant to your students relies on knowing them well and building relationships with them. Thus, the domain of relationships sets the stage for successful instruction by motivating students as well as by helping teachers select relevant curriculum and instruction.

Similarly, as we mentioned in Chapter 5, the domain of classroom management provides the structures necessary for students to engage with curriculum and instruction. Without minimally effective management of the classroom, students will not have access to relational or instructional interactions and activities.

At the same time, when teachers maintain high expectations for learning through effective instruction, they can motivate trust and care in the domain of relationships, which also supports students' cooperation in the domain of classroom management. You may recognize these connections from our previous description of **warm demanding**. In this chapter, we put warm demanding to work in the service of high-quality learning experiences in the domain of curriculum and instruction.

Remember from Chapter 2 that after engaging the **habits of mind**, Ms. Nash stated her dilemma as: *Students do not enter the classroom quickly and do not start working on the posted assignment.* This **dilemma statement** was focused on her observation about students' behaviors related to **rules** and **routines**, which is why, in Chapter 3, we noted that she positioned it in the domain of classroom management. However, when we prompted her to further engage the **Habit of Deliberate Interpretation** by describing more of her **observations** about what was happening before, during, and after the dilemma occurred, she noticed other possible issues related to it as well. These new observations had to do with what was taught (curriculum) and how it was taught (instruction) by focusing on whether students understood or could relate to the warm-up assignments that they were supposed to complete upon entering class. When we discussed with Ms. Nash the possibility that students did not understand or relate to the content, she **frame shifted** her dilemma statement to the domain of curriculum and instruction, generating new dilemma statements and their related **focus questions** (see Table 6.2). In this chapter, we will focus on identifying teacher moves that address her **driving question** by answering her focus questions within the domain of curriculum and instruction. In the sections below, we build upon research literature to discuss issues relevant for teachers who may be addressing dilemmas like this one that are framed in this domain. In order to focus your reading, review the focus questions you wrote in Exercise 3.4 when you frame shifted your dilemma to the domain of curriculum and instruction.

TABLE 6.2 *The Dilemma Statements and Focus Questions Ms. Nash Generated When Frame Shifting to the Domain of Curriculum and Instruction*

Ms. Nash's Driving Question: "How do I structure the transition into class so students quietly and quickly finish the warm-up and we smoothly transition into the lesson?"

Ms. Nash's Dilemma Statements in the Domain of Curriculum and Instruction	Focus Questions
Students do not understand the content of the warm-up assignments.	How do I create warm-up assignments that are accessible?
Students do not relate to the content of the warm-up assignments.	How do I create warm-up assignments that are relatable?

Curriculum

Curriculum is the "what'" that we teach. It includes the requirements given to teachers by governmental and district oversight bodies, the materials provided to meet those requirements such as textbooks, software, and practice exercises, and the additional materials we create or find to supplement those that are provided. These things make up the **explicit curriculum**, the facts and messages that are directly communicated when students encounter the materials. There is also the implicit or **hidden curriculum** that makes up the messages that are also communicated to students but not explicitly stated within the materials or as part of the lesson or classroom interactions. Table 6.3 gives an example of the difference between the explicit and hidden curricula.

> **Key Terms**
> *Explicit Curriculum*: The facts and messages that are directly communicated when students encounter the materials.
> *Hidden Curriculum*: The messages that are communicated but not explicitly stated within the materials or as part of the lesson or classroom interactions.

TABLE 6.3 *Example Showing the Difference Between Explicit and Hidden Curricula*

Explicit Curriculum	Hidden Curriculum
From the science textbook: "The greenhouse effect has to do with the heating and trapping of carbon dioxide in the atmosphere."	The illustrations accompanying the section explaining the greenhouse effect show White men in lab coats conducting experiments, the natural release of carbon dioxide into the atmosphere, and a diagram of how gases are trapped in the atmosphere between the earth and the sun.

You can see in the left-hand column an example sentence that you might find directly in a science textbook. This sentence describing the greenhouse effect appears neutral, and students might experience it as far removed from their lives. The images alongside this explicit statement communicate messages that suggest that science is a White- and male-only endeavor and that downplay the role of human-made emissions in the greenhouse effect by not portraying them in the illustrations. These implicit messages are the hidden curriculum. Teachers may not notice or be fully aware of the hidden curriculum, but students often are and may be reacting to it even when teachers do not realize it. If you have originally framed your dilemma with a focus on curriculum within the domain of curriculum and instruction, it likely has to do with the explicit curriculum. But if you have attempted to reframe it here and perhaps are not exactly sure how it might fit, then your dilemma might have more to do with the hidden curriculum than the explicit one. Both types of curriculum are always active in classrooms and may affect all domains of teaching.

Explicit Curriculum

No curriculum is neutral. There is always a set of beliefs and values undergirding the explicit curriculum. In their work on curriculum, Jeannie Oakes et al. (2018) described two different opposing perspectives or positions that may guide curricular requirements and the development of different types of curricular materials. They named these positions **traditionalist** and

progressive. These positions are rooted in different philosophies about the purpose of education. Philosophies about the purpose of education also define the role of the teacher and the role of the student. We won't go into too many details about curriculum theory where these debates about curriculum are had, but we will define these two positions briefly because dilemmas related to curriculum have their roots in them. It is likely that one of these positions resonates more closely than the other with your own perspectives about teaching and learning as well as the purpose of schools.

Key Terms

Traditionalist: Perspective about curriculum that focuses on the role of teaching and learning as creating a foundation of factual knowledge upon which students can continue to build throughout their educational careers and lives.

Progressive: Perspective about curriculum that focuses on the role of teaching and learning as creating a foundation of thinking skills or capabilities that students can apply within various contexts.

As you read about each of the positions below, consider how you might be able to adopt or adapt the one that feels less comfortable to you if your dilemma ends up requiring that. Just as we advised in the previous chapter when we discussed **classroom management** moves, trying on a perspective and its affiliated teacher moves that feels a bit uncomfortable may be required to solve your dilemma. That does not mean that you have to give up your convictions or compromise your core values, but it means you have to figure out how bring your convictions into alignment with new teacher moves. Remember that we take a pragmatic approach in this book, meaning that we are asking teachers to use new **habits of mind** and try on different teacher moves to address dilemmas that they have not yet been able to solve using their tried-and-true methods. The **Habit of Deliberate**

Interpretation can be helpful in creating space between your values themselves and the ways you have previously **interpreted** them in your teaching. Perhaps a new interpretation will better serve you and your students.

Traditionalist and Progressive Positions Related to Explicit Curriculum

Traditionalists generally focus on creating a foundation of factual knowledge upon which students can continue to build throughout their educational careers and lives. They support the goal of education to socialize students into a shared body of core cultural knowledge in order to promote social cohesion (Biesta, 2009). From a traditionalist perspective, the role of the teacher is to impart facts and procedures related to this foundation and the role of the student is to learn them. "Back to basics" curriculum movements, rote memorization, and extrinsic motivation are based in traditionalism.

Progressives generally focus on creating a foundation of thinking skills or capabilities that students can apply within various contexts. They support education that develops the individualized capacity, skills, and interests of each student, with the goal of meeting the needs, and developing the capabilities, of a diverse student population. Like traditionalists, progressives also support the goal of social cohesion but take an approach to cohesion through diversity and understanding rather than through shared knowledge and experience. From a progressive perspective, the role of the teacher is to facilitate student inquiry and development. Student-led inquiry and project-based learning may play prominently in the instructional activities associated with progressive approaches to curriculum. Multicultural and multilingual education, and anti-racist pedagogy are based in progressive positions related to curriculum (Oakes et al., 2018).

You might recognize how these two positions play a role in the "phonics (*traditionalist*) versus whole language (*progressive*)" and "old math (*traditionalist*) versus new math (*progressive*)" debates as well as in current movements to limit students' exposure to curricular content related to race, gender, and sexual diversity. If you are required to teach certain standards, you can most likely identify which of these two philosophies are most reflected in those standards. We know that many teachers do not have, or do not feel like they have, much freedom when it comes to choosing the curricular requirements they must meet. As curriculum gets sucked in to "culture wars" in various global contexts, teachers' choices might be even more limited, such as in US states that now prohibit teachers from having certain types of books or materials in their classrooms. Nevertheless, we encourage you to engage the **Habit of Personal Attribution** to consider how you might leverage your autonomy in the area of **explicit curriculum**. The reason we think this might be important is because students' reactions to curriculum based on these different positions might be at the core of your dilemma. We explore this idea further in the sample scenarios in Table 6.4. In each scenario, the teachers have similar dilemmas that can be framed in the **domain of curriculum and instruction**. The curricular tasks related to those dilemmas reflect the traditionalist and progressive positions described above.

In both scenarios described in Table 6.4, a student does not begin an activity. As we have explained throughout the book, most dilemmas, including this one, can be framed within each of the three **domains of teaching**. If we narrow our focus to explore possible connections to curriculum and curricular approach, we can see that an overreliance on rote learning that students do not find relevant can cause a dilemma as it did for Mr. Fox, whereas an attempt to create student-centered activities might also cause a dilemma as it did for Ms. Monroe. In both scenarios, the teacher's ability to create balance between approaches might better support their students in engaging in the activity. Mr. Fox could shorten the duration of rote practice (*traditionalist*) and contextualize it within a real-world issue that Jamila cares about (*progressive*). Ms. Monroe could increase her directive role in the student-centered project (*progressive*) by creating a fact sheet about World War I that lists important details for Max to review as well as step-by-step suggestions for getting started (*traditionalist*). Considering the philosophical underpinnings of your curricular materials and objectives can also yield additional possible teacher moves, as it does for Mr. Fox and Ms. Monroe.

TABLE 6.4 *Scenarios Connecting Classroom Dilemmas to Curricular Positions*

Scene	Connection to Curricular Position
Mr. Fox: *Let's practice our multiplication tables. I've passed out each of your practice sheets. See if you can finish more problems today than you finished yesterday.* Mr. Fox sets the timer for five minutes. He notices Jamila put her head on her desk like she does most days when it is time for practicing multiplication.	Rote memorization of multiplication tables reflects a traditionalist position related to curriculum. Jamila may put her head down because she does not see meaning in, or feel successful at, the memorization activity.
Ms. Monroe: *Today we will start a project of your choosing that has to do with World War I. Your task is to explore the websites I have provided in our web quest and then choose one of the following activities*: a) *Select a country involved in the war and choose a topic that is important to that country's involvement.* b) *Build an argument for who the most important hero OR villain was during the war.* c) *Make a case that if the League of Nations had existed before the war began it either could OR could not have prevented the war.* *You may choose the format you would like to use to present your project. I have outlined the requirements for different types of products in our class web portal.* Ms. Monroe releases the class to start working. She notices Max put his head on his desk like he does most days when it is time for independent work.	The student-centered projects that Ms. Monroe provides reflect a progressive position related to curriculum. Max may put his head down because he does not have the foundational knowledge that he will need to succeed in the task—for example, he may shut down when he hears "League of Nations" if he cannot remember what that was—or he may be overwhelmed by the options or the organizational skills necessary to even be able to start the task.

Use Exercise 6.1 to further explore and practice identifying traditionalist and progressive curricular approaches in your context.

Pedagogical Content Knowledge

To be able to make decisions about how to balance the focus on different skills and curricular purposes, you will need to have strong pedagogical content knowledge. In his early formative work on the topic, Lee Shulman (1987) distinguished **pedagogical content knowledge** from **pedagogical knowledge** and **content knowledge**, which he said are also required for effective

> **Exercise 6.1** *Exploring the Role of Curricular Positions in Your Dilemma*
>
> 1. What evidence do you see of the traditionalist and/or progressive position in the explicit curricular materials and activities you are given to teach?
>   a) What impact does that position have on your students' experiences with the curriculum?
>   b) How might your curricular materials and activities change if the curricular position underlying them were to shift (i.e., traditionalist-oriented materials were to become more progressive-oriented and vice versa)?
>   c) How might such a change affect your students' experiences with this revised curriculum and activities?

teaching. Pedagogical knowledge has to do with how to teach—the general principles and skills of teaching, such as those related to classroom management. Pedagogical knowledge also includes information related to the particular developmental, social, emotional, and cognitive needs of your students. Content knowledge relates specifically to knowing your subject or subjects well. Pedagogical content knowledge "represents the blending of content and pedagogy into an understanding of how particular topics, problems, or issues are organized, represented, and adapted to the diverse interests and abilities of learners, and presented for instruction" (Shulman, 1987, p. 8). In this definition, you see how curriculum and instruction become inseparable during teaching.

> **Key Terms**
>
> *Pedagogical Knowledge*: The general principles and skills of teaching.
>
> *Content Knowledge*: Knowledge of the teacher's subject area, how subject-specific knowledge and skills deepen and build upon each other, and how the subject relates to other subjects.
>
> *Pedagogical Content Knowledge*: The blending of pedagogical knowledge and content knowledge that allows the teacher to organize and adapt curriculum and instruction to their particular students.

Pedagogical content knowledge empowers teachers to be able to make conceptual connections from one part of a lesson to another. Mr. Fox can use his pedagogical content knowledge as he balances traditionalist and progressive perspectives to explain to Jamila how rote practice of multiplication will be required for the upcoming community-focused project about food deserts. Ms. Monroe can use her pedagogical content knowledge to break the complex synthesis of ideas needed for the project on World War I into discrete and simpler facts for Max. Pedagogical content knowledge also allows you to choose appropriate levels of difficulty for your students in terms of what they learn and how they learn it. When you (re)frame your dilemma in the domain of curriculum and instruction, consider whether fine-tuning your pedagogical content knowledge might be helpful. Use Exercise 6.2 to help you.

Exercise 6.2 *Evaluating Your Pedagogical Content Knowledge*

Directions

Consider the following questions in evaluating your own pedagogical content knowledge:

1. How robust is my pedagogical knowledge?
   a. What more could I learn about effective teaching in general?
   b. What more could I learn about the specific developmental, social, emotional, and cognitive needs of my students?
2. How robust is my content knowledge?
   a. What topics could I further strengthen?
   b. How could I develop my own ability to connect topics to each other and to explain these connections to students?

3. To what extent does my pedagogical content knowledge enable me to select and use appropriate curricular materials, in terms of both topic and level of difficulty, and to know when and how to modify those materials if necessary?
   a. Can I think of ample examples of when I was able to make a curricular topic easier for students who did not understand?
   b. Can I think of ample examples of when I was able to make a curricular topic more complex for my most advanced students?
   c. Do I accurately anticipate when I will need to make a curricular topic easier or more complex?
4. How well can I describe connections between curricular topics?
   a. Can I think of ample examples of when I have been able to articulate these connections in ways that students understood?
   b. Can I think of ample examples of when I have been able to explain to students how they will use each curricular topic in the future?

Focus on Culture 12: Diversity Pedagogical Content Knowledge

Recent research has introduced the concept of *diversity pedagogical content knowledge* (Dursun et al., 2021). This concept adds diversity knowledge as an additional knowledge base to Shulman's (1987) original **content knowledge** and **pedagogical knowledge**. It combines *general diversity knowledge* with *diversity content knowledge* and *diversity pedagogical knowledge*. *General diversity knowledge* is what a teacher knows about race, culture, and social power, and is contextualized in particular geographical and sociocultural regions. It includes knowledge of one's own racialized experience, as well as knowledge about the role culture plays in one's beliefs and identity. General diversity knowledge also includes an understanding of culture as a dynamic phenomenon that is embedded in and shapes society in ways that are not equally fair to all groups. Dursun et al. (2021) measured teachers' general diversity knowledge in Flanders by asking respondents about the Muslim population in Belgium, other ethnic and linguistic groups in Belgium, other questions related to Islam, and conceptual questions about immigration and assimilation.

Diversity content knowledge is knowledge about how issues related to culture and power appear in one's subject area content. Dursun et al. (2021) specifically examined how White European identity, history, norms, and values are reflected in different content areas. Examples of specific questions that they used to measure this had to do with teachers' knowledge of Belgian colonization, the history of Muslims in Europe, knowledge about China, and knowledge about the Roman Empire. These questions largely focus on history and relate specifically to the geographical context of their work but might also inform other content areas and contexts as well.

Diversity pedagogical knowledge is knowledge about how students' cultural backgrounds and identities shape appropriate instructional approaches. Questions assessing a teacher's diversity pedagogical knowledge might have to do with ethnic identity development, how students learn to identify discrimination, and how societal colorblindness affects students who are perceived as racially nondominant.

Diversity pedagogical content knowledge, then, combines these three bodies of knowledge and describes the dispositions and knowledge that teachers need to have to effectively teach students from different cultural backgrounds. The research on this topic provides specific information about teachers' bases of knowledge that support their abilities to use culturally responsive classroom management, which we discussed in Chapter 5, and culturally responsive pedagogy, which we will further discuss below.

Privileged Knowledge and the Hidden Curriculum

We began the previous section on **explicit curriculum** by stating that no curriculum is neutral. After making that statement, we introduced the different philosophical beliefs and positions that undergird any curriculum. What we have not yet discussed is the specific content of the curriculum, such as which knowledge counts as worthy of teaching and learning. Topics, perspectives, facts, and skills that are included in the explicit curriculum and selected for instruction and assessment are considered **privileged knowledge**. Meanwhile, other possible topics, perspectives, facts, and skills are either neglected or actively left out by policymakers, publishers, and teachers. This situation can lead to generations of students lacking knowledge about particular topics, creating societal blind spots that may result in the harming or exclusion of certain groups. For example, in Western European countries that participated in the slave trade but did not engage in slavery on their own soil, students may not be required to learn about their country's role in slavery (Wekker, 2016). This lack of knowledge creates and supports a false societal narrative of innocence and fairness within which contemporary discrimination can more easily be ignored.

> **Key Terms**
>
> *Privileged Knowledge*: Topics, perspectives, facts, and skills that are included in the explicit curriculum and selected for instruction and assessment.

Teachers might originally frame classroom dilemmas in the **domains of relationships** or **classroom management** that actually result from students' resistance to curriculum. Certain omissions of topics, perspectives, facts, and skills can also fuel student resistance if what is left out is something students consider vital to their identities or their community's or family's norms and values (Toshalis, 2015). In Chapter 4, we discussed how achieving justice in the classroom means not requiring students to accept their own erasure from the content of their lessons in order to succeed in class. We also established that teachers can minimize microaggressions related to societal discrimination through their curricular choices. In Exercise 6.3 (also see the extended version in the online Study Guide), we explore situations in which students' encounters with explicit curriculum might cause conflict or fuel resistance. Consider how the curricular topic or circumstance described in the left-hand column might affect the student described in the middle column. There is a blank column on the right for your notes, and we have included suggested answers in the online Study Guide.

In addition to the explicit curriculum containing and omitting particular content and perspectives, the **hidden curriculum** does so as well. Hidden curriculum consists of the messages, ideas, norms, and values that are not explicitly taught in curricular

---

Exercise 6.3 *Exploring Students' Experiences with Explicit Curriculum*

Explicit Curricular Topic or Circumstance	Description of a Student in the Class	*How might this student experience this circumstance?*
In order to teach a middle school math standard about using algebraic equations to solve everyday problems, Ms. Garcia goes over a word problem about three students selling candy bars to raise money for their school club.	Gus' parents immigrated to the US from Germany nine months ago. The family has paid for extra English tutoring and Gus does well with learning content in English. Ms. Garcia often forgets that he is an immigrant. When his teacher presents this word problem, Gus has no idea what it is about since German students do not do fundraisers for the school.	

materials but that students learn anyway. Kevin Kumashiro (2015) calls these "unintentional ways of teaching" (p. 37) and collected examples from his teacher education students by asking them how they encountered gender in school. He then divided their answers between explicit and hidden curriculum, and the list of examples that were "hidden" or unintentional far exceeded the list of those that were explicit. An example of how students explicitly learned about gender was in celebrating Women's History Month when students learned about women's roles or achievements that have benefitted society at large. Examples of how gender was taught as a binary in the hidden curriculum included boys and girls being segregated or singled out as two distinct groups, such as in seating arrangements, school uniform requirements, during classroom transitions like lining up, or being named "prom king and queen." The fact that there was a Women's History Month conveyed the "hidden" message that all other months focused on men's historical accomplishments. Similar types of unintentional teaching occur related to race, language, national origin, socioeconomic status, gender identity, sexual orientation, and other social identifiers that might shape students' experiences. We have provided Exercise 6.4 (also see the extended version in the online Study Guide) to help you identify some example situations where hidden curriculum may negatively affect students.

We explain these concepts here because teaching dilemmas that address the appearance of student disengagement, opposition, or resistance could have their roots in explicit or hidden curriculum that is exclusionary or even rejects certain groups of students. Being able to gauge whether this situation might be occurring with your students requires not only a keenly reflective and critical stance on your curriculum but also sufficient knowledge of your students, which connects this domain back to the domain of relationships, as we mentioned at the beginning of the chapter. When you engage in the teacher moves associated with developing teacher–student relationships that we discussed in Chapter 4, such as developing communication with parents or getting to know students' lives outside of school, you not

Exercise 6.4 *Exploring Students' Experiences with Hidden Curriculum*

Hidden Curricular Topic or Circumstance	Description of Student in Class	What Is the Hidden Message this Example Is Sending?	How Might This Student Experience This Circumstance?
During silent reading time in their third-grade classroom, students can choose any book they want to read from the class library. Mr. James has worked hard to select books that range in difficulty and topic, including picture books and chapter books, and books with themes having to do with friendship, family, adventure, and science fiction, among others.	David goes to the bookshelf to choose a new book to read for silent reading. He loves to make new selections and dive in to new books! But lately he has been noticing that none of the families in the picture books he loves so much look like his family.		

only invest in the relationship, but you also gather information about how to make **curriculum and instruction** most relevant to students.

Making Curriculum Matter to Students

Many teachers would be able to empathize if a colleague reported that students are constantly asking, "When will I ever need to know this in *real* life?" Dilemmas framed in the **domain of curriculum and instruction** are often connected to students not feeling that they have sufficient answers for this question. In order for students to experience curricular relevance, teachers need to tap in to students' **frames of reference**, connect curriculum to students' **funds of knowledge** and **funds of identity**, and just generally make curriculum interesting. In Ms. Nash's case in Chapter 2, we described how her warm-up questions, such as the one we first observed that asked students about the resources in Antarctica in honor of Antarctica Day, might not tap in to relevant or relatable content to students, which is what she aimed to address by reframing her dilemma in this domain. Next, we discuss specific ways for teachers to make curriculum more relatable to students.

> **Key Terms**
> *Frames of Reference*: Objects, events, or experiences shared by a particular group of people, such as those belonging to a particular cultural group, generation, or geographical location.
> *Funds of Knowledge*: Mastery of facts, processes, or ways of being based on cultural upbringing that is embedded in family histories and circumstances.
> *Funds of Identity*: "Significant people, institutions, cultural artifacts, geographical spaces, and meaningful practices, passions, and interests embedded in a learner's definition of themself" (Esteban-Guitart, 2021, p. 4).

Frames of Reference

Frames of reference are objects, events, or experiences shared by a particular group of people, such as those belonging to a particular cultural group, generation, or geographical location. We first gave examples of frames of reference in Chapter 2. We all have frames of reference and we share different references with different groups to which we belong. Students, like all of us, have hundreds of references that they draw upon on a daily basis, mostly unaware of them. These include familiarities incorporated into daily routines and yearly rituals, some intimately connected to culture, others more associated with immediate context, and some both. For example, students who ride the same school bus route share frames of reference to particular local businesses they see each day, roads they take, even the bus driver's favorite radio station. In Table 6.5, we list five frames of reference that come to

TABLE 6.5 *Examples of Brianna's and Amy's Current Frames of Reference*

Brianna's Frames of Reference	Amy's Frames of Reference	Brianna and Amy's Shared Frames of Reference
Utrecht canal path ("The Singel")	Oviedo rails-to-trails path	The 13th street tunnel
The Pasadena Tournament of Roses	The Athens Wild Rumpus Parade	The UF-UGA annual college football game
Los Angeles Unified School District	New College of Florida	The train stops at the Atlanta airport
Distinctly "Dutch" phrases *gezellig* and *lekker*	University of Georgia words *Double Dawg* and *Triple Dawg*	US education-related acronyms such as IEP, FAPE, ATE, AERA
The Inland Empire	East Orlando	Gainesville, Florida
Being jammer on the roller derby team	Playing mahjong	Training dogs

mind from both of various living situations and contexts over the years, and then, in the third column, we list frames of reference that we have come to share while working together. We duplicate this table with an additional blank column for you to add your own frames of reference in the activities at the end of the chapter.

Teachers can make curriculum relevant by connecting content to students' frames of reference. We will use our first shared example to illustrate how a teacher might do this. The first in our examples of shared references is also one that we share with all education students and faculty at the University of Florida where there is a tunnel path leading under Southwest 13th Street that connects the College of Education to the rest of the campus. Designers of this path installed unattractive, zigzagging railing leading into the tunnel in order to slow down bicyclists who would otherwise pose a danger to pedestrians. Local students who come to the university on field trips also share this frame of reference, which local teachers could use in discussing various laws of physics. The tunnel also contains graffiti and posters announcing protests or perspectives about social issues, which could be addressed in various social studies courses.

In Ms. Nash's Earth Science class, she learned that her students knew a lot about household cleaners because they were responsible for keeping their homes clean. They knew which cleaner worked best on which types of dirt, stain, or surface. Household cleanliness was a strongly held cultural value, one that Ms. Nash did not experience as strongly in her own culture and one that she did not consider much since it was normal in her neighborhood for families to hire people to clean for them. Once she learned about this frame of reference that her students shared, she could create meaning in the curriculum by relating cleaning products to the geographical concept of erosion, which was otherwise not very intrinsically interesting to her students.

One difficulty teachers may encounter in connecting students' frames of reference to curriculum is that not all students might share a particular reference. In the example in Exercise 6.3, Gus experienced a disconnection between his own frame of reference as a German and the frame of reference shared by his US-born classmates. Ms. Garcia did an excellent job connecting the content of algebraic equations to candy bar fundraisers, a reference nearly all students shared, and she noticed that most of them eagerly engaged in solving this problem because they had actually been in similar situations when trying to sell candy bars.

But Gus did not know what was going on. That does not mean that Ms. Garcia should not have included this word problem. It only means that she needed to be aware of the situations in which not all students would share a reference and she needed to provide a sort of "translation" for them. She might do this by saying something like, "Okay, in this word problem, students are fundraising by selling chocolate bars. But let me check in with Gus for a moment. Gus, did students raise money for school clubs in this way in your schools in Germany?" This question would give Gus a moment to explain something about his own experience and then Ms. Garcia could say, "So Gus doesn't have this experience raising money by selling chocolate bars. Can someone quickly explain what that's about?" In this way, the students would get to know each other a bit better, learn to recognize that not all experiences are shared, have their differences normalized, and be on the same footing for addressing the word problem at hand. Note that in order for Gus to feel comfortable with Ms. Garcia asking this question in front of the class, there would need to be a positive and safe classroom climate. Ms. Garcia would then be modeling for students what one can do to welcome a new student into a space and learn more about them. Here again, we see the **interdependence** of the **domain of relationships** and the **domain of curriculum and instruction**.

This situation is also an example of how curriculum and instruction overlap. Ms. Garcia first tried to relate the **explicit curriculum** to students' shared frames of reference and succeeded in the case of most students. However, she also realized that Gus might not understand this example, and so, through her instruction, she created a connection between Gus' understanding and that of the rest of the students. Even if Ms. Garcia had not been able to create her own curricular example, she could still use instruction to create a shared frame of reference for the students that she could then connect to a specific curricular idea or exercise. Drawing upon students' frames of reference, creating shared frames of reference, and using small connections are ways for teachers to exercise curricular autonomy even in contexts where there is not a lot of flexibility to be responsive to student differences or to waver from curricular requirements.

Funds of Knowledge and Funds of Identity

Each student's cultural upbringing is embedded in their family histories and circumstances, in which they develop funds of knowledge (Moll et al., 1992). These funds of knowledge include numerous frames of reference and also include the meaning made when various frames of reference are put in relation to each other. For example, when studying funds of knowledge, Luis Moll and his team (1992) visited households of public-school students who lived in the border region of Tucson, Arizona. Many students in the southwestern US who have ties to Mexico travel there regularly with their families and have family members who still live there. One particular student of focus in this research, Carlos, traveled to a family ranch during each summer vacation. While there, he played with bows and arrows, rode horses, and went fishing. Each of these experiences are frames of reference that a teacher could relate to particular **content knowledge**. When taken together as part of Carlos' funds of knowledge, these three separate frames of reference gain additional meaning as parts of Mexican ranch life. Carlos' fund of knowledge about ranching included all of these discrete activities among others, which were embedded in linguistic practices, culinary traditions, and intergenerational and community relations that Carlos also came to recognize as "ranch life." Through deep learning about students' funds of knowledge, teachers can make relevant curricular connections, but they can also discern relevant communication styles, norms, and values that students have that also inform the development of teacher–student relationships and culturally relevant **classroom management**. Once again, the activities teachers can use to get to know students pertain to all three **domains of teaching**.

More recently, funds of knowledge research has been criticized for two reasons. First, it can essentialize and overgeneralize students' experiences. For example, teachers who do not themselves have ranching in Mexico as a fund of knowledge might assume that riding horses and fishing are the essential activities that make up ranching, or these teachers could fail to understand certain elements of those activities related to the care of the land that are integral to those cultural practices. Or, it could have turned out that Carlos' family owns a ranch and his brothers like to visit there, but Carlos does not like to go and so he does not go often. Teachers would be in error, in that case, to presume that ranching is one of Carlos' funds of knowledge. It could also be the case that Carlos' peer group and popular culture on the US side of the border are far more important to his identity than his family's ranch in Mexico. The original funds of knowledge research does not address this situation. The second reason that funds of knowledge research has been criticized is because there lacks a practical and accessible way for teachers to learn about students' funds of knowledge. Funds of identity research has addressed these two criticisms.

Funds of identity may include funds of knowledge but also broadens the focus of the relevant knowledge and experiences that students bring to the classroom from outside of school that may be important for teachers to connect to curriculum. Moises Esteban-Guitart (2021) defined funds of identity as, "Significant people, institutions, cultural artifacts, geographical spaces, and meaningful practices, passions, and interests embedded in a learner's definition of themself" (p. 4). Funds of identity research positions young people as informants about their own lives, allowing them to tell educators what things are important to them. Recent research has also suggested additional ways that teachers can learn about students' funds of knowledge and funds of identity other than making home visits ('t Gilde & Volman, 2021). Those include having conversations with parents, colleagues, and students, creating assignments designed to discover students' funds of identity, and paying careful attention to things students casually share or examples they give during classroom interactions (Esteban-Guitart, 2021; 't Gilde & Volman, 2021). Learning about students' frames of reference, funds of knowledge, and funds of identity can help teachers create and connect curriculum to interest students.

> **Focus on Culture 13: Rethinking "Cultural Capital": Community Cultural Wealth**
>
> Pierre Bourdieu and Jean-Claude Passeron (1990) explained that certain cultural experiences and social networks are given value by the dominant cultural group while other experiences and networks are not. When children have the cultural experiences valued by dominant culture, they are said to have *cultural capital*. When they have connections to people who have power to successfully navigate within the dominant culture, such connections may help them get in to prestigious colleges, get more lucrative and desirable jobs, have better access to medical care, and obtain other desired resources. These connections are called *social capital*. Bourdieu and Passeron critiqued this situation but their ideas are sometimes used in education to make the case that educators need to give children from marginalized backgrounds more cultural and social

capital. This distortion of Bourdieu and Passeron's original critique supports the **deficit perspective** that children from these backgrounds do not have valuable cultural and social capital. Bourdieu and Passeron might instead argue that everyone has culture and social connections but that some cultures and social connections are undervalued within the context of a stratified society with one main dominant group.

More recent educational research has focused on changing this deficit orientation toward students from marginalized backgrounds by identifying the various sources of capital these communities do have (Neri et al., 2021). Tara Yosso (2005) named additional types of capital that socially marginalized communities have that together form *community cultural wealth*. These types of capital are aspirational, navigational, linguistic, familial, and resistant capital. From each type of capital developed and maintained within the contexts of their communities, students also gain **funds of knowledge** and **frames of reference**. Here is a definition of each type of capital that belongs to community cultural wealth and a guiding question to support teachers in finding out more about their students' capital.

a) *Aspirational capital*: Stories and advice that help young people maintain hope in the face of an unjust system.
   ◆ What family or community members inspire your students and how do they do that?
b) *Navigational capital*: Skills to maneuver through social institutions.
   ◆ How do your students' families learn about what they need to do to enroll children in school, visit the doctor, or obtain social services?
c) *Linguistic capital*: Communication and social skills learned as a result of being multilingual and multicultural.
   ◆ What unique circumstances do your students face as a result of crossing linguistic and cultural boundaries and what are they able to do as a result of that?
d) *Familial capital*: Kinship ties that extend beyond direct relatives and provide the context in which shared history and culture are nurtured and maintained.

> ♦ What kinship networks do your students have and what role does kinship play in their lives?
> e) *Resistant capital*: Knowledge and skills used to understand, critique, and fight against unjust laws, policies, and practices that disadvantage the community and individuals in it.
>   ♦ In what ways have members of your students' communities been resistant to injustice? What sense do your students make of this?
>
> In addition to these five types of capital, Yosso (2005) also redefines social capital to include the helpful networks that students have. She argues that these networks are a form of wealth even if they are not recognized as the same social capital that is valued by the powerful majority. Better understanding community cultural wealth and students' various forms of capital can support teachers' engagement of the **Habit of Asset Identification** as well as contribute concrete examples that teachers can apply to make **curriculum and instruction** relevant to students.

Developing Critical Thinking

Meaningful curriculum also offers students opportunities for developing critical thinking, which is in turn necessary for developing social consciousness and taking social action. Students often find such activities to be highly relevant, especially if they see connections with their own communities. Esteban-Guitart (2021) points out that sometimes when we talk about funds of knowledge, we focus only on ways of connecting teacher practices to students' lives outside of school without also developing students' critical thinking or **critical consciousness**. He discusses how, in addition to funds of identity, there are also **invisible funds of identity**, norms that people engage in and re-create that shape their thinking and behavior often without them realizing it. He argues that an appropriate curricular goal is to teach students to be able to identify these invisible funds of identity in order to make both personal and societal change.

To move toward this goal, teachers can intentionally push students toward higher order thinking more often.

> **Key Terms**
> *Critical Consciousness*: The ability to recognize and analyze social systems that systematically disadvantage certain groups and to commit to try to change these.
> *Invisible Funds of Identity*: Norms that people engage in and re-create that shape their thinking and behavior often without them realizing it.

There are several models of cognitive complexity in use today that teacher's may be familiar with, including Bloom's taxonomy and Webb's Depth of Knowledge. These models help teachers understand how instructional tasks may be scaffolded to help students build foundational knowledge and develop and apply that knowledge in more complex ways. These models can support teachers as they attempt to balance **traditionalist** and **progressive** curricular approaches as Mr. Fox and Ms. Monroe did in Table 6.3. Bloom's taxonomy of cognitive complexity distinguishes between **lower order thinking** and **higher order thinking** (Krathwohl, 2002). Lower order thinking involves tasks related to remembering and understanding, which is often a focus of traditionalist curriculum. Once students can understand and remember, they can engage in the slightly more complex task of applying their learning. With this foundation of remembering, understanding, and applying, students can then analyze, evaluate, and create. These tasks engage and develop critical thinking and are often the focus of progressive curriculum. Figure 6.1 shows an example of how Ms. Nash transformed a lower order warm-up question that did not relate to students' lives to a higher order warm-up question that connected to students' funds of knowledge. This transformation allowed her to better meet the learning objective because it addressed a more complex aspect of the content while also tapping in to something personally familiar to students.

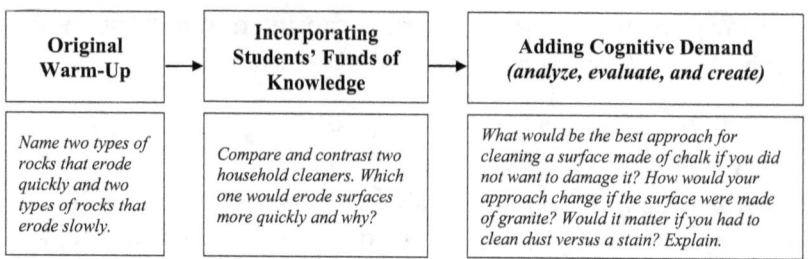

Figure 6.1 Transforming Ms. Nash's Original Warm-Up Activity to Include Students' Funds of Knowledge and Develop Higher Order Thinking.

> **Key Terms**
>
> *Lower Order Thinking*: Remembering and understanding.
> *Higher Order Thinking*: Analyzing, evaluating, and creating.

If students are not used to being asked by teachers to engage in cognitively demanding tasks and if they are not held responsible for doing so, they may resist a teacher's efforts to challenge them. In Chapter 2, we explained Haberman's (1991) term "pedagogy of poverty," which he used in explaining the unspoken trade-off he observed in classrooms that had large percentages of low-income students. In this trade-off, students offered behavioral compliance in return for teachers not asking them to think hard or work hard. In her chapter discussing the importance of teachers developing critical thinking among their students from marginalized backgrounds, Lisa Delpit (2012) borrowed Mike Schmoker's term "the Crayola Curriculum" to describe this same phenomenon of teachers not challenging their low-income students (but instead allowing them to color). Ms. Nash expressed how it can feel when a teacher tries to introduce complex concepts and tasks in a setting where students have not been prepared to engage with and master them. Remember that she stated:

...I really want to figure out how to make this work, but it seems much easier to just put it all away and read from the textbook instead. At least that way, they might sit still, be quiet, and have some work to show for it at the end of the period. I don't want to resort to this, but I'm at a loss for how to make this work.

When scaffolding high levels of student learning and navigating students' hesitation in taking on tasks for which they feel unprepared, teachers may be tempted to water down curriculum or simplify tasks. This situation may occur most quickly in contexts where students lack the self-efficacy to tackle these tasks and teachers simultaneously lack the **teacher efficacy** to scaffold these activities effectively. If you and your students experience a lack of self-efficacy, you can develop it through small steps and with a lot of support. Although students may at first resist teachers' efforts to increase cognitive demands, they ultimately equate teachers' high expectations with care and are motivated by it. Adding cognitive demand and requiring students to think critically is part of **warm demanding** and connects the domain of curriculum and instruction with the domain of relationships.

Focus on Culture 14: Understanding the Three Tenets of Culturally Relevant Pedagogy

Diversity pedagogical content knowledge, discussed above, adds to our understanding of culturally responsive pedagogy (CRP), an effective approach for teaching students from nondominant racial backgrounds. We first introduced CRP in Chapter 2, where we also discussed the pedagogy of poverty and the importance for teachers to challenge, and hold high expectations for, students from marginalized backgrounds. CRP has particular relevance for **curriculum and instruction** as well (Powell et al., 2016). It has often been reduced to teacher moves such as displaying flags representing certain groups or countries or to vague nods to culture such as through exchanges about food or clothing (Oakes et al., 2018). However, implementation of CRP that stays closer to its origins and comprehensiveness addresses social justice through anti-racist curriculum and instruction (Milner, 2017).

In her development of CRP, Gloria Ladson-Billings (1995, 2017) laid out its three tenets. The first tenet is a focus on student learning. Although CRP is based on strong **relationships** between students and teachers, teachers keep the focus on learning. The point of CRP isn't to make students feel good about themselves, but rather to support learning and student achievement. In describing her own **observations** as well as the observations of other teachers and teacher educators, Delpit (2012) describes a pervasive, low level of academic work in classrooms with large percentages of students who are not White. She argues that such classrooms may look well managed as students sit compliantly filling in worksheets or doing puzzles or coloring activities. However, overly simplified curriculum only disadvantages students who particularly need to be challenged at school to think critically.

The second tenet of CRP is to develop cultural competence by learning more about your own culture and others'. Teachers then use this knowledge to support students in continuing to develop and maintain knowledge about their own cultures while also being able to operate strategically across cultures. For example, teachers applying this tenet might support students in being able to speak in vernacular during class discussions and then also use academic English in their formal writing. In order to enact this tenet, teachers need diversity pedagogical content knowledge as discussed above (Dursun et al., 2021).

The third tenet of CRP is to develop students' **critical consciousness**, which means teachers must be critically conscious as well (Ranschaert & Murphy, 2020; Sensoy & DiAngelo, 2017). We discussed earlier how helping students identify **invisible funds of identity** promotes critical thinking that can address social injustice. This third tenet of CRP focuses on that. We want students asking questions about power and to be

> investigating issues that matter to them because when they care about what they're studying, then their learning is accelerated. To promote the development of students' critical consciousness, teachers can select curricular materials and instructional activities that present multiple perspectives and shed light on how social marginalization functions (Oakes et al., 2018). With critical consciousness, students can then apply these higher levels of learning in ways that lead to a more just society. Teachers can use the tenets of CRP to further consider possible teacher moves framed in the domain of curriculum and instruction, especially if they are teaching in settings with many students from marginalized backgrounds.

Instruction

Once we know what we're going to teach (*curriculum*), we need to determine how we are going to teach it (*instruction*). Remember that each **domain of teaching** we are addressing in Part II has already been the focus of hundreds of research studies, books, and articles over many decades of time and across geographical regions. Our goal is not to summarize all there is to be known about each domain. Instead, we are using our focus on dilemmas related to classroom teaching, and the key concepts and skills needed for frame shifting, to guide our decision-making about what topics to synthesize in each chapter in this part. The final topic we will address in this chapter is instruction.

When we think back to Ms. Nash's **dilemma description**, we can identify several details that indicate that instruction might be a relevant domain to explore in order to identify teacher moves to address it. Recall that students did not get to work right away on the warm-up activity and that Ms. Nash's reframed **focus question** in the **domain of curriculum and instruction** is: "How do I structure the first ten minutes of class so students are engaged in activities that access their prior knowledge?" When **frame shifting** the dilemma to the focus on instruction in the domain of curriculum and instruction, we can explore whether the causes of this situation have to do with students not understanding the relevance of the activity, not making links between the activity and the other class activities, or maybe not understanding the specific instructions or outcomes of the activity. If we think about how a teacher plans instruction, we can imagine layers from the macro to micro levels of planning. Each of the potential issues occurring in Ms. Nash's dilemma relates to a different part, or layer, of instructional planning. In this section, we present a model for understanding these layers, and then we consider each one in turn, exploring terms and concepts that can inform teacher moves to address dilemmas in this domain.

We will use the following terms to discuss instructional planning from the "big picture" (macro-level) goals to the minute task steps (micro-level ones): **instructional design, instructional sequence, instructional formats**, and **activity components** or steps. Instructional design is the overall planning and execution process related to instruction. It usually addresses a whole unit and the connections between units. Teachers enact their instructional design of units using instructional sequences. These sequences include whole lessons as well as parts of lessons. We can think of instructional sequences as strings of instructional activities put together in a strategic way to support the outcomes identified during instructional design. Each instructional activity is made up of components or steps that can be further examined for the roles they may play in a persistent dilemma. Figure 6.2

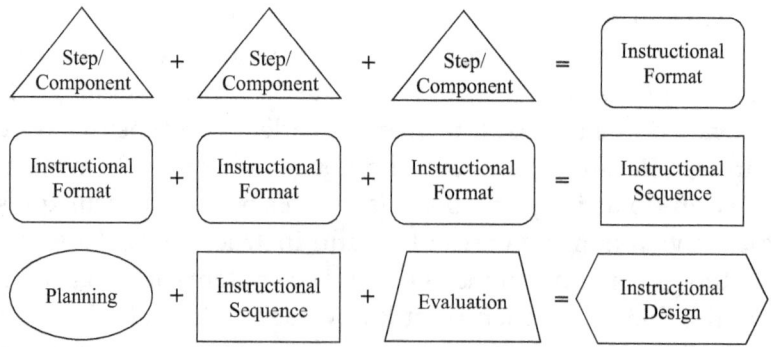

Figure 6.2 Relationships Between Terms Used to Describe Instruction.

illustrates the relationship between these four terms, showing how the activity components build up toward the overall instructional design.

Key Terms

Instructional Design: The overall process of thinking through, planning for, implementing, and evaluating instruction.
Instructional Sequence: A set of instructional formats or activities in which one activity leads to the next.
Instructional Format: Task, experience, or activity through which students access curriculum.
Activity Component: Discrete part of an instructional activity, such as the directions or steps students take to complete it.

Dilemmas may occur if instructional activities are not aligned or effectively scaffolded, and students may be missing connections, not understanding concepts, or losing motivation. Thus, we begin with a description of key concepts that guide a teacher's instructional design. We then provide an overview of instructional sequencing followed by descriptions of various instructional activities as they may relate to instructional design and potential teaching dilemmas, such as if individual activities do not connect with each other. Recall from the section above that both curricular and instructional decisions reflect particular philosophical positions related to the overarching goals and purposes of education. For example, when Ms. Nash gave us more information about her context and her own beliefs about teaching science, she told us that she believed scientific understanding requires authentic explorations of the content. Therefore, she put her **progressive** philosophy to work by trying to incorporate lived experience in the field in her instructional activities. Her design and lesson planning required tightening, but we encouraged Ms. Nash to maintain her core values related to science instruction while also breaking things down into more concrete steps for students, which is a **traditionalist** approach. We similarly encourage you to make connections between your core values, your curricular philosophy, and the instructional processes we describe next.

Instructional Design

When you **frame shift** your dilemma to the focus on instruction within the **domain of curriculum and instruction**, we encourage you to take a systematic look at the entire instructional sequence as it relates to your dilemma so that you can make connections between any potential issues and streamline your approach to resolving them. We begin this systematic look by examining your **instructional design**. As shown in Figure 6.2, instructional design is made up of planning, instructional sequences, and evaluation. We're going to present you with two models that for the instructional design process, Shulman's **Model of Pedagogical Reasoning** and **backwards design**. As we present these models, we will explain the relevance of each step for overall instruction and possible instruction-related dilemmas. Exploring these models in detail may help you figure out if the cause of your dilemma might be related to missing or short-changing a step in the sequence.

Key Terms

Model of Pedagogical Reasoning and Action: Steps teachers take to determine, plan, implement, and evaluate the content of a lesson. These steps include: 1. Comprehension, 2. Transformation, 3. Instruction, 4. Evaluation, 5. Reflection, 6. New Comprehensions.

Backwards Design: Instructional design that begins with identifying learning objectives, followed by creating assessments to evaluate students' performance on the objectives, and then designing the instructional activities required for students to meet those objectives.

Shulman's Model of Pedagogical Reasoning

In an earlier section of this chapter, we reviewed Shulman's (1987) concept of **pedagogical content knowledge**. He first defined pedagogical content knowledge as one of the core competencies that teachers need in order to make effective instructional decisions. He embedded these competencies within a model of the decision-making process which he called the Model of Pedagogical Reasoning and Action. We think this model can be especially useful for teachers whose dilemma is (re)framed within this domain because it breaks into steps all of the decisions teachers make during instruction which could make it easier to identify where different teacher moves might be possible. First we describe each step in detail, then in Figure 6.3, we summarize how each step may pertain to addressing particular teaching dilemmas. The steps are:

1. *Comprehension*: The teacher first has to understand and have mastery of the content that they will teach to the students. This mastery needs to include how the content develops within a field and how subject matter connects across fields. Shulman names this competency **content knowledge**, as we discussed above. Ample content knowledge can equip teachers to answer students' questions about particular topics like "Why do we need to know this? How does this relate to my life? When will we ever use this in the real world?" If you recognize such questions to be part of your dilemma, a focus on developing your content knowledge might be useful.
2. *Transformation*: This is the step where the teacher makes the content accessible for students. It's called transformation because it requires teachers to apply their content knowledge to knowledge that will be relevant to students. You may recognize this skill as **pedagogical content knowledge**, which we introduced earlier in the chapter. Turning curricular content into effective instructional activities requires an accurate understanding of what students might find difficult. Sometimes teachers encounter problems with instruction when they assign a task that is too difficult for students or when students are not yet prepared for the task. When this

happens, students need **scaffolding** which consists of the supports students need to accomplish a certain goal.

> **Key Terms**
>
> *Scaffolding*: Supports students need to accomplish a certain goal.[1]

In addition to being able to provide appropriate scaffolding, teachers also need to be able to help students transfer knowledge across contexts. Transfer is perhaps the most difficult skill for students of all ages and subject matters. You can recognize a problem related to transfer when a surprised and exasperated teacher exclaims, "But you already learned this!" In such a situation, it may be the case that the students do not recognize a particular task, activity, problem, or context as one in which they should put a particular skill to use. Teacher educators face such difficulties when teacher candidates move from teacher training to the full-time induction phase of the first three years of teaching independently. That is the time when new teachers suddenly have to transfer all of the knowledge they have learned to their own classrooms and be able to do everything all at once. It is the new teacher's limited capacity related to transferring so many ideas and skills at once that make the first years of teaching so challenging. Students of all ages need help with recognizing how the knowledge they have and the skills they know fit in to new situations. We might even say that transfer needs to be scaffolded. Teaching dilemmas at all levels of education may be related to students' needs for more effective teacher scaffolding of content or of transfer. Scaffolding and transfer are part of teachers' considerations when transforming content knowledge into instructional activities in the context of Shulman's (1987) Model of Pedagogical Reasoning and Action.

3. *Instruction*: This is the action step when teachers actually teach the content they have transformed. We will discuss frequently used instructional activities below, particularly with a view

toward how these activities might be involved in particular teaching dilemmas.
4. *Evaluation*: In this step, teachers check for understanding and see how well the instruction is going. While evaluation can include both formative and summative assessment, effective formative assessment is particularly important in preventing instruction-related dilemmas from growing in size and complexity. It serves as an early warning system that can alert the teacher to student difficulties as they occur and allow the teacher to correct course before students become agitated, receive a low grade, lose focus, or any of the other effects that occur as a result of a lack of competency and mastery and may ultimately cause classroom conflict. Formative assessment results feed back into further transformation (step 2) and instruction (step 3) and might even require the teacher to develop additional content knowledge (step 1) before proceeding.
5. *Reflection*: The teacher learns from both their students' and their own performance. They ground their conclusions in evidence.
6. *New Comprehensions*: The teacher takes stock of their new understanding related to content knowledge, pedagogical knowledge, and pedagogical content knowledge in order to improve future teaching. You might recognize the power of the **Habit of Personal Attribution** in teachers' continued motivation to keep learning and improving throughout their careers.

Backwards Design

Shulman's (1987) entire model presumes that the teacher has clear learning objectives in mind that drive the teacher's process through the steps. However, if your dilemma is related to low student achievement, it may be related to a lack of alignment between curricular objectives, assessment, and instructional activities. Grant Wiggins and Jay McTighe (2005) address potential instructional misalignments in their framework called backwards design. In describing their framework, they discuss the importance of how the teacher transforms content knowledge to promote effective student understanding. They refer to backwards design because the teacher should begin this process by first identifying the desired outcomes by asking: *What should*

234 ◆ The Domains of Teaching

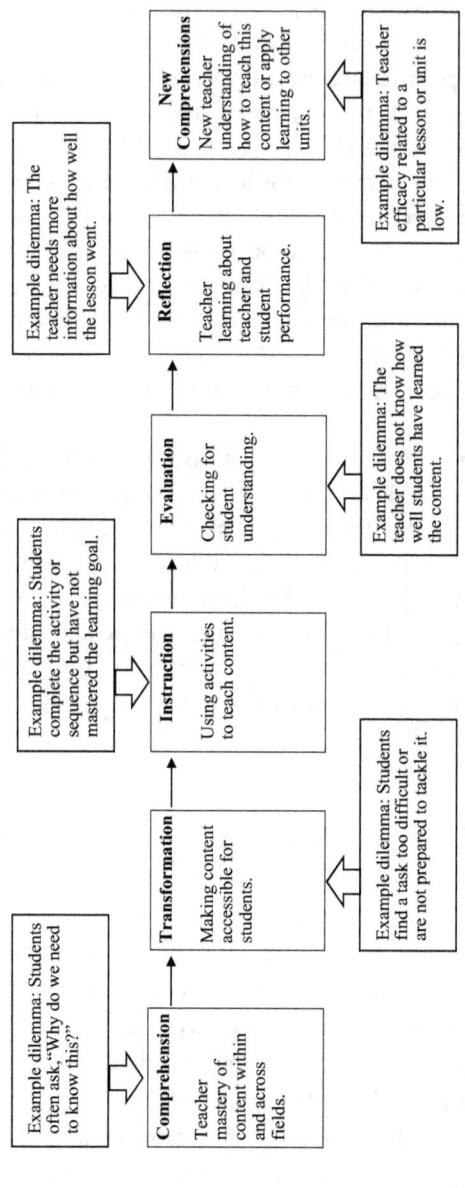

Figure 6.3 Connecting Shulman's Model of Pedagogical Reasoning and Action to Addressing Teaching Dilemmas.

students be able to know, do, and understand at the end of this lesson/instructional sequence? Next, the teacher identifies appropriate assessment by asking: *How will students demonstrate that they have mastered this goal?* It is only after giving these first two stages thorough attention that the teacher then begins to plan instruction, which is the third and final stage in backwards design. It answers the question: *What will I do to support students in being able to develop and demonstrate this mastery?* Ideally, teachers will be selecting from various possible instructional activities "with the end in mind." You may notice that backwards design and the Model for Pedagogical Reasoning and Action fit nicely together. Thinking with the end in mind can shape teachers' decision-making at each step in Shulman's model.

If we return back to Ms. Nash's original dilemma description, she expressed frustration that students were playing with materials for the solar cars project rather than completing the steps for building the cars that she laid out for them at the beginning of the lesson. Her reframed **dilemma statement** had to do with students' completion of the warm-up activities that came as the first task of the lesson that would then transition into the next steps in the solar cars project. However, when we asked Ms. Nash what the specific lesson goals were and how the warm-up connected to the instructional activities that came later in the lesson, we noticed that she was not clear about the learning goals, which was why she could not articulate the connection between the warm-up and the learning goals. She had a vague notion about what she hoped students would learn, but the objectives were not clear and tight and, therefore, the alignment between objectives, assessment, and activities was off. This lack of alignment prevented her from maintaining a sense of academic press, which is necessary for **warm demanding**. In order to be a warm demander, the teacher has to have a clear sense of what to demand and how to demand it. Ms. Nash did not have this at the moment of her dilemma. Strengthening her skills related to pedagogical reasoning and backwards design could address this gap. Once Ms. Nash was clear about the learning goals and how each step of her instruction contributed to those goals, she could press students toward these goals with a sense of purpose that also inspired **teacher efficacy** and conveyed **withitness**. Here again, we see the connections between **domains of teaching**.

Instructional Sequences

An **instructional sequence** is a set of instructional activities in which one activity leads to the next. In Ms. Nash's **dilemma description**, she complained that her instructional sequence of starting with the warm up then moving on to the solar car activity did not lead to a desired outcome. We identified above that part of the issue she faced might have been that her learning outcome was unclear. This is an issue related to instructional design. An additional difficulty she may face even after clarifying her ultimate objective could be related to her instructional sequencing. An instructional sequence combines instructional activities to guide students to the objective.

Beginning teachers might be so consumed with **classroom management** or **relationship** building that their instructional sequences look more like a collection of time-filling activities rather than a sequence of activities in which one activity builds upon the previous ones. In Ms. Nash's case, her first warm-up activity was about Antarctica Day, but that had no conceptual link to her subsequent focus on solar cars. She had two distinct instructional activities. The quality of those activities can be considered separately in the next section, but even with high-quality individual activities, the lack of strategic sequencing to connect these activities into a logical whole can be at the root of a teaching dilemma. Because this is not a book about instructional design, we will only briefly explain one example of instructional sequencing that we ourselves use to scaffold your learning in Part III. Other examples might include design-based learning or organizing a sequence around a K-W-L chart, but we will not go into detail about these additional examples.

Gradual Release of Responsibility Model

In Chapters 7 and 8, we will use the instructional sequence called the **gradual release of responsibility model** to guide your practice of **frame shifting** (Fisher & Frey, 2021). In this instructional sequence, the teacher begins by explaining content in a primarily teacher-led instructional activity. Douglas Fisher and Nancy Frey (2021), the creators of the gradual release model, refer to this step as the "I do" step because the teacher is doing most of the activity by modeling what to do and sharing their thinking. The teacher is active while the students listen and observe. As in any instructional sequence, the teacher may use formative assessment to determine when to move on to the subsequent step, "we do." In this step, the teacher and students practice the content or skill together. The teacher selects an appropriate instructional activity or group of activities to structure and scaffold this practice. Again relying upon formative assessment, the teacher then determines when to release students to work with peers for further practice in the "we do together" step. In the final step, students work independently to solidify and demonstrate their individual understanding. This is the "you do" step.

> **Key Terms**
>
> *Gradual Release of Responsibility Model*: An instructional sequence that begins with teacher modeling followed by activities in which the student has increasing autonomy in, and responsibility for, completing the task.

Notice that the teacher can choose any specific instructional activities that are appropriate for the content and for the students. Instructional sequencing does not necessarily tell us which activities to choose only that the activities should be strategically chosen to link one to the next and build toward student mastery. This is also true if the teacher is using a different instructional sequence than the gradual release of responsibility model.

Instructional Formats

The vast majority of time spent lesson planning goes into the selection, design, and preparation of **instructional formats** and activities. As we have already discussed, the selection and design of activities should always be aligned with each other in the **instructional sequence** and with the overall lesson and unit goals in the **instructional design**. There are many possible activities a teacher can choose from, depending on their learning outcomes and how they plan to assess students. We have selected several formats to discuss based on those we have identified as relevant to most teaching dilemmas. To streamline our discussion, we provide an overview of the instructional formats we have selected in Table 6.6 and list potential dilemmas that might arise with the use of that format. Then, in the body of this section, we expand on each instructional format specifically with regard to these dilemmas and teacher moves that might address them.

Direct Instruction

Direct instruction may serve the important goal of allowing the teacher to share explicit and discrete content with the entire class at the same time. Teachers may introduce several moves to prevent or address the possible dilemmas that may arise in relation to direct instruction, which are listed in Table 6.6. For example, to maintain student attention and keep students engaged in content, the teacher can incorporate **interaction routines** and activities into whole class instruction. Spencer and Miguel Kagan (2009) describe a series of interaction activities in their book on cooperative learning which can be adapted for learners of all ages. They name individual activities **structures**, which are interaction activities that have different applications but are all designed to maximize student engagement. Structures can be applied to different content, so once students know how to do them, the teacher can use them over and over. These structures can be used as part of a **whole-class cooperative learning system**, or they can be adapted for the teacher to use as discrete interaction routines. Here, we argue that structures provide an effective way for teachers to prevent dilemmas during direct instruction. As an example, we describe the structure Think-Pair-Share.

TABLE 6.6 Overview of Selected Instructional Formats

Instructional Format	Definition/Description	Instructional Goals/Purposes	Dilemmas That May Arise
Direct Instruction	Teacher-led exposition on a topic.	• Deliver information. • Model problem-solving. • Demonstrate a procedure. • Articulate a thought process (i.e., think-aloud).	• Students whisper to each other or do other things as the teacher talks. • The teacher may focus on students' recall of lower order facts without scaffolding higher order thinking. • Students may learn to over-rely on the teacher for "correct" answers, making it less likely that gain skills and confidence to work independently.
Whole-Class Discussion	Students contribute ideas one at a time about a given topic. They listen to each other and build upon the ideas and arguments of those who spoke before them.	• Build multi-perspectival understanding of a topic. • Support students' development of their own, evidence-based opinions. • Give students tools for, and practice with, listening, speaking, and justifying their opinions. • Raise questions for future lessons and learning.	• The teacher may lead with an unclear question or one that students do not find compelling. • Specific curricular objective may be unclear, resulting in disconnected contributions or a lack of learning. • Students may talk over each other or fail to listen carefully to others. • The same students may repeatedly contribute while others are completely silent.

(*Continued*)

TABLE 6.6 *(Continued)*

Instructional Format	Definition/Description	Instructional Goals/Purposes	Dilemmas That May Arise
Group Work	Students work together on a shared activity or project.	• Scaffold student learning through heterogeneous or homogeneous grouping. • Allow students to create or gain exposure to a topic more broadly or deeply than they would be able to do alone. • Provide the social interaction required for learning. • Allow more students to talk simultaneously in the classroom.	• Student participation within the group may be imbalanced, with some students doing most or all of the work and others doing little or none of the work. • Students may not get along with each other or may bicker in their groups. • Teachers cannot supervise all groups simultaneously and may miss important moments where teacher scaffolding is needed.
Centers	Different activities targeting the same content are set up in the classroom and small groups of students move at designated times from one activity to the next. At each center, the activity may require members of the small group to work together or independently.	• Give students independent practice while providing peer support. • Allow the teacher to meet with small groups of students to provide targeted scaffolding. • Provide variety across a range of practice activities all focused on the same content.	• Students may look at answer keys before trying or completing each format. • When the teacher is working with one group, the other groups may lose focus, thus dividing the teacher's attention between instructing one group while trying to monitor the others. • Groups may leave center materials disorganized, making it hard for the next group to begin. • The teacher may face challenges related to the time required to create so many new materials.
Independent Work	Students work alone to learn new content, develop an idea or product, or practice a skill.	• Receive formative assessment of the progress of every student. • Give each student the same opportunity to practice.	• Students may lose motivation or focus. • Students may not understand what to do and since they are supposed to work alone, may do nothing instead of getting help. • Multiple students may require the teacher's individual help at the same time

> **Key Terms**
> *Direct Instruction*: Instructional format containing teacher-led exposition on a topic.
> *Structures*: Interaction sequences that have different applications but are designed to maximize student engagement.
> *Whole-Class Cooperative Learning System*: Physical and interactional design of all class activities using intentional and consistent student groupings in which all students are equally responsible and accountable for task completion, and group and class success.

Think-Pair-Share is a common interaction structure that ensures that all students have an equitable opportunity to share. When one student is sharing at a time during direct instruction, then only a very small percentage of the class is actively participating. In a room full of 20 students, for example, only 1/20th (or 5%) of students are sharing at a time. However, when we use a structure such as Think-Pair-Share, we increase simultaneous participation to 50%, as half of the class is speaking and half is listening at the same time (Kagan & Kagan, 2009). To prevent repetition of **lower order** recitation questions during direct instruction, teachers can prepare several **higher order** questions to sprinkle in to the instruction and build in explicit **scaffolding** between lower order skills and higher order questions during the teacher directed sequence.

Think-Pair-Share and other interaction structures require effective classroom management for their success. You may notice that we discussed interaction routines in Chapter 5 along with other classroom management practices, and here we are discussing interaction structures that could be used during direct instruction. Just as interaction routines require explicit instruction, so do interaction structures. Teachers need to engage strategies such as precorrection, explicit timing, and withitness to ensure the success of these interaction structures, which again shows the **interdependence** of the domains of teaching. If a certain instructional format or interaction structures does not "work" for you, consider how looking at the domain of classroom management might be a pre-requisite for success.

> **Focus on Culture 15: Using Cooperative Learning Structures to Support Language Learning**
>
> By assigning each student a role and increasing engagement and accountability, Kagan cooperative learning **structures** have particular benefits for learners who speak a different native language than the language of instruction. By providing ample opportunities to talk with partners and small groups, these structures lower the stakes of speaking in class, which gives students the practice they need with academic language while minimizing their anxiety about making mistakes in front of everyone. Interaction structures also allow for highly verbal or highly distractable learners to have more positive and teacher-approved opportunities for involvement with curricular content and class activities. Therefore, these structures have particular importance in providing equitable education for diverse learners. Although Kagan materials look like they target an elementary audience, we currently adapt them successfully at the university level and believe they hold promise for learners of all ages.

Whole-Class Discussion

Effective **whole-class discussions** can be challenging. Our first question for teachers who have dilemmas related to whole-class discussion is whether the activity is truly a discussion or whether it is more of an interaction routine during direct instruction. For example, a teacher may think that they are facilitating a discussion when in reality they are using a string of IRE sequences in which the teacher initiates (I) with a question, a student responds (R), and the teacher evaluates (E) the quality of the response. In authentic whole-class discussion, the teacher tries to build student understanding and critical thinking by helping students critically listen to and respond to each other. During discussions, students should develop and express their own perspectives while relying upon verifiable evidence to support their positions. To avoid many of the pitfalls of this instructional format, the teacher should have a clear goal for the discussion and should be able to accurately anticipate the various points that might be raised and how one point might lead to the next critical question that the teacher will need to pose. A successful whole-class discussion requires the teacher to have robust **content knowledge, pedagogical knowledge,** and **pedagogical content knowledge.**

> **Key Terms**
>
> *Whole-Class Discussion*: Instructional format in which students contribute ideas one at a time about a given topic. They listen to each other and build upon the ideas and arguments of those who spoke before them.

Even when this is the case, teachers may find that the same students contribute a lot while others say nothing. Teachers may balance student contributions more effectively if they allow students time either before or during the discussion to think independently and prepare what they would like to say. For example, a teacher might say,

> Okay, I hear Jolene's point that [teacher summarizes point]. Next I am going to ask a follow up question that I would like you all to consider. After I ask the question, we are going to sit in silence for thirty seconds so that everyone has time to think about their answer. If you feel like you can't hold your answer in that long and might blurt it out, write it down on a piece of paper. Then after the time is up and everyone has had an opportunity to think about their answer, I will pull out an answer stick and the person whose name is on the stick will have a chance to share their answer.

In this example, the teacher is introducing wait time, using **precorrection**, and engaging a specific **interaction routine** that evenly distributes whose voice is heard. Here we see the **interdependence** of classroom management and instruction in preventing or addressing this instructional dilemma related to carrying out an effective whole-class discussion.

Group Work

To set students up for success with **group work**, all of the students in the group need to feel comfortable working with each other. As part of their curriculum that helps teachers establish and implement **whole-class cooperative learning** in their classrooms, Kagan and Kagan (2009) include suggestions and structures for class building and team building. We described one such structure, Quiz-Quiz-Trade, as a method for building student–student **relationships** in Chapter 4. Just as we mentioned there, team-building activities do take some time to complete—time that could be spent on academics—but we assert that this time is well spent in the service of learning. When students know each other, respect each other, and laugh together, they learn better together and collaborate better with one another which are the ultimate goals of group work. We first made this argument when discussing the importance of student–student relationships and we now see the relevance of that domain for effective instruction.

In order to be able to succeed as a team, students should be intentionally grouped according to the teacher's goals for the activity. **Heterogeneous groups** have the advantage of allowing students with different skills, abilities, and perspectives to work together, but may create a situation where the most academically capable student carries more weight than the others while the least academically capable student feels left out or behind the group. **Homogeneous groups** have the advantage of allowing students with similar skill levels and interests to support each other. Very advanced groups can move quickly or tackle a more complex topic while the students in the groups that might work more slowly can also move together toward a shared goal. Teachers should take other factors into account when grouping students as well in order to create the best possible situation for groups to succeed in meeting the instructional goals.

> **Key Terms**
>
> *Group Work*: Instructional format in which students work together on a shared activity or project.
> *Heterogeneous Groups*: The teacher forms groups of students with differences that are important for the goals of the activity.
> *Homogeneous Groups*: The teacher forms groups of students with similarities that are important for the goals of the activity.

In addition to being able to form a productive team, successful group work also requires students to be able to break a task into parts and divide those parts evenly among group members, know how to approach and complete all parts of the task, and work persistently toward completion. Depending on the developmental level and specific needs of students, the teacher may need to provide explicit direction for each of these sets of skills and introduce individual accountability as group members carry out their designated tasks. Since the teacher cannot help every group navigate their difficulties simultaneously, there might be specific moments when the teacher asks for attention from the whole class and does a quick formative check in. For example, the teacher might use an attention getter and when the class is quiet, say, "Group leaders, raise your hand if your group has already completed subtask 1." After canvasing the room, the teacher might say, "Okay, if your group has completed subtask 1, please continue. Your goal is to complete subtask 2 in 20 minutes. Leaders of groups that have not completed subtask 1, I would like a one-sentence description of what you need in order to complete task 1." After hearing from the groups, the teacher could then prioritize the order to circulate to these groups that are not yet finished. Alternately, each group might have a short, frequent appointment with the teacher throughout the project to report on progress. Of course, the teacher's approach might be different in different educational levels or for different content but these teacher moves demonstrate ways to address possible dilemmas related to group work.

Centers

Centers is an instructional format in which different activities targeting the same content are set up in the classroom and small groups of students move at designated times from one activity to the next. Running successful centers hinges not only on having compelling content and activities (**curriculum and instruction**), but also on the effective creation of routines to guide center time (**classroom management**). Challenges with using centers as an instructional format occur if the teacher has not developed and practiced tight **routines** with students when setting up centers. Reinforcing expectations can also be challenging during centers if one of the centers is led by the teacher because the teacher's ability to provide small group instruction depends on the other groups working completely independently. Students need to get along with their small group members in order to work smoothly at each center (**relationships**) and they need to know the teacher's expectations related to handling materials and submitting completed tasks (classroom management). Again, the three **domains of teaching** are **interdependent** here.

> **Key Terms**
>
> *Centers*: Instructional format in which different activities targeting the same content are set up in the classroom and small groups of students move at designated times from one activity to the next.

Independent Work

Time in class with the teacher is valuable time for students to engage in teacher-facilitated learning activities. Teachers may strategically choose to have students do **independent work** in class so that the teacher can help individual students. To facilitate successful independent work time, teachers should explain the goals of the independent work to the students. Several challenges related to independent work may fuel dilemmas. Students may be overwhelmed by the quantity of exercises or size of the task they are being asked to do or they may be under challenged by tasks that do not align well with the instructional goals or that do not tap in to their **higher order thinking**. For example, one teacher we worked with stated her dilemma as wanting students to produce higher-quality work during independent work time. When we asked for a description of the situation, the learning objective, and an example of work that she considered to be of low quality, she explained that the instructional goal was to practice map skills by labeling the geographical locations and features of countries in the Middle East. She then produced a student work sample of a colored map with mountain ranges, rivers, and capital cities labeled. She said that the student had not colored neatly and had not imitated the example of the giant colored map that the teacher had posted on the board. We wondered about the alignment between the instructional goal and the instructional activity. Students did not actually need to learn more about the geography of the Middle East to complete the activity, and the teacher was not evaluating the effectiveness of the independent work according to what students learned but rather according to how well they copied and colored. This exercise had characteristics of the "Crayola Curriculum" and we were not surprised to learn that this teacher faced other classroom management dilemmas from students who did not feel respected and academically engaged by her.

Key Terms

Independent Work: Instructional format in which students work alone to learn new content, develop an idea or product, or practice a skill.

Another challenge that can occur when a teacher assigns independent work as an instructional format is that students may simultaneously need teacher support to complete the work. In some cases, students may opt out of a challenging task by putting their head on their desk or engaging in other activities besides the one assigned. If the teacher has carefully chosen independent work as the appropriate instructional format and verified a connection between the activity and the instructional goals, then the teacher might address student disengagement by organizing an impromptu small group of disengaged students that can sit near the teacher's desk as they work. In that way, the teacher can easily provide academic support as well as **active supervision** to all of these students at the same time.

Steps or Components of Instructional Formats or Activities

We have given a general overview of several common instructional formats and discussed teacher moves that can prevent or address common dilemmas that can arise in these formats. We can further break down an instructional format by examining its steps or components that students encounter and move through as they engage in the activity. Taking Ms. Nash's warm-up activity as an example, students have to complete the steps of sitting down, taking out a pencil and their journal, reading the prompt, answering the prompt, and sharing their answer. The components involved in this activity are the subtasks of reading, writing, and speaking, all in relation to the specific prompt. Making the distinction between steps and components is less important than generally considering how these individual parts of an instructional activity may be where an instructional dilemma lies.

In Ms. Nash's case, we discussed earlier how she could improve the transition between the warm-up and the main activity by creating an **instructional sequence** in which these two activities are linked. That means that the content of the warm-up and the main activity are connected and Ms. Nash intentionally develops the complexity of students' understanding of the day's instructional objectives across these activities. Examining the steps of each activity can point her to further possible teacher moves for addressing her dilemma. For example, one component of the warm-up was a requirement for students to copy down lengthy directions and sets of answer choices before selecting and justifying a correct answer. When we asked why students were required to write the question, Ms. Nash reasoned that this procedure allowed her to understand which warm-up question the student was answering and it also allowed the student to go back over their own work and quickly evaluate it.

Since Ms. Nash's dilemma statement was about students quickly engaging in the warm-up after entering class, we wondered if changing the directions to make the task more intellectually engaging and less physically laborious might be useful. We suggested dropping the requirement for students to copy lengthy questions or else providing the questions to them as handouts or in a format where the question was already listed. Such adjustments would not require a change in the selection of instructional format or in the development of the instructional sequence, although those things did turn out to be important as well. Instead, they would involve only a small change in the components required to complete the activity, which could have a big impact on how easily and how well students engage with the warm-up.

Key Takeaways: Teacher Moves to Address Dilemmas Related to Curriculum and Instruction

We have named teacher moves throughout the chapter as we have discussed different topics related to **curriculum and instruction**. As we stated at the beginning of the chapter, many of these teacher moves address curriculum and instruction at the same time since those two parts of this domain of teaching are integrated. We list here for review all of the teacher moves we have discussed in this chapter:

- Consider whether your **explicit curriculum** reflects more of a **traditionalist** or **progressive** approach and if introducing more balance between the approaches might improve curriculum and instruction in your practice.

- Make curriculum relevant by connecting content to students' **frames of reference, funds of knowledge,** and **funds of identity**. Create shared frames of reference among students when necessary.
- Move students toward **higher order thinking** more often.
- Incorporate Think-Pair-Share or other **structures** into direct instruction.
- Prepare several higher order questions to sprinkle in to **direct instruction** so that there is explicit **scaffolding** from students' lower order skills to higher order thinking in teacher questioning.
- Have a clear goal for **whole-class discussions**.
- Anticipate the various arguments that will be raised during class discussions and how one argument might lead to the next critical question you will pose.
- Allow students time either before or during a discussion to think independently and prepare what they would like to say.
- Spend time on team building.
- Group students intentionally, based on your instructional goals.
- Provide explicit direction for the skills and steps needed in order for students to succeed at group work.
- Check in with groups often and hold them accountable for progress.
- Practice **routines** for centers.
- Explain the goals of **independent work** to students.
- Align independent work tasks to curricular goals and assessments.
- Form an impromptu group of students who are disengaged from an independent activity so that you can address their questions and needs simultaneously.

When we return to Ms. Nash's dilemma and how she **frame shifted** it to the **domain of curriculum and instruction**, we recall that she identified two versions of her **dilemma statement**:

Frame Shifting to the Domain of Curriculum and Instruction ◆ 251

Students do not understand the content of the warm-up assignments, and *Students do not relate to the content of the warm-up assignments.* She phrased her **focus questions** as: "How do I create warm-up assignments that are accessible?" and "How do I create warm-up assignments that are relatable?" Looking back on what we have discussed in this chapter, we can identify several teacher moves she can make within the domain of curriculum and instruction to address both of these dilemma statements (see Figure 6.4). We first advised Ms. Nash to develop her **pedagogical content knowledge** to assess why students might not understand the content of the warm-up assignments. She realized that her slides were too visually cluttered and used terms that students did not remember from previous lessons. She decided to reduce the amount of content on each warm-up slide and to add supportive information such as the definition of key terms that the warm-up used.

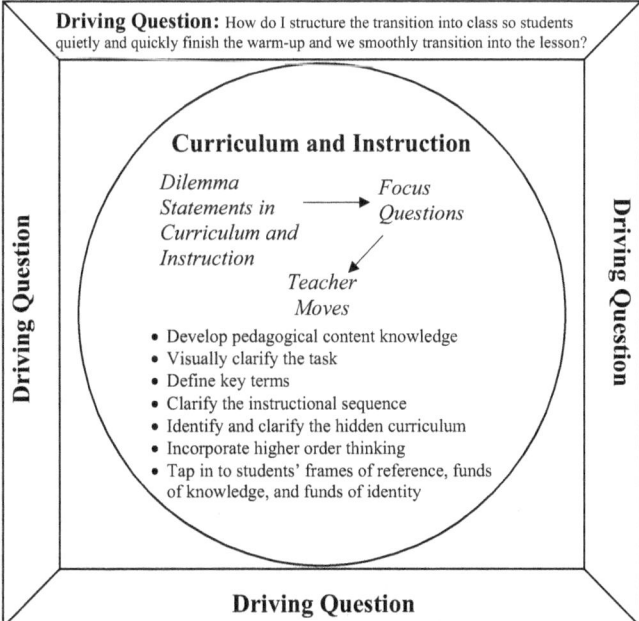

Figure 6.4 Teacher Moves Ms. Nash Identified in the Domain of Curriculum and Instruction Using the Zoomed In Frame.

We also asked Ms. Nash how she was scaffolding her students' experiences to engage in higher order thinking. Together we discussed how the pedagogy of poverty had impacted her students' motivation to this point since they belonged to the main program at the school where teachers' academic expectations of students were low. Ms. Nash decided to add think-alouds to the discussion she had with students about the warm-up each day so that she could model higher order thinking for them. She began to prompt them to do this for themselves over time, thereby scaffolding their abilities to tackle higher order exercises and boosting their self-efficacy for doing so independently.

Ms. Nash also noticed that she could ensure that the content of the warm-ups taps in to students' **frames of reference, funds of knowledge,** and **funds of identity.** She had already begun to learn more about students' lives outside of school as she contacted parents more regularly and attended students' extracurricular activities. One example of how she applied the knowledge she learned about her students was by changing her warm-up question about erosion to a focus on how household cleaners cause erosion. When considering students' engagement in the warm-up in light of her **instructional sequence,** Ms. Nash ensured that her learning goals were clear, that the specific objectives from the warm-up tied in to the objectives of the next activity, and that the sequence of activities worked together to build toward student mastery of the lesson objectives. For example, as the unit on solar cars continued, Ms. Nash began to narrow down and clarify a daily learning objective and then ensure that the warm-up activity supported foundational knowledge about that objective that the next activity would build upon.

By clarifying her daily learning goals and tightening her own understanding about the instructional sequence, Ms. Nash could provide the academic press necessary to be an effective **warm demander.** As students experienced this academic press, they began to rise to the challenge of engaging in increasingly difficult warm-ups. They demonstrated more respect for Ms. Nash for holding them to high standards, which benefitted both her relationships with them as well as her classroom management. Ms. Nash had not originally considered these as possible moves for answering her **driving question**, but she now saw their relevance. Frame shifting to the domain of curriculum and instruction could indeed help her answer: "How do I structure the transition into class so students quietly and quickly finish the warm-up and we smoothly transition into the lesson?"

Now let's return to your dilemma. When you (re)frame your dilemma within the domain of curriculum and instruction, consider your how your dilemma might be impacted by your instructional design, instructional sequences, instructional activities, and the steps or components of those activities. Then, decide which teacher moves might generate the changes you would like to see. Try Exercise 6.5 to help you.

Exercise 6.5 *Identifying Teacher Moves in the Domain of Curriculum and Instruction*

1. Jot down the focus questions you listed in the domain of curriculum and instruction in Exercise 3.4 in the left-hand column below.
2. Using the information presented in this chapter, use the right-hand column to identify one or more teacher moves that answer each focus question and that you have not tried before.

Focus Questions in the Domain of Curriculum and Instruction	Teacher Moves to Try

For Discussion and Practice

1. In one of the *Focus on Culture* boxes in this chapter, we described the concept of diversity pedagogical content knowledge. Consider the following questions in evaluating your own diversity pedagogical content knowledge:
    - What general diversity knowledge would be relevant in your teaching context? How knowledgeable are you about it?
    - What diversity content knowledge is relevant in the subjects you teach? How knowledgeable are you about it?
    - What diversity pedagogical knowledge is relevant to the ages and groups of students you teach? How knowledgeable are you about it?
    - How would you characterize the current level of your diversity pedagogical content knowledge?
2. To what extent do you recognize the situations in Exercise 6.3 and 6.4? Have you witnessed them in your teaching? What could the teacher do in each scenario to better include all students?
3. Identify the hidden curriculum in the following examples. See suggested answers in the online Study Guide.
    a) First grade math problem: *Joey went upstairs to get a clean pair of socks out of his drawer. He didn't find any, so he went into his brother Carter's room where he found five pairs of socks, two pairs of pants, and a sweatshirt folded in a neat pile and left on the bed by their housekeeper. How many pieces of clothing did Joey find on Carter's bed?*
    b) Maria entered her history classroom and noticed that in celebration of Black History Month, her teacher had changed the bulletin board by removing White heroes from World War II and replacing them with Black heroes from the US Civil Rights Movement.
    c) As the students sat in the morning circle, Ms. Jones asked each one to share one exciting thing they had done during the weekend. Jared and Jennifer each shared that their soccer teams had won their games

and Ms. Jones seemed thrilled. Peter shared that he had attended his French lesson where they learned how to make croissants. Ms. Jones enthusiastically explained how important it is to learn a foreign language. Hearing that, Muhammed shared that he attended Arabic lessons at his mosque and learned a new verse from the Quran. Ms. Jones nodded her head and looked quickly at the next student in the circle whose turn it was to share.

4. Identify three frames of reference that you share with all of the teachers at your school but not with teachers at other schools.
5. Identify five frames of reference that you had as a child that a teacher could have used to relate curriculum more effectively to your life. The examples we listed in the chapter are duplicated here to get you started.

Table for Activity #5

Brianna and Amy's Shared Frames of Reference	Your Frames of Reference	How a Teacher Could Connect Your Frame of Reference to Curricular Content
The 13th street tunnel		
The UF-UGA annual college football game		
The train stops at the Atlanta airport		
US education-related acronyms such as IEP, FAPE, ATE, AERA		
Gainesville, Florida		
Training dogs		

6. Investigate Kagan interaction structures using online resources and videos. Identify one (new) Kagan interaction structure that you think could support your instruction. Discuss with a colleague how you will plan and prepare students for using this structure. Then, try it out and debrief with a colleague, coach, or your PLC how it went and why you think it had that outcome.

Note

1 Vygotsky (1978/2009) described scaffolding as the supports needed to help students extend what they can do independently to the more complex cognitive tasks that they can accomplish with more skilled peers or adults. We also use the term scaffolding in a more general sense to describe supports students need to accomplish a certain goal.

References

Biesta, G. (2009). Good education in an age of measurement: On the need to reconnect with the question of purpose in education. *Educational Assessment, Evaluation and Accountability*, 21(1), 33–46. https://doi.org/10.1007/s11092-008-9064-9

Bourdieu, P., & Passeron, J. C. (1990). *Reproduction in education, society, and culture* (2nd ed.). Sage.

Delpit, L. (2012). *Multiplication is for White people*. The New Press.

Dursun, H., Claes, E., & Agirdag, O. (2021). Diversity pedagogical content knowledge: A new conceptual framework and assessment across different teacher education programmes. *Multicultural Education Review*, 13(4), 303–322. https://doi.org/10.1080/2005615X.2021.2006118

Esteban-Guitart, M. (2021). Invisible funds of identity in urban contexts. *Urban Education*. [Advance online publication]. https://doi.org/10.1177/00420859211016536

Fisher, D., & Frey, N. (2021). *Better learning through structured teaching: A framework for the gradual release of responsibility* (3rd ed.). ASCD.

Haberman, M. (1991). The pedagogy of poverty versus good teaching. *Phi Delta Kappan, 92*(2), 81–87. https://doi.org/10.1177/003172171009200223

Kagan, S., & Kagan, M. (2009). *Kagan cooperative learning*. Kagan.

Kennedy-Lewis, B. L. (2012). What happens after students are expelled? Understanding teachers' successes and failures at one alternative middle school. *Teachers College Record, 114*(12), 1–38. https://doi.org/10.1177/016146811211401207

Krathwohl, D. R. (2002). A revision of Bloom's taxonomy: An overview. *Theory Into Practice, 41*(4), 212–218. https://doi.org/10.1207/s15430421tip4104_2

Kumashiro, K. K. (2015). *Against common sense* (3rd ed.). Routledge.

Ladson-Billings, G. (1995). But that's just good teaching! The case for culturally relevant pedagogy. *Theory Into Practice, 34*(3), 159–165. https://doi.org/10.1080/00405849509543675

Ladson-Billings, G. (2017). The (R)Evolution will not be standardized. In D. Paris & H. S. Alim (Eds.), *Culturally sustaining pedagogies* (pp. 141–156). Teachers College Press.

Milner, H. R. (2017). Where's the race in culturally relevant pedagogy? *Teachers College Record, 119*(1), 1–32. https://doi.org/10.1177/016146811711900109

Moll, L. C., Amanti, C., Neff, D., & Gonzalez, N. (1992). Funds of knowledge for teaching: Using a qualitative approach to connect homes and classrooms. *Theory Into Practice, 31*(2), 132–141. http://www.jstor.org/stable/1476399

Neri, R. C., Zipin, L., Rios-Aguilar, C., & Huerta, A. H. (2021). Surfacing deep challenges for social-educational justice: Putting funds, wealth, and capital frameworks into dialogue. *Urban Education. 58*(7), 1443–1448. https://doi.org/10.1177/00420859211016520

Noddings, N. (2005). *The challenge to care in schools: An alternative approach to education* (2nd ed.). Teachers College Press.

Oakes, J., Lipton, M., Anderson, L., & Stillman, J. (2018). *Teaching to change the world* (5th ed.). Routledge.

Powell, R., Cantrell, S. C., Malo-Juvera, V., & Correll, P. (2016). Operationalizing culturally responsive instruction: Preliminary findings of CRIOP research. *Teachers College Record, 118*(1), 1–46. https://doi.org/10.1177/016146811611800107

Ranschaert, R., & Murphy, A. (2020). Developing preservice teachers' critical consciousness and understanding of community contexts. *School-University Partnerships, 13*(3), 85–101. https://napds.org/wp-content/uploads/2020/11/6-ranschaert-article.pdf

Sensoy, O., & DiAngelo, R. (2017). *Is everyone really equal?* (2nd Ed.) Teachers College Press.

Shulman, L. (1987). Knowledge and teaching: Foundations of the new reform. *Harvard Educational Review, 57*(1), 1–23. https://doi.org/10.17763/haer.57.1.j463w79r56455411

't Gilde, J., & Volman, M. (2021). Finding and using students' funds of knowledge and identity in superdiverse primary schools: A collaborative action research project. *Cambridge Journal of Education, 51*(6), 673–692. https://doi.org/10.1080/0305764X.2021.1906845

Toshalis, E. (2015). *Make me! Understanding and engaging student resistance in school*. Harvard Education Press.

Vygotsky, L. (1978/2009). Interaction between learning and development. In M. Gauvain & M. Cole (Eds.), *Readings on the development of children* (5th ed.) (pp. 29–35). Worth.

Wekker, G. (2016). *White innocence*. Duke University Press. https://doi.org/10.1215/9780822374565

Wiggins, G., & McTighe, J. (2005). *Understanding by design* (2nd ed.). ASCD.

Yosso, T. J. (2005). Whose culture has capital? A critical race theory discussion of community cultural wealth. *Race Ethnicity and Education, 8*(1), 69–91. https://doi.org/10.1080/1361332052000341006

Part III
Putting It All Together

In this final part of the book, we put all of the pieces of the frame shifting approach together to see how they function and interact in teachers' dilemmas. Throughout the book we have worked step by step through Ms. Nash's and your dilemma, starting with engaging the **habits of mind** and **frame shifting** in Part I. Then, in each chapter of Part II, both you and Ms. Nash were able to identify teacher moves in each **domain of teaching** that answered **focus questions** and contributed to the ultimate answering of the **driving question**. In the figure below, we put together all of the teacher moves Ms. Nash identified (a collection of Figures 4.1, 5.1, and 6.4). Before we move on to Part III, we want to tell you how our work with Ms. Nash unfolded and how she relied on the **habits of mind** and used these teacher moves to answer her driving question: "How do I structure the transition into class so students quietly and quickly finish the warm-up and we smoothly transition into the lesson?"

In the **domain of relationships**, Ms. Nash began calling caregivers with positive reports and greeting students at the door. These moves maintained the positive climate that supported her work in the other domains. In the **domain of classroom management**, Ms. Nash worked on combining her use of **explicit timing**, the consistent use of seating charts, and attention getters. When we concluded the PLC, she was still working on developing

260 ◆ Putting It All Together

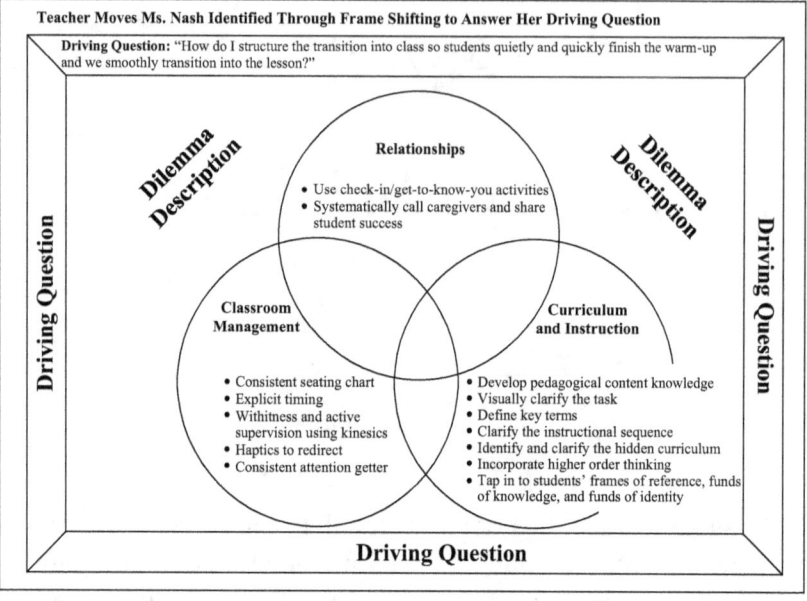

withitness because she noticed that that was the move that needed to be implemented along with the others in order to make them work. In the **domain of curriculum and instruction**, Ms. Nash was adjusting her warm-up questions to be more engaging and relevant—the requirements for completion to be meaningful—and the visual presentation of the warm-up to be simpler. She noticed incremental improvements that indeed made the transition into class smoother and the students more interested in the warm-up activity. It was then easier for her to connect the warm-up to the next activity in the lesson, which also contributed to a smoother transition.

As Ms. Nash found, and as you may also find, there was no one silver bullet. The reason these are persistent dilemmas, and the reason we do not offer tips and tricks to solve them, is because these moves are interlocking and complex. They require the continual engagement of the habits of mind, and they rely on your successful simultaneous implementation of multiple new moves. Ms. Nash did not master this right away, but just because a move did not work the first time did not mean that she was not on the right track. We encouraged her, and we encourage you, to stick with it. To help you continue to make progress, we present example cases in this part that you can use to practice the frame shifting approach.

In Part III, we combine the foundational concepts of frame shifting presented in Part I with the specific content related to teacher moves within each domain of teaching presented in Part II. In this final part, we illustrate the key concepts of the book by presenting an extended example about a dilemma faced by Mr. Lee that we use to walk the reader through this approach. Because our chief purpose in writing this book is to help teachers develop a conscious approach to their persistent challenges, we use conversations between Mr. Lee and his instructional coach to demonstrate the complexity in how a teacher might think through the frame shifting approach. First, in Chapter 7 we help the reader develop and engage the habits of mind by applying them to Mr. Lee's case. In Chapter 8, the reader practices **frame shifting** Mr. Lee's dilemma to different domains of teaching and identifying relevant teacher moves for addressing their driving question in a new way.

In formatting this part, we were inspired by the **gradual release of responsibility model** of instruction discussed in Chapter 6 to scaffold the reader's practice (Fisher & Frey, 2021). In both Chapters 7 and 8, we provide explicit guidance about how to apply the habits of mind and then frame shift using Mr. Lee's case narrative as an example. We offer the reader extended opportunities for practice by providing two more cases in the online Study Guide. The Study Guide includes the case narrative of second-grade teacher Ms. Cohen, in which we give the reader more opportunities to practice by pausing the description at key points and asking the reader to complete exercises that help you think about next steps before proceeding. After Ms. Cohen's case, we provide the case of high school Spanish teacher Ms. Ortega, which is left for the reader to apply the approach independently.

Suggested answers are provided for both of these cases in the online Study Guide. By the end of Part III, you should be able to:

- Talk a colleague through the frame shifting approach in response to any persistent dilemma they raise.
- Apply the frame shifting approach to your own future dilemmas.

7
Practicing Engaging the Habits of Mind

The frame shifting approach consists of two foundational sets of practices: engaging the **habits of mind** and **frame shifting** across **domains of teaching**. In this chapter, we practice the first foundational set of practices: engaging the habits of mind. We present the case of Mr. Lee whose seventh-grade students do not meet his expectations for completing a group project and use his case to help you practice the three habits of mind presented in Chapter 2. Some of the frustrations faced by Mr. Lee have to do with his beliefs about his own ability to effect any change related to the dilemma, the students in his class, and/or the source of the problem. At the end of his **dilemma description**, we include Mr. Lee's initial **driving question** and **dilemma statement** which we will engage with throughout the chapter and ultimately revise after practicing all three habits of mind in preparation for frame shifting in Chapter 8.

When teachers first approach a persistent dilemma, we encourage starting with engaging the **Habit of Personal Attribution** which helps teachers position their dilemma so that it is within their control or sphere of influence to change. Next, we recommend practicing the **Habit of Asset Identification** which helps teachers first determine if they have described their dilemma in a way that blames students, their families, or their communities, and then guides teachers toward an asset-based view of students so that they can productively engage in frame shifting. Engaging these two habits are prerequisites for the final habit of mind, the **Habit of Deliberate Interpretation**. This habit helps teachers consciously and intentionally separate **empirical** observations from **interpretations** and **judgments** in order to identify the dilemma's source and respond to it differently.

We introduced each of the habits of mind separately in Chapter 2 because each is a process of its own. In practice, though, teachers may engage the habits in a different sequence depending on a particular case, or sometimes they may engage them simultaneously. We will demonstrate how this might look in Mr. Lee's case presented here and in the two other case studies provided in the Study Guide. Throughout this chapter we refer to handouts teachers can consult when engaging the habits of mind. These "handouts" are reproductions of tables or exercises first presented in earlier chapters and listed in the Table of Contents and List of Tables.

We want to make a final note before we begin practicing the habits of mind with the sample case studies. We have found in our own teaching and in our work with educators of all levels that our core dilemmas are often similar across different age groups. For example, teachers of six-year-olds, sixteen-year-olds, and college students alike sometimes face dilemmas related to group work, as seventh-grade teacher Mr. Lee does in the case you are about to read. In fact, we used a dilemma similar to his in a frame shifting exercise in Chapter 3 focused on postsecondary education. Rather than providing different examples for every educational level after each of the three cases, we provide examples in the Study Guide in which we demonstrate how teachers of different levels might frame shift a dilemma similar to Mr. Lee's. We present examples of teachers from primary school through postsecondary education who face dilemmas with group work, and we show how each of these teachers might engage the habits of mind similarly to how Mr. Lee did when addressing their dilemma with their students. We then ask you to use these examples as models to consider how you can apply key takeaways from each of the three cases to your own work with students regardless of the educational level you teach.

Sample Case: Group Projects in Mr. Lee's Class

Mr. Lee was in his fifth year of teaching at Valley Oak Middle School. He primarily taught students who were selected for the accelerated track based on teacher recommendations and test scores. Mr. Lee was a first-generation Korean American, and his students were primarily White and from upper-middle class backgrounds. The students in his seventh-grade life science class entered the classroom one Monday to learn that they would be concluding their unit on ecosystems by starting a weeklong group project related to environmental issues in the rainforest. Mr. Lee explained the project and let students know they would have group work time each day of the week until the project was due on Friday.

Students counted off by 7's to create seven groups of four students each. Mr. Lee used this grouping strategy to ensure the groups would be heterogeneous and that students would not be working with those who they were already sitting next to. Once students got into their groups, he assigned each group a particular issue to explore. Wanting to instill independence and task management skills in his students, he told them he trusted them to figure out who would take the lead on various tasks and to make sure each student was contributing equally.

By the end of the first day of the project, some groups were struggling to even get started. When Mr. Lee visited Group A, he heard them arguing over who would complete each task. Group B had the opposite issue: instead of dividing up the tasks, each student worked on the same task at the same time and then planned to combine their work. Mr. Lee feared this group would never finish by Friday. A couple of students vocally complained about their assigned topics because they were more interested in other groups' topics, and one student boldly questioned, "What does this even matter to us? We don't even live near the rainforest!" Annoyed with this response, Mr. Lee thought to himself, "Some kids can be so entitled and think that they should be able to call the shots in my classroom."

By Wednesday, students in group A were continuing to bicker, this time arguing over whose cover art for the project was the best. Meanwhile, it was clear that one student was carrying the weight of Group D while other students in the group talked and played with each other. In fact, each day several students were out of their own groups and hanging out with their friends in other groups. By the time Friday came around, Mr. Lee was exasperated. He had designed the project for students to have an inquiry-based project and an opportunity to collaborate with their peers but instead he threw up his hands and in a moment of frustration told the students, "This is the last time we will be doing group work in this class. You clearly cannot handle it."

But Mr. Lee felt uneasy with this decision because what he really wanted was for his students to be able to do the task he'd assigned. He wanted some help and decided to ask his instructional coach, Ms. Brown, if she would work with him. She had recently facilitated professional learning sessions for the entire faculty about frame shifting and offered to work individually with any teachers who wanted to practice frame shifting with a persistent dilemma they were experiencing. Mr. Lee reached out to her and they came together over the course of several meetings to practice frame shifting together. Prior to their first meeting, Ms. Brown asked Mr. Lee to review the materials she shared with the faculty about **frame shifting** and to draft **a dilemma statement** and **driving question** that they would discuss. When they met for the first time to discuss this dilemma, he recounted what happened with the group project and after describing everything that happened, he identified his driving question as, "How can I get my students to approach group projects with maturity?" and he stated his dilemma as, *My students cannot handle group work* (see Table 7.1). During their first meeting, Ms. Brown guided him through the **habits of mind** to help him home in on the source of his dilemma.

TABLE 7.1 *Mr. Lee's Original Driving Question and Dilemma Statement*

Mr. Lee's Driving Question	Mr. Lee's Dilemma Statement
How can I get my students to approach group projects with maturity?	My students cannot handle group work.

Engaging the Habit of Personal Attribution with Mr. Lee's Dilemma

Engaging the **Habit of Personal Attribution** helps teachers position their dilemmas as within their realm of control. Remember that the Habit of Personal Attribution has two parts: first, positioning the dilemma as **proximal** rather than **distal**, and second, adopting an **internal attribution** for addressing it. If a teacher's dilemma is outside of their power to change, then it is a dead end: there is nothing they can do to effect change. Similarly, if they do not believe that they are the ones who can or should improve it, they are similarly left at a stand-still. As we discussed in Chapter 2, oftentimes teachers can reposition their dilemmas so that they are within the teacher's sphere of influence and so the teacher can garner resources to improve their **teacher efficacy** for addressing them. In our case study, Ms. Brown started her conversation with Mr. Lee by focusing on proximal positioning. We pause the conversation at key points to elaborate on how Ms. Brown is coaching Mr. Lee to engage the **habits of mind**.

> "Thank you for sharing this description of your dilemma with me," Ms. Brown began, "and for coming to our meeting having already written a **driving question** and **dilemma statement** so that we have somewhere to start. Group projects can be challenging for many teachers because there are so many moving pieces happening at once. To start the process of **frame shifting**, I think it's important to start with the Habit of Personal Attribution because we want to make sure that we have a dilemma that we can do something about. You are far too busy and

overworked to spend time on a dilemma that is completely out of your hands. I want to help you zero in on what part of your dilemma is within your sphere of control." Ms. Brown asked Mr. Lee to get out the handouts she provided at the previous faculty meeting which included questions to help develop the Habit of Personal Attribution (see Handout 1, also Exercise 2.2).

Handout 1   *Developing the Habit of Personal Attribution*
Directions
Consider these questions in developing personal attribution.

Diagnosing a distal approach

- Am I dependent on a change in policy or some other part of the situation that I cannot impact before I would be able to solve the dilemma?
- What else is preventing me from solving the dilemma?

Adopting a proximal position

- What part of the dilemma can I affect in the classroom?

Diagnosing an external attribution

- When I think about how I have described my dilemma up until now, who has the power to solve it?
- Who do I think is responsible for solving the dilemma?
- Have I given up on, or already dismissed, my ability to solve the dilemma because I do not have the knowledge or skills to solve it?

Adopting an internal attribution

- What personal characteristics do I have that might help me solve the dilemma?
- What additional knowledge or skills might I need to develop? How can I do that?
- What material resources do I have that might help me solve the dilemma?
- How can others in my immediate environment help me?

"First let's look at whether you have positioned your dilemma as something within your control to impact (we call that a proximal dilemma) or outside of your control (that's called a distal dilemma). Distal dilemmas are going to be those big dilemmas that require a change in policy or outside forces in order to impact change, like social media's impact on kids. That is outside of an individual teacher's sphere of influence as a problem on its own. Proximal dilemmas are ones that are within reach for us to change. So, let's examine your dilemma statement and driving question to determine if they are distal or proximal dilemmas. You stated, Students can't handle group work, and your driving question is, 'How can I get my students to approach group projects with maturity?' What do you think? Is this a distal or proximal dilemma?" Mr. Lee thought for a moment, "My gut reaction is that it's distal because I can't help if students are mature or not…but I think it's actually proximal because group work in my classroom is something that's in my purview to impact."

Mr. Lee made an important distinction between distal and proximal dilemmas. His initial reaction was that he had a distal dilemma because he could not control students' maturity levels. However, once he shifted the focus away from students' developmental maturity to his responsibility to facilitate group work in his classroom, he positioned the dilemma as a proximal one that was within his sphere of influence to impact. But, had he described his dilemma in a way that put the responsibility of that change on himself or on someone else? Mr. Brown next asked him to focus on the second part of the Habit of Personal Attribution: internal attribution.

Ms. Brown asked, "When you think about how you have described your dilemma up until now, who has the power to solve it? In other words, who do you think is responsible for solving the dilemma?" Mr. Lee reflected on how he had thought about and talked about the students' behavior up to this point. As he thought out loud with Ms. Brown, he realized that when he said things like students "can't handle" group work, it suggested that any resolution to the problem relied on students shifting their behaviors before they could participate in any more group projects. He also realized that he had no control over students' maturity, "Although I want my students to act more maturely, I guess when I'm honest with myself I know they are seventh graders and it's to be expected that they would have some immature behaviors. I guess I can't really fix that, so it's out of my hands." Ms. Brown commented on his response, "First, that is a really useful observation because if you're relying on the students to change in order to move forward with your dilemma, then that's not very productive because it means you can't really do anything until they do something first. I also want to note that what you've just explained is a great example of how sometimes teachers identify proximal dilemmas—something that's within their realm of control—but they maintain an external attribution, which means that they attribute the solution to someone or something outside of themselves. You had just positioned your dilemma as proximal because group work is in your realm of control, but when asked who was responsible for solving the problem, you initially said your students. A key step in the Habit of Personal Attribution is believing that you as the teacher are responsible for addressing the instructional dilemma you've identified."

If Mr. Lee believed the students could not participate in group work because they "cannot handle it," then he would have also been preventing himself from considering new ways to think about and effect change in the dilemma. The Habit of Personal Attribution helps teachers focus their dilemma within the realm of their control. Through his conversation with Ms. Brown, Mr. Lee noticed that he had interpreted his dilemma in a way that placed the onus of change on the students, thus assigning **external attribution** to the dilemma: if it is outside the teacher's control or if the teacher has a sense of hopelessness toward solving the dilemma, then they will not see a purpose in trying to make any changes. Perhaps unintentionally, this is a way of letting oneself off the hook for examining their own practice and how their teacher moves may be impacting the classroom in ways they do not intend. In Mr. Lee's case, it meant he was waiting on students to develop capacities on their own before they could effectively work on group projects.

Another factor that sometimes contributes to a teacher using external attribution is a low sense of **teacher efficacy**, which can lead to hopelessness about one's power to change a situation. Ms. Brown discussed this with Mr. Lee.

> Before they moved on to the next habit of mind, Ms. Brown wanted to see if Mr. Lee believed in his own ability to effect change in his classroom. She said, "Mr. Lee, I want to check in with you before we discuss the next habit of mind. It's one thing to go through the process of developing the Habit of Personal Attribution and to recognize intellectually that you can reposition how you think about the dilemma so that it's in your control. It's another thing altogether to actually believe that you, as a teacher, have the ability to positively impact change in the classroom. How are you feeling about that right now? Do you have confidence in your ability to turn this around so that next time you'll have a more successful experience with group projects?" Mr. Lee thought for a moment, "I guess I would say it's a bit of a mixed bag. On one hand I generally think I'm an effective teacher, which is why this group project going awry bothers me so much. But on the other, I feel like I've tried everything and I'm not really sure where to go with that." "That's why I'm so glad you reached out to me," Ms. Brown said. "It can definitely be daunting to figure out what you might need to do differently…and even how you might need to think

differently." She asked him to get out the handout on building teacher efficacy (see Handout 2, also Exercise 2.1) and asked him to identify dispositions, knowledge, skills, and resources he already possessed that could help him as he worked on his dilemma.

Mr. Lee noted that his willingness to learn and self-reflect had always been strengths of his and are what led him to seek out Ms. Brown as a resource in the first place. He felt strong in his **content knowledge** as a science teacher, but because he was trained in a secondary science teacher education program that tended to focus on high school education, he did not learn a lot about young adolescents and did not always know how best to reach them. He was curious and open to learning more about the students he taught, as well as new approaches that might improve the effectiveness of his teaching. Upon hearing Mr. Lee share these insights, Ms. Brown said, "You have a lot of strengths on your side that will help you as you move forward with making changes to your teaching practice. Also, I believe your confidence will be bolstered as we work through the other habits of mind because they will help you break down the dilemma so that it doesn't seem so big."

Engaging the Habit of Personal Attribution is key to positioning Mr. Lee's dilemma in a productive manner and, along with the other habits of mind, will influence how he revises his original driving question and dilemma statement.

Engaging the Habit of Asset Identification With Mr. Lee's Dilemma

The next **habit of mind** Ms. Brown talked through with Mr. Lee is the **Habit of Asset Identification**. This habit helps teachers to be aware of how they think about and position their students and their students' families and communities. If teachers find

Handout 2 *Building Teacher Efficacy*

Directions
Consider which of the following you already have and/or can draw upon as you approach your dilemma:

Dispositions	Knowledge	Skills	Resources
☐ Curiosity ☐ Optimism ☐ Persistence ☐ Courage ☐ Commitment ☐ Openness ☐ Friendliness ☐ Honesty ☐ Willingness to learn ☐ Self-reflection ☐ Other:_____	☐ Content area ☐ Student developmental levels ☐ Students' personal and learning needs ☐ Student activities and interests ☐ Community strengths and resources ☐ Parent and family backgrounds, values, and approaches ☐ Other:_____	☐ Collaboration ☐ Learning new things ☐ Practices of reflection ☐ Insightfulness ☐ Attention to detail ☐ Building connections with students and families ☐ Other:_____	☐ More skilled colleagues ☐ School and district leaders ☐ Community, parent, and/or university partners ☐ Trade journals ☐ Professional organizations ☐ Professional development opportunities ☐ Other:_____

themselves assigning blame to students for the dilemmas they face, then they may be using **deficit thinking**. Ms. Brown gently guided Mr. Lee to examine whether deficit thinking was present when he talked about his students.

> We've already worked through the first habit of considering whether you've attributed the source of the dilemma as outside of yourself or within your control. You noted that by suggesting that the issue is due to students' 'immaturity' you have given the problem an **external attribution**. The **Habit of Personal Attribution** works somewhat in parallel with the other habit of mind we discussed at the faculty meeting last month, the Habit of Asset Identification. Flip back through the resources I provided at that meeting and find the handout for Developing the Habit of Asset Identification (see Handout 3, also Exercise 2.3). Take a couple minutes to read through it and share what stands out to you about this habit of mind.
>
> Mr. Lee took some time to refresh his memory and then shared, "Okay, so from what I can remember, this habit of mind is about how we think about students, like if we see them in a negative light or not. I don't know that I need to practice this habit because I really do love my students." Ms. Brown valued this response and offered a delicate reply, "Of course you care about your students. The fact that you took the time to come up with a project about rainforests, which you thought your students would enjoy, shows that you care about them. Sometimes, though, we don't realize how the language we use to think and talk about our students might actually be deficit thinking. Deficit thinking is when we blame our dilemmas on something that's wrong with our students. Now look, we know that students obviously play a role in whether a lesson works or not, but that's different from squarely assigning blame to them when something goes wrong, as there may be something else that's contributing

Handout 3 *Developing the Habit of Asset Identification*
Directions:
Consider these questions in adopting a focus on assets.

Evaluating your current beliefs about students:

- Do I fully believe that no student really wants to fail if they believe they can succeed?
- Do I sometimes lower my expectations for some students out of "pity?"
- Do I fully believe that every student wants to make their caregiver or other significant adults proud if they believe that is possible?
- Do I fully believe that every caregiver loves their child?

Diagnosing deficit thinking:

- When I think about my dilemma, what do I think is wrong with the students?
  - How is my cultural or social position shaping my perspective about what might be wrong with the students?
  - What assumptions am I making based on cultural stereotypes?
- When I think about my dilemma, what do I think is wrong with the students' caregivers for situations outside of school?

Identifying assets:

- What strengths do I notice in my students?
- What strengths do I notice in caregivers and in students' communities?
- How could I build upon students' and caregivers' strengths to solve my dilemma?

to the dilemma. Let's look at the questions on the handout that helps us see if you may be using deficit thinking without realizing it. First, we'll look at the first questions that address teachers' core beliefs about students. Do any of these resonate with you?" Mr. Lee replied, "Some of these questions do resonate with me because sometimes when I see students not doing their work, I think they are okay with failure, which I do not understand or relate to at all. As the son of Korean immigrants, it was instilled in me my whole life that one must always do their absolute best and that failure is a dishonor on the family. So, when I see some of my students not working up to their potential, it makes me wonder what they have been taught about success. Many of my students have benefited from generational wealth and sometimes I think that makes them not care as much about working hard because they think success will just be handed to them." "I appreciate your honesty," Ms. Brown said, "and know it can be challenging when we teach students who do not share our cultural norms or backgrounds. Let me ask you this: Do you really think your students' caregivers would be okay with them not doing their work?" "Well, actually no. I have a lot of caregivers who email me asking for updates on their child's progress and who I know get frustrated with their children when they fall behind because they aren't trying as hard as they could to do well in school. I guess to be fair, they want their kids to succeed as much as my parents wanted me to succeed, they just may go about it in a different way."

It is important for teachers to examine their core beliefs about students and caregivers because they impact how we treat our students. In Mr. Lee's case, he realized through talking with Ms. Brown that his cultural background shaped some assumptions he had about his students and their caregivers. Next, he and Ms. Brown discussed the questions related to deficit thinking.

Examining the Habit of Asset Identification handout together, Ms. Brown said, "One question asks, 'When you think about your dilemma, what do you think is wrong with the students?' To get us thinking about this question,

I want to draw your attention to how you described students and their behaviors a few minutes ago. Sometimes we talk about our students in ways we don't even realize, and this happens more often when we are frustrated. For example, when you initially described your dilemma, you said you were a bit offended that some students complained about their topic and you described your students as 'entitled' for thinking they should have a say in their particular topic. This describes the students in a way that suggests there is something inherently wrong with them." Ms. Brown stopped to give Mr. Lee a moment to collect his thoughts and then asked him what he thought about what she had shared. Mr. Lee said, "Honestly, it kind of makes me feel bad because I don't actually think something is wrong with my students. I love them and don't mean to speak about them in a negative way. Like you said, I guess I was speaking out of frustration."

Ms. Brown then asked Mr. Lee to look at his driving question and dilemma statement and asked, "Do you see any deficit thinking reflected in either of these?" Mr. Lee replied, "Yeah, I can see that when I say things like students are 'immature,' I'm putting them in a negative light." Ms. Brown picked up this thread, "That's a good example of deficit thinking, and I think it connects to your original statement that your students 'cannot handle group work.' How do you see those two things as related?" Mr. Lee ventured a guess, "Maybe because both of them are saying that the heart of dilemma is that something is wrong with the students. That's not really helping me move forward, I guess." Ms. Brown thought this was a breakthrough, "Bingo! You hit the nail on the head, Mr. Lee! Deficit thinking is clouding your ability to take control of the problem."

The deficit thinking Mr. Lee used when blaming students' shortcomings for his group work dilemma works in tandem with **external attribution** because by blaming the problem on the students, he is also placing responsibility on the students for changing the dilemma. Here we see how engaging the **Habit of Personal Attribution** paves the way for engaging the Habit of Asset Identification because Mr. Lee has already committed to positioning his dilemma as **proximal** by not waiting for students to change their behavior before he tries to solve the problem. These first two habits of mind work together and sometimes, engaging the Habit of Asset Identification may be a necessary first step for engaging the Habit of Personal Attribution.

Now that Mr. Lee recognized that he had unwittingly been using deficit language about his students when describing his dilemma, Ms. Brown wanted to see if he could use **asset-based thinking** to identify his students' positive attributes that could be seen as beneficial when solving his dilemma.

> Ms. Brown continued, "Like you said earlier, you do care about your students and want to think favorably about them. When we're mired in a dilemma, though, sometimes it can be easier to see what's wrong with the situation than to recognize the strengths and positive assets our students bring to the table. The Habit of Asset Identification helps us make an intentional effort to recognize our students' positive traits. When you think about the students in your class, what strengths do you recognize in them?" This question gave Mr. Lee some pause. "I have to admit, it was kind of easy to notice when I used deficit thinking, but it's harder to identify positive traits when my students are doing things like arguing about who's going to do what task in their groups." Ms. Brown rephrased the question, "If students are arguing because they're not sure how to divide up the work, what does that say about their investment in their learning?" Mr. Lee had an 'a-ha' moment, "Oh, I think I see what you're getting at. Well, I can see that they care about their learning. If they didn't care, they wouldn't be arguing about the work. And also, it seems that they want to be responsible

contributors to a group project. I wish they hadn't argued about it, but now I can see some positive traits in them despite the arguing." Ms. Brown wanted to emphasize the significance of what Mr. Lee shared, "This is a really, really important insight, and I want to take a moment to highlight why it's so important. When you can identify assets in your students that are beneficial to resolving your dilemma, then you can build upon these assets when you decide what your teacher moves will be."

Shifting toward asset-based thinking has other advantages, as well. Educators such as Mr. Lee who work hard to create instructional activities that will interest their students do not want to be riddled with negative thoughts about them, the very young people they work hard for. The Habit of Asset Identification has the big advantage not only of helping teachers shift their thinking about their students, but also of helping them feel good about the work they do over time which can help to avoid burn-out. The act of consciously changing how teachers think about their students also affects their desire to help them, which bring us back to the Habit of Personal Attribution. When we position the problem as residing with our students (or their caregivers or communities), then the problem is out of our hands; we cannot effect any change and we may even see students as adversaries. A deficit perspective about students paired with an external attribution that places responsibility for the problem on students can have a negative impact on **teachers' efficacy** as well as their motivation to keep trying. But when teachers intentionally work to see their students' assets that can contribute to solving the problem, then they are closer to feeling like change is really possible and that can strengthen their confidence. When Mr. Lee recognized that his students were arguing not because they were immature, but because they cared about their work, it buoyed his own self-efficacy in believing that he could make a change that helps the dilemma since students also want group work to go differently.

Engaging the Habit of Deliberate Interpretation With Mr. Lee's Dilemma

Engaging both the **Habit of Personal Attribution** and the **Habit Asset Identification** sets teachers up to approach their dilemmas anew. Pairing a sense of empowerment as we see the dilemma within our realm of control with a positive focus on students' strengths provides a strong foundation for the final **habit of mind**, the **Habit of Deliberate Interpretation.** This habit helps teachers think about how they identify, think about, and make sense of their dilemmas by slowing down the process by which they arrive at a conclusion about why the dilemma exists. They then can diagnose the source of the dilemma more accurately so that more productive interpretations and judgments can be made and actions taken. To review, the Habit of Deliberate Interpretation involves four steps: 1) **observation**, an **empirical** description of the situation, 2) **interpretation**, how we make sense of the observation, 3) **judgment**, our internal response to our interpretation, and 4) **decision**, our conclusion about whether to take action and which actions to take. The hectic pace of the school day often gets in the way of teachers taking the time to deeply examine their observations and interpretations of their dilemmas, and thus they often initially position their dilemma in judgment before critically evaluating their initial observation. Using the Habit of Deliberate Interpretation helps us identify when we have made judgments in our **dilemma description**, **driving question**, and **dilemma statement** that prevent us from moving forward in our desire to resolve the dilemma. This is an instinctual impulse, to make judgments about what we experience before we think through the situation that led to the judgment. Because this **habit of mind** requires us to pause and critically reflect on our automatic impulses, we have found in our work that it can be the most challenging for teachers to develop.

To help you see how a teacher might wrestle with this habit, we return to the discussion between Mr. Lee and Ms. Brown to see how she guided him through the Habit of Deliberate Interpretation.

"Alright," Ms. Brown said, "I think we're making really good progress so far. You've used the Habit of Personal Attribution to consider what is within your control to change related to your dilemma, you have recognized some deficit thinking, and you have identified students' strengths that relate to the dilemma. These are important steps to get us ready for the last habit of mind, the Habit of Deliberate Interpretation. As you work through this last habit, you will need to draw upon your internal attribution of the problem and think about how you can build on your students' assets." Ms. Brown explained why the habit is critical for teachers when they're examining their dilemmas, "The reason we call this the Habit of Deliberate Interpretation is because too often we as educators begin in a place of judgment without realizing it. This habit helps us see if we need to check our statements to see if they contain judgments—and, if so, to restart the process by using all four steps with intentionality." Mr. Lee turned to the next page in his handouts from the faculty meeting and found the four steps in the habit of deliberate interpretation (see Handout 4, also Figure 2.2) as well as the handout that included questions to guide teachers in developing this habit of mind (see Handout 5, also Exercise 2.5). Ms. Brown explained that they would go through the questions on Handout 5 step by step as they worked through this habit of mind together.

Handout 4 *Steps in the Habit of Deliberate Interpretation*

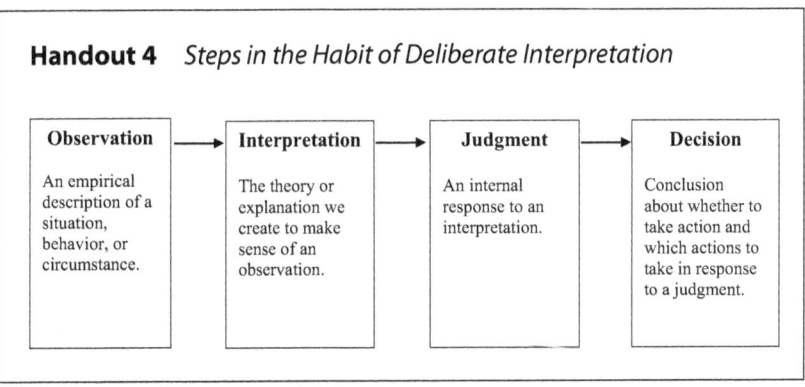

Observation	Interpretation	Judgment	Decision
An empirical description of a situation, behavior, or circumstance.	The theory or explanation we create to make sense of an observation.	An internal response to an interpretation.	Conclusion about whether to take action and which actions to take in response to a judgment.

"Let's start by having you repeat your dilemma statement and driving question that you started with. After you have done that, we're going to assess whether your statement is based on a neutral observation, an interpretation, or a judgment." Mr. Lee read aloud, "Okay, so my dilemma statement is, Students cannot handle group work," and my driving question is, 'How can I get my students to approach group projects with maturity?'" Ms. Brown said, "Thank you. Now let's look at Handout 4 which has the four steps on it. Which of these four steps do you think your dilemma is currently positioned in?" Mr. Lee thought for a moment then said, "You know, had you asked me this question when we started this conversation, I would've said that my statement is an observation because I can see that students can't handle group work. But after talking about how the statement reveals some deficit thinking and also places the responsibility for change on the students' shoulders, I can see how it's not neutral. I think my statement may actually be a judgment." Ms. Brown was impressed with Mr. Lee's critical self-reflection, "That's really perceptive and you can see how engaging the first two habits of mind make this last one easier. When we say things like students are 'immature' and 'can't handle group work,' we are actually making judgments, not observations of what we see."

This deliberate process helps teachers identify when they are unintentionally describing an observation or dilemma statement with judgment and asks them to return back to the first step of observation so that they are starting from a neutral position. The purpose of this entire process is to create new options for a solution. Thus, when teachers start working on the dilemma from a position where they have already judged the cause of the problem, they have narrowed the ways it needs to be solved. Since this is a persistent dilemma, those solutions have not worked. Rather than just trying more things, engaging the Habit of Deliberate Interpretation allows for a reinterpretation of what is happening when the dilemma occurs, which ultimately helps teachers identify different possible teacher moves to address it.

Handout 5 *Developing the Habit of Deliberate Interpretation*

Directions

Consider these questions in developing deliberate interpretation.

Reflecting on your starting point

- What feelings do I have about the dilemma?
- What judgments am I making that cause these feelings?
- How is my cultural or social position affecting my interpretation and judgment of the dilemma?
- What assumptions am I making based on cultural stereotypes?

Observation of empirical facts

- What information about the dilemma can I actually observe with my senses?
- Is my observation empirical (neutral and focused specifically on what I see and hear without interpretation or judgment)?
- Which part of my framing of the dilemma results from my observation and which part results from my interpretation?
- What other important information might exist that I have not yet observed or paid attention to?

From observation to interpretation

- How could I interpret the information I observe differently?
- How do these new interpretations make me feel about my ability to effect change with this dilemma?

From interpretation to judgment

- What new judgments might result from these new interpretations?
- How are these judgments different than the ones I had before?

From judgment to decision

- What new conclusions can I identify now?
- How are these conclusions different than the ones I was coming to before?

Developing Empirical Observations

If teachers find, like Mr. Lee did, that their dilemma statement and driving question are a judgment or interpretation, then they need to make their way backward in the Habit of Deliberate Interpretation by slowing things down and starting with a neutral observation about the dilemma. Ms. Brown helped Mr. Lee do this next.

> Ms. Brown continued, "Since your dilemma is currently positioned in judgment, let's make a deliberate step to back up and start with the observation step. Look at Handout 5 and we'll go step by step through some of the questions on the handout that help us engage the Habit of Deliberate Interpretation. First, what did you observe happening during the group project?" Mr. Lee responded, "I observed that students were incapable of completing group work." "Hmm," Ms. Brown replied, "I think that is actually an interpretation because that's a way that you're making sense of what happened. Observations should be strictly what we experience with our senses. We can't see or hear that students are incapable of group work, for example. When you describe your observations, you'll want to make sure they are empirical. That is, what exactly did you see students doing? What did you hear them saying?" Mr. Lee replied, "I saw some students bickering loudly with each other in their groups. I heard other students being rude by complaining about the topic they were assigned. I saw students taking their time by wasting two class periods to complete something that should've been done on day 1." As Mr. Lee spoke, Ms. Brown wrote down his statements so they could look at them together (see Table 7.2).

When Mr. Lee attempted to describe his observation based on what he saw and heard, he was still describing students' behaviors in a subjective and negative manner, which shows that he was continuing to interpret what he saw and heard. To work

TABLE 7.2 *Mr. Lee's Initial Observation*

Original dilemma statement:
Students cannot handle group work.

What Mr. Lee described observing:

- Students bickered loudly with each other in their groups.
- Some students were rude by complaining about the topic they were assigned.
- Other students took their time and wasted two class periods to complete something that should've been done on day 1.

toward an **empirical** observation, it can be helpful for teachers to strip their observation of words that are not neutral.

"Okay, now we have a list of observations based on what you saw and heard and I wrote them down so we can look at them more closely. I noticed that some of these descriptions include words that carry negative connotations, and it sounds like you've already tried everything you can think of to change that behavior but are feeling like you are out of options. This goes to the heart of your feelings of **teacher efficacy** to address the dilemma. We can use this habit of mind to identify how to get some options back. If you can be more neutral in describing what you see and hear, then you might be able to see what other things going on in the classroom might actually lead us to other possible causes of the dilemma. So, let's try that by peeling back what you've said a little bit more so that we're avoiding any words that suggest a judgment. This will help us focus in on what we can objectively see and hear so that we have the option to interpret those facts differently." Ms. Brown asked Mr. Lee to focus on the questions on the handout about teachers naming observations of empirical facts.

She began, "The first two questions help you get at the feelings you have about the dilemma and your judgments that arise from the feelings. One way to approach these questions is by noticing where you have used adjectives and adverbs to describe students' behaviors because often those words suggest interpretations and judgments. Where do you see adjectives or adverbs in the observations you made initially?" Mr. Lee joked, "Hey, I'm a science teacher, not an English teacher!" Ms. Brown laughed and said, "Of course! It's been a long time for all of us that don't teach English. An adjective is a word that describes a thing and an adverb is a word that describes an action. Adverbs often end in -ly." Mr. Lee said, "Oh yes, it's coming back to me now!" Then he noted that words such as loudly and slowly were adverbs and rude was an adjective. He saw how those words suggested judgment towards the students' behaviors. Ms. Brown agreed with Mr. Lee then joked back with him, "To continue our little English lesson, another way to check if your statement has judgment is to examine the verbs because sometimes verbs can carry negative connotations. For example, the word 'berate' doesn't just mean to criticize someone, but to do so angrily and at length. What words do you see in your dilemma statement that might carry a negative connotation?" They discussed how words like bickered, complaining, wasting time have negative connotations and determined other verbs that could be used to describe what was happening in a neutral manner, such as "taking time" rather than "wasting time."

"Now that we've gotten rid of words that suggest judgments," said Ms. Brown, "let's look again at what you observed. Without putting any of your personal judgments on what you saw, objectively describe what you observed when students were supposed to be working on their group projects." Mr. Lee thought about his words carefully as he said, "Okay, let's try this again. I saw some students arguing with each other in their groups. I heard other students saying they wish they'd been assigned a different topic, and I saw some students taking a couple days to complete tasks that should've taken a short amount of time." Ms. Brown wrote these down

TABLE 7.3 *Comparison between Mr. Lee's Initial and Revised Observation Statements*

Mr. Lee's Initial Observations	Mr. Lee's Revised Observations
Students **bickered loudly** with each other in their groups. Some students were **rude** by **complaining** about the topic they were assigned, and other students **wasted** time by taking two class periods to complete something that should've been done on day 1.	Students **disagreed** with each other about who's going to do what in the project. Some students **said** they wish they'd been assigned a different topic, and other students **took a couple days** to complete tasks that should've taken a short amount of time.

beside his initial observation statements (see Table 7.3). She explained, "This is a good new starting point because when we work with the observation you originally made, we end up a bit in a dead end. Remember when we talked about the Habit of Personal Attribution and how teachers need to have a sense of ownership for addressing the dilemma? When we look at your initial observation about students 'bickering,' it not only conveys judgment but at the same time puts the onus on students to change. A neutral observation allows you to start fresh with solving your dilemma because it gives you space to consider other clues that give you a little more information about what you observed."

Although this may seem like a laborious process, it is essential when developing the Habit of Deliberate Interpretation to critically evaluate how we have described our dilemmas so that we can start from a neutral observation when we turn to the second step in this habit, interpretation.

From Observation to Interpretation

Interpretations are how we make sense of what we have observed. Now that Mr. Lee has made a set of observations that fit the criteria of being empirical and without judgment, he can move on to the next step in the Habit of Deliberate Interpretation by forming other plausible interpretations of his observations.

"Let's look at the next section of the handout which will help us think through how you're interpreting your observations," said Ms. Brown. "This is a key step because however we interpret what we see in the classroom informs our judgments, which then impact our actions. They're all related. To start with, you observed, 'Some students disagreed with each other in their groups about who was going to do what in the project.' How do you make sense of that? Why do you think this was happening?" After thinking for a moment, Mr. Lee shared, "I think students were arguing because it's the only way they know how to resolve conflict." Ms. Brown wrote that down as a plausible interpretation and commented, "I can see how this is one way to make sense of why students were arguing. Something I notice, however, is that this interpretation has a negative connotation to it. You've stated it as a deficit of the students, and sometimes when teacher do that, they also think of those deficits as external to their control. We'll talk more about that in a little while, but for now, just notice that this kind of thinking likely isn't going to get us anywhere in solving the issue of students arguing during group work because it's something that students need to change. Let's continue peeling back your observation to see if there are any other clues that maybe you've not considered that can help us get to the bottom of why they were arguing."

Considering additional clues they may not have initially noticed related to their dilemmas can help teachers identify new explanations for their dilemmas. Let's return to Mr. Lee and Ms. Brown's conversation to hear what this might sound like as Mr. Lee seeks additional clues related to his observation.

Ms. Brown began, "Okay, since we've determined that your initial interpretation has not helped you move closer to making productive changes in your classroom, let's back up a bit and address the last question related to making an observation on the handout to see if there is anything you may not have paid attention to before that can help us: 'What other important information might exist that I have not yet observed or tried to observe?' For example, when you heard students arguing, did you hear what they were arguing about?" Mr. Lee replied, "Well, I did notice that in a couple of the groups, more than one member the groups wanted to complete the same parts of the project and that caused conflict." "Okay," Ms. Brown replied, "now we have more information about your observation. This is useful because it may lead to interpretations that are helpful for resolving the situation."

Here Mr. Lee returned to the step of observation to look for other clues that might inform his observation. Previously he had not paid attention to why students were arguing; he was only paying attention to the fact that they were arguing in general. However, this new fact gives important information about the dilemma that can inform how he works to solve it.

Ms. Brown probed, "How can you interpret this new information about students arguing? In other words, why do you think this issue about group members wanting to do the same tasks would cause conflict?" "Hmm," Mr. Lee thought, "Maybe because they weren't sure how to divide up the work among group members? I provided a large packet of tasks to be completed by the end of the week but maybe they didn't know how to divide up the tasks on their own." Ms. Brown applauded this interpretation, "This is really helpful because now you have an interpretation based on your observation that is going to move you closer to a productive solution." As they continued to talk about additional clues or details that Mr. Lee hadn't paid attention to before, Mr. Lee noted that other groups were working slowly through each task without seeing how each task fit into the bigger picture of the whole project, which meant that they were not going to finish the project on time. He recognized that previously he thought students were procrastinating, but now he interpreted their slow progress as a sign that they needed more structure to complete the project. As he thought back in an effort to consider new clues about why the group project was not successful, he also remembered that some students expressed that they wanted a different topic. Previously he had chalked this up to students being entitled or just wanting to be in groups with their friends, but when he recalled what students said when they complained, he remembered that they said they wanted to study an environmental issue that mattered to them rather than one far away in the rainforest. Considering this, he now interpreted the students' comments about wanting to be in a different group as students wanting to feel a connection to what they learned. Ms. Brown captured these new plausible interpretations (Table 7.4).

TABLE 7.4 *Examining Different Plausible Interpretations of Mr. Lee's Observations*

Observation	Plausible Interpretation	A Different Plausible Interpretation
Students argued with each other about who's going to do what in the project.	Students do not know how to resolve conflict without arguing.	Students are unsure of how to divide up the work among group members.
Some students said they wish they'd been assigned a different topic.	Students want to be in groups with their friends.	Students want to study a topic that connects to their lives and that matters to them.
Other students took a couple days to complete tasks that should've taken a short amount of time.	Students procrastinate.	Students do not know how to pace the tasks within the project.

Observation	Initial Plausible Interpretation	A Different Plausible Interpretation
Students argued with each other about who's going to do what in the project.	Students do not know how to resolve conflict without arguing.	Students are unsure of how to divide up the work among group members.
Some students said they wish they'd been assigned a different topic.	Students want to be in groups with their friends.	Students want to study a topic that connects to their lives and that mattered to them.
Other students took a couple days to complete tasks that should've taken a short amount of time.	Students procrastinate.	Students do not know how to pace the tasks within the project.

These interpretations reflect external attributions.

These interpretations reflect internal attributions.

Figure 7.1 Using Empirical Observations to Identify Different Plausible Interpretations in Mr. Lee's Case.

Ms. Brown wanted to highlight a common difference between Mr. Lee's initial interpretations and his new interpretations and made some notes underneath the table she had made (see Figure 7.1).

"There's something interesting I'd like to point out to you. By making empirical and neutral observations, we can now make different interpretations that also allow for internal attributions. To notice this difference, we need to reengage the Habit of Personal Attribution to consider where the locus of control lies for solving the problem. Look at the three initial interpretations you made in the middle column. What kind of attribution do those have?" Mr. Lee read down the column and said, "Looks like they all have external attributions because they're all focused on change being in the students' realm of control, not mine. I can already guess where you're going next – you probably want me to do the same thing for my new interpretations?" "You got it! What do notice when you read all of your different plausible interpretations together in the right column?" After reading through those responses, Mr. Lee said, "Wow, yeah, I can see that they all have an internal attribution now. I didn't mean to do that on purpose. It's kind of neat to see how considering new evidence helped me come up with new interpretations that empower me to change something in my classroom."

The initial interpretations Mr. Lee made reflected an **external attribution** by placing the onus of responsibility for changing on the students. However, when we consider the new plausible interpretations, we can see that these have an **internal attribution** because they are within Mr. Lee's control to change.

From Interpretation to Judgment

After making interpretations of what we observed in our dilemmas, the next step in the Habit of Deliberate Interpretation is to articulate our judgments about these interpretations. A judgment is our internalized response to an event. Earlier we mentioned that teachers often start from a place of judgment, as many people do when they are faced with a challenge. By developing this habit of mind, teachers can be more deliberate about their judgments to ensure that they are derived from empirical, neutral, observations and from thoughtful interpretations. Ms. Brown helped Mr. Lee as he worked on this step.

> As she finished writing down Mr. Lee's different interpretations, Ms. Brown said, "The strength of the Habit of Deliberate Interpretation is that it helps us be intentional in how we think about our persistent challenges. For example, looking at the chart we developed, you first interpreted students' arguing as their not being able to resolve conflict. What is your gut response to students' behavior based on this interpretation?" This question was easy for Mr. Lee to answer, "I think they're too immature to handle group tasks." Ms. Brown replied, "Right, we're back to the issue of maturity which we talked about earlier when we talked about deficit thinking. It also brings us back to the Habit of Personal Attribution because we again see a dead-end to our dilemma if it's something that's out of our hands to address.

So, let's consider your new interpretation and see where that gets us. When you interpret students' arguing as a sign that students weren't sure of how to divvy up the work among group members, then what do you think of the behavior then? What judgment do you make about the behaviors now?" Mr. Lee thought a moment and ventured, "I guess what I think about their behaviors based on that interpretation is that students need direction about how to allocate tasks across the group members." They continued this process as Mr. Lee articulated the judgments that arose based on the new interpretations he had made. Ms. Brown captured these ideas in a new column of the chart she had made (see Table 7.5).

TABLE 7.5 *Mr. Lee's Different Interpretations Lead to Different Judgments*

Observation	Plausible Interpretation	Judgment	Different Plausible Interpretation	Different Judgment
Students disagreed with each other about who's going to do what in the project.	Students do not know how to resolve conflict without arguing.	*Some students are too immature to handle group tasks.*	Students are unsure of how to divide up the work among group members.	*Students need direction about how to allocate tasks.*
Some students said they wish they'd been assigned a different topic.	Students want to be in groups with their friends.	*Some students care more about socializing than learning.*	Students want to study a topic that connects to their lives.	*Students care about their learning.*
Other students took a couple days to complete tasks that should've taken a short amount of time.	Students procrastinate.	*Some students are lazy.*	Students do not know how to pace the tasks within the project.	*Students need more guidance about how to structure the project.*

The key word in the Habit of Deliberate Interpretation is *deliberate*. We have to slow down a process that often begins in judgment and make a deliberate observation and deliberate interpretations of that observation. By being open to new interpretations at this step, Mr. Lee was able to form judgments that were productive in helping him address his dilemmas. This step of making a new interpretation and judgment also helped Mr. Lee see how he could have some control over changing the dilemma. The Habit of Personal Attribution set Mr. Lee up for being open to this process. The Habit of Deliberate Interpretation also strengthened Mr. Lee's Habit of Personal Attribution because he could then see more clearly the parts of the dilemma that he could control.

From Judgment to Decision

To determine how Mr. Lee might go about changing his dilemma, we turn next from judgment to decision. This final step in the Habit of Deliberate Interpretation is where we conclude whether and how to take action based on the judgments we have made about the dilemma.

> Ms. Brown explained, "The reason we want to take the time to think through different interpretations and judgments is because those inform the decisions we make. For example, let's play out your first interpretation and judgment you made about the students arguing to see what decision that might lead to. You said you could interpret the arguing as students not knowing how to resolve conflict and your judgment of that behavior is that students are too immature to handle group tasks. If you think the argument happened because students are immature, then what would you do about that? Another way of thinking about this is, what will you decide to do as a result?" Mr. Lee replied, "Well, in the future I'd avoid group projects because I've decided that students are too immature for them…this isn't really what I'd prefer to do because I believe collaboration is important. But

if they're too immature for it, then maybe it's easiest just not to fight it." Ms. Brown nodded and said, "This habit works with the Habit of Personal Attribution because as a teacher who wants to make things work in your classroom, it's not productive for you to stop collaborative projects when there could be something in your power to change that would help you meet your original goals. When you reinterpreted the students' arguing, you saw that it was about students' being uncertain about how to divide up the work and you judged that as students needing direction. What decision would you make as a result of this new awareness of the dilemma? You don't have to be very specific here because we'll get into the details of your teacher moves in our next meeting when we meet to talk about the domains of teaching. But in general, what kind of decision might you make if you have judged that students need more direction about the tasks?" After taking a moment to consider this question, Mr. Lee responded, "I think it'd be helpful for the students if I made the assignment's tasks and roles a little clearer so they wouldn't be arguing trying to figure that out on their own." "Great!" Ms. Brown said, "That's something that's definitely in your realm of control and it's doable." They continued to discuss decisions Mr. Lee could make as a result of his new judgments, which Ms. Brown wrote down for them (see Table 7.6).

Engaging All of the Habits of Mind to Describe Mr. Lee's Dilemma

Once teachers have engaged each of the three **habits of mind**, they are ready to revisit their initial **driving question** and **dilemma statement** in case these need to be revised to reflect an **internal attribution**, an **asset orientation**, and deliberate **interpretation**. This is a vital step before frame shifting the dilemma

TABLE 7.6 *Examples of How Different Judgments Lead to Different Decisions in Mr. Lee's Dilemma*

Observation	Plausible Interpretation	Judgment	Decision	Different Plausible Interpretation	Different Judgment	Different Decision
Students disagreed with each other about who's going to do what in the project.	Students do not know how to resolve conflict without arguing.	*Some students are too immature to handle group tasks.*	Stop assigning group work.	Students are unsure of how to divide up the work among group members.	*Students need direction about how to allocate tasks.*	Make assignment tasks and roles clearer for students.
Some students said they'd been assigned a different topic.	Students want to be in groups with their friends.	*Some students care more about socializing than learning.*	Assign more independent work so students are not interacting with friends.	Students want to study a topic that connects to their lives.	*Students care about their learning.*	Provide choices that are in line with the assignment's learning objectives.
Other students took a couple days to complete tasks that should've taken a short amount of time.	Students procrastinate.	*Some students are lazy.*	Deduct points from group project grade for tasks that were incomplete.	Students do not know how to pace the tasks within the project.	*Students are confused about the structure of the project.*	Breaks tasks down and give a suggested timeline for each task.

to the different domains of teaching. To prepare for frame shifting, Mr. Lee and Ms. Brown workshopped his initial driving question and dilemma statement.

> As they neared the end of their meeting that day, Ms. Brown reminded Mr. Lee that his original driving question was, "How can I get my students to approach group projects with maturity?" and his dilemma statement was, My students cannot handle group work. "The last thing we'll do in today's meeting is consider how we might reword your driving question and dilemma statement so that they are positioned within your control, avoid deficit language, and reflect the interpretations you made earlier. Let's look back at the notes I took and see if we can craft a more productive driving question that gives you some direction for change." Mr. Lee ventured an attempt, "How can my students work better together on group projects?" Ms. Brown asked him, "Who has control over this?" Mr. Lee immediately saw that the driving question he came up with had an external attribution because it was something that students needed to change, not him. He reworded it so it was within his realm of control, "How about, 'How can I structure group projects to help students work together effectively?'" Ms. Brown clapped, "This is perfect! Now we have a driving question that will really guide our path towards determining your next steps."

Developing the habits of mind takes practice, and we see here that Mr. Lee slipped into external attribution without meaning to when he was developing a revised driving question. His new driving question is productive because it focuses on what he can do and provides a focus that will drive his teacher moves. Next, he and Ms. Brown worked on revising his dilemma statement.

> Ms. Brown asked, "When we consider the issues that arose during the group project, such as students wanting

a different topic and students taking more time than you thought was necessary to complete components of the project, what is a unifying issue they all have in common?" They played with different wording and eventually came to the dilemma statement, When students are placed in heterogeneous groups for projects, they do not know how to collaborate effectively. "This is an excellent dilemma statement because it's something that's in your control to change. The next time we meet we'll start by looking at your new driving question and dilemma statement (see Table 7.7) and will consider them within the domains of teaching. I look forward to it!"

Here Mr. Lee has crafted a new dilemma statement that gets at the root of why the group project was not effective: students did not know how to collaborate effectively. This is a productive dilemma statement because it deals with students' lack of knowledge or skills, which is something Mr. Lee can address through various teacher moves we will discuss in Chapter 8. This is different from his previous dilemma statement, *Students cannot handle group work*, because that positions the problem as rooted in students' lack of development or their personality traits, which he cannot do anything about.

As illustrated in Mr. Lee's case, engaging the habits of mind helps us peel back our dilemmas so we can more clearly

TABLE 7.7 *How Mr. Lee Changed His Original Driving Question and Dilemma Statement after Developing all Three Habits of Mind*

	Before Applying Habits of Mind	After Applying Habits of Mind
Driving Question	"How can **I** **get my students** to approach group projects with maturity?"	"How **can I structure** group projects to help students work together effectively?"
Dilemma Statement	*My students **cannot** handle group work.*	When students are placed in heterogeneous groups for projects, **they do not know how** to collaborate effectively.

examine how we think about them. In Chapter 8 we will return to Mr. Lee's situation and will see how he could practice reframing his dilemma into the different domains of teaching in order to identify different things he could do to answer his driving question.

For Discussion and Practice

Before completing the discussion and practice activities for Chapter 7, we recommend completing the exercises for the additional two practice cases provided in the Study Guide, where you will also find additional discussion and practice activities related to these cases.

1. After having practiced engaging the habits of mind in this chapter, reflect on the following:
   a. How is each habit important for addressing a persistent teaching dilemma in a new way?
   b. Which habit seems most important for you to develop and practice? Why? How will you do that?
2. Imagine you are sharing with a colleague how you engaged the habits of mind to help you identify your beliefs about a persistent teaching dilemma you have encountered in your practice. After you share what you have done, the colleague says, "I have a dilemma that is nagging me, too. When my students are practicing their math exercises during independent work, the same three students keep hitting each other and playing. They really don't care if they fail." How would you guide this colleague through each of the habits of mind. The steps to include are below and exercises related to each step are in the study guide for Chapter 7:
   a. Habit of Personal Attribution
   b. Habit of Asset Identification
   c. Habits of Deliberate Interpretation
3. In each of the example cases in this chapter, issues related to differences in cultural and socioeconomic backgrounds

between students and teacher may be relevant for each teacher's habits of mind as Mr. Lee and Mr. Brown discussed. How might your or your students' cultural, linguistic, socioeconomic, or other social positions (e.g., gender, gender expression, sexual orientation) be playing a role in your dilemma? How might these issues affect how you engage the habits of mind?

8
Practicing Frame Shifting to the Three Domains of Teaching

Throughout this book we have introduced readers to the **frame shifting** approach to solving persistent teaching dilemmas. Recall that frame shifting relies on two foundational practices that work together to help teachers thoughtfully (re)consider how they approach their dilemmas. First, teachers explore their beliefs about their dilemma by engaging the three **habits of mind**: the **Habit of Personal Attribution**, the **Habit of Asset Identification**, and the **Habit of Deliberate Interpretation**. Ideally, the habits of mind become just what the name implies: habits that teachers engage automatically as they encounter new dilemmas. Engaging the habits of mind helps teachers peel back the layers of their dilemma to arrive at a **driving question** and **dilemma statement** that are within the teacher's control to change; use **asset-based thinking** toward students, their caregivers and communities; and are based on **empirical observations** and intentional **interpretations** of these observations.

DOI: 10.4324/9781003301806-11

We introduced these foundational habits in Chapter 2 and then practiced applying them to in Chapter 7. In that chapter we met Mr. Lee, who had concerns about using group projects in his seventh-grade science class. To help readers develop their habits of mind, we used the **gradual release of responsibility model** by modeling here how to engage the habits of mind using Mr. Lee's case. In the Study Guide, we then used Ms. Cohen's case to give the reader the opportunity to complete exercises on their own accompanied by our explanations, and finally asked readers to complete the exercises independently using Ms. Ortega's case.

In this chapter we focus on the second foundational practice of the **frame shifting** approach: reframing dilemmas in the different **domains of teaching**. When crafting driving questions and dilemma statements for their persistent dilemmas, teachers often unconsciously situate their dilemma in one of the three **domains of teaching: relationships, classroom management**, and/or **curriculum and instruction** (see Key Figure 3). Recall that in Chapter 1, you began by describing the context and details related to your persistent dilemma. We then suggested using the metaphor of the frame to focus on the dilemma and that our initial framing contained all the dilemma's details. The three domains of teaching help us to further focus on and understand what is happening in the classroom during the dilemma. In Key Figure 3, all three domains of teaching are positioned within the frame, meaning that they are all within view. We continued to build upon Key Figure 3 in Chapter 3, and you will see it, and its related figures, again here as we practice the final step in the frame shifting approach.

As we first described in Chapter 3, the step of frame shifting, or reframing dilemmas in the different domains of teaching, can help us see how teacher moves we hadn't previously considered might be the key to finally answering the **driving question**. As a first step, it is often productive to zoom in on the domain in which the teacher has already framed their dilemma to see if there are issues related to that domain that have not been contemplated. For example, we saw how Ms. Nash used the frame shifting approach to identify new teacher moves in the domain of classroom management, which was also the original domain in which she had placed her dilemma (shown in Figure 3.1 in

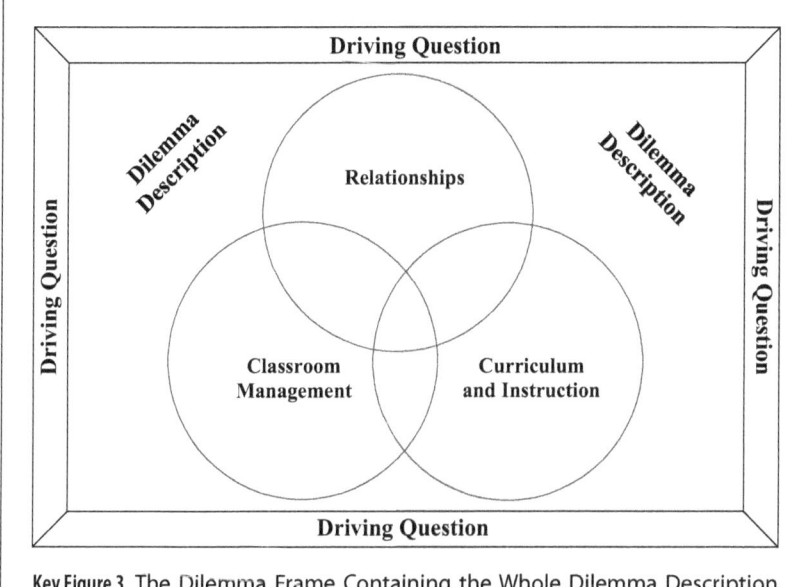

Key Figure 3 The Dilemma Frame Containing the Whole Dilemma Description With All Three Domains of Teaching.

Chapter 3). The greatest impact of frame shifting may occur, however, when teachers discover that they can shift the frame of focus to a different domain of teaching and thereby open up a host of possibilities not yet considered for how they can answer their driving question.

In this chapter, we will return to Mr. Lee's case from Chapter 7 to demonstrate how teachers can shift their dilemma's frame of focus to other domains of teaching. We will begin this process by determining in which domain of teaching he has already framed his dilemma based on the driving question and dilemma statement he crafted after engaging the habits of mind. We will stay in this domain initially to establish if there are other, more specific, dilemma statements and resulting **focus questions** might then help him answer his driving question. The last step in this process is to identify teacher moves within this initial domain that can answer the focus questions. Key Figure 4 illustrates how we will zoom the frame in on one domain of teaching and then identify dilemma statements, focus questions, and teacher moves within that domain.

Key Figure 4 Using the Zoomed In Frame as a Focus for Generating Dilemma Statements, Focus Questions, and Teacher Moves Within Each Domain of Teaching.

Once we have finished focusing on the initial domain of teaching, we will shift the frame so that it brings into view another domain of teaching. We explore the relationship between this next domain and the dilemma description and repeat the steps above. Ultimately, we will arrive at a set of teacher moves within each domain of teaching that may contribute to solving the teacher's persistent dilemma. To identify teacher moves, we will rely on those discussed for each domain in Part II. However, as we previously noted, there is a plethora of resources available to teachers related to each of the domains of teaching to identify additional moves as well.

Although we will address each of the three domains separately for the sake of clarity throughout this chapter, we want to reemphasize that these domains operate **interdependently**, as teacher moves in one domain affect the other domains as well. As we did in the previous chapter, we will use the **gradual release of responsibility**

model to support readers' development of frame shifting skills. We first model how Mr. Lee might approach frame shifting by rejoining his conversation with his instructional coach, Ms. Brown. Then, in the Study Guide we provide opportunities for you to practice frame shifting by returning to Ms. Cohen's dilemma about students talking over one another during whole-group discussion and Ms. Ortega's dilemma about technology use in her Spanish II class. In the Study Guide we also revisit the dilemmas from different educational levels related to group projects and model how you can apply key takeaways from each of the three cases in this section to your own work with students, regardless of the educational level you teach. In these examples, we show how each of these teachers might frame shift and identify new teacher moves similarly to how Mr. Lee did when addressing their dilemma with their students.

Frame Shifting Mr. Lee's Dilemma

We begin by returning to Mr. Lee's dilemma in which he encountered challenges with a group project in his seventh-grade life science class. We encourage you to reread his dilemma from Chapter 7 prior to practicing **frame shifting** so that relevant details are fresh in your mind. As we did with the **habits of mind**, we will illustrate how Mr. Lee worked through his dilemma by following his conversation with his instructional coach, Ms. Brown. Below we listen in on their next conversation to see the process Mr. Lee went through to determine the **domain of teaching** in which he had originally framed his dilemma. After working through this framing, Ms. Brown walks him through frame shifting to other domains in order to open up possibilities for identifying different teacher moves relevant to his **driving question**.

How Mr. Lee Initially Framed His Dilemma: Domain of Curriculum and Instruction

In their last meeting, Mr. Lee and Ms. Brown practiced the **habits of mind** which helped Mr. Lee refine the **driving question** that summed up his dilemma, as well as his **dilemma statement** that described the core of the issue. Now it was time to

TABLE 8.1 Mr. Lee's Driving Question and Dilemma Statement after Engaging the Habits of Mind

Driving Question	Dilemma Statement
How can I structure group projects to help students work together effectively?	*When students are placed in heterogeneous groups for projects, they do not know how to collaborate effectively.*

determine which domain his dilemma was framed in, as this would determine the teacher moves he could make to answer his driving question. Ms. Brown had facilitated a session defining and describing the three **domains of teaching** at the previous month's faculty meeting and built on this in their conversation. She started the conversation by asking Mr. Lee to read aloud the driving question and dilemma statement he developed after engaging the habits of mind (see Table 8.1).

Ms. Brown started, "Alright, so today we'll focus on **frame shifting** your dilemma to the different domains of teaching. Here's another copy of the packet I gave everyone at the last faculty meeting that includes handouts we'll need during our conversation. Let's review the process of frame shifting by looking at Key Figure 3. This figure depicts how your driving question guides your entire inquiry around your dilemma. Your driving question, "How can I structure group projects to help students work together effectively?" will stay with us the entire time we are frame shifting. Within the frame here you see the three domains of teaching. We will zoom in to each of these domains one by one to see how that domain is impacting your dilemma and what can be done about it to help answer the driving question. Before we go any further, what questions do you have about this process?" Mr. Lee thought for a moment then asked, "Since this is a Venn diagram, that means that sometimes what we do in classroom management, for example, might also affect relationships, right?" "Exactly. We call that **interdependence**. As we start talking about specific teacher moves, we'll definitely come up with some teacher moves to address your issue that affect more than one domain at a time. Are you ready to get started?" Mr. Lee responded enthusiastically, "No time like the present!"

Ms. Brown laughed, "Alright then, let's get started by first figuring out what domain of teaching you have already situated this dilemma in. Look at Handout 6 (also Tables 3.1 to 3.3) which includes indicators for each of the domains to help you determine how that domain might be relevant to your dilemma. Take a couple of minutes to refamiliarize yourself with the domains by reviewing the indicators for each of them. Keep your driving question and dilemma statement in mind as you read through the indicators and mark indicators that relate closely to your dilemma."

As Mr. Lee looked at the indicators for each of the three domains, he gravitated toward the indicators for the domain of **curriculum and instruction**. "Looking through these questions, it seems like curriculum and instruction are most relevant to my dilemma. One of the indicators is 'non-completion of assignments' which definitely has to do with what happened in my case because students procrastinated and were a bit lazy which meant they didn't complete the tasks in the project in a timely manner. It also mentions 'unequal participation among students' which definitely happened because some students let others bear the brunt of responsibility for doing the work. And it mentions 'student complaints that the class is not relevant.' Some students did complain that they wished I could have given them some choice in the topic they were assigned. So, I feel pretty confident that my dilemma is currently framed in the domain of curriculum and instruction."

Since this was the first time Mr. Lee was practicing frame shifting, Ms. Brown was pleased that he determined the framing of his dilemma correctly and independently so quickly. She complimented his thinking, "I think you're right—your dilemma is currently framed in the domain of curriculum and instruction. What the frame shifting approach helps us do is to zoom into a particular domain to determine teacher moves perhaps we have not tried that will help us solve our driving question and dilemma statement."

Handout 6 *Indicators for Each Domain of Teaching*

Directions

Use the indicators below to determine in which domain of teaching your dilemma is originally framed.

Indicators of the Domain of Relationships

Does your dilemma involve:
- ☐ Students' perceptions about each other's backgrounds and current lives?
- ☐ Students' perceptions about each other's unique characteristics and abilities?
- ☐ Students' and teachers' responses to each other's limitations?
- ☐ How students treat each other?
- ☐ How students treat the teacher?
- ☐ The quality or nature of the communication between students?
- ☐ The quality or nature of the communication between teachers and students?
- ☐ The quality or nature of teachers' communication with students' families?
- ☐ The behavior of students' families?

> **Indicators of the Domain of Classroom Management**
>
> Does your dilemma involve:
> - ☐ Students' movements through the classroom?
> - ☐ Students' use of materials?
> - ☐ Unruly transition periods or transitions that take too long?
> - ☐ Students talking out of turn?
> - ☐ Students not complying with class rules or norms?
> - ☐ Students' off-task behavior?
> - ☐ How students interact during group work?
>
> **Indicators of the Domain of Curriculum and Instruction**
>
> Does your dilemma involve:
> - ☐ Student misunderstanding of material?
> - ☐ Student disengagement?
> - ☐ Non-completion of assignments?
> - ☐ Student complaints that the class is boring?
> - ☐ Student complaints that the class is not relevant?
> - ☐ Student underperformance or failure?
> - ☐ Unequal participation among students?
> - ☐ Challenges related to heterogeneous student (dis)abilities?

The way Mr. Lee had described his dilemma was, indeed, in the domain of curriculum and instruction. Specifically, his dilemma had a focus on instruction within the domain of curriculum and instruction because it dealt with the activities designed and used to support the students' learning of the curriculum. This positioning is also confirmed when we look back at the **interpretations, judgments**, and **decisions** that arose when Mr. Lee undertook the **Habit of Deliberate Interpretation** in Chapter 7 and realized that part of the source of students' disengagement related to the open-ended nature of the project he assigned. Figure 8.1 illustrates how Mr. Lee's initial framing has zoomed in to a focus on curriculum and instruction. Notice that the domains of **relationships** and **classroom management** are also still present since they will affect aspects of curriculum and instruction as well. As

310 ◆ Putting It All Together

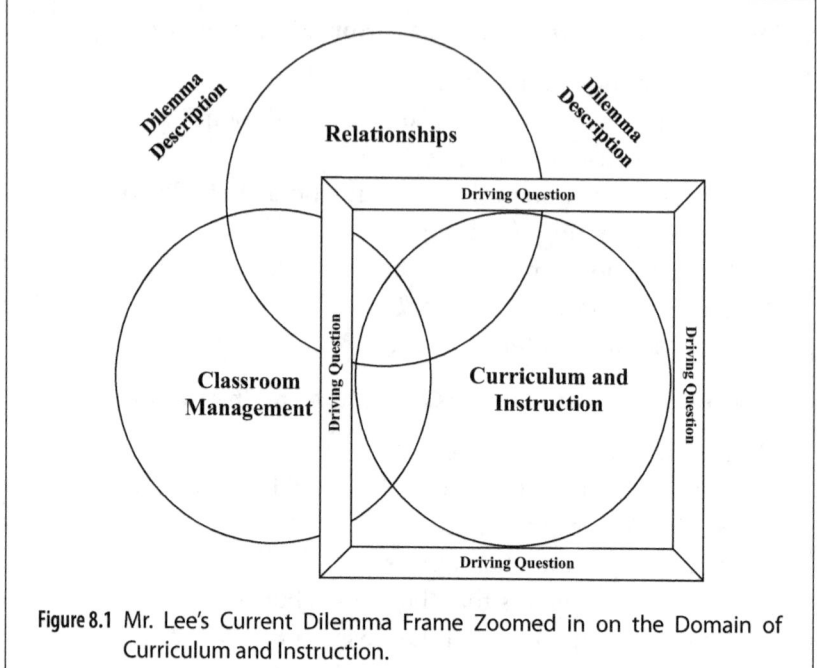

Figure 8.1 Mr. Lee's Current Dilemma Frame Zoomed in on the Domain of Curriculum and Instruction.

a first step, though, Ms. Brown will help Mr. Lee look within the frame just at the domain of curriculum and instruction.

While Mr. Lee was describing his thought process in determining his dilemma's frame, Ms. Brown noticed how he had engaged the habits of mind.

> "Before we look further at the domain of curriculum and instruction, I want to comment on what I noticed just now related to the habits of mind. When you talked about the students who complained about how the topic wasn't relevant to them, you noted that they wanted more choice which is something you can do something about. We previously talked about the **Habit of Personal Attribution** and how it's important to adopt an **internal attribution** for the dilemma so that it's within your realm of control. You did this just now when you talked about how you have some control over whether students have choices in their assignment topic, which is really great." Next

Ms. Brown wanted to address something she heard from Mr. Lee that required a tactful approach, as she did not want to alienate him from the process. "I want to point out something else I heard when you were talking through the indicators. I believe this was unintentional, but you used some language just now that sounded a bit like it was blaming students for the dilemma, such as describing the students as being 'lazy' and procrastinating. This is easy to do when we're frustrated and not being intentional in our thinking. We've all been there, believe me! Let me look through our notes from last time we met so we can remind ourselves of how you worked through this last time when we practiced the Habit of Deliberate Interpretation."

Mr. Lee was a little embarrassed for what felt like a step backwards in his progress, "Oh geez, I can see what you're saying. I didn't even realize I was saying that again." Ms. Brown reassured him, "It takes time and practice to develop the habits of mind so that they become automatic habits that shift our thinking and how we talk about students, so I don't want you to think I'm criticizing you at all. That's why I'm here: to help you as you work through this process. When we learn any new skill, we have to really think about it when we're practicing it before it becomes instinct." Reflecting on this, Mr. Lee said, "Yeah, that reminds me of learning to drive stick shift and having to think about every move before I did it, and now it's just automatic for me." Ms. Brown said, "Exactly, that's a perfect example! Now, looking back at the work you did last time we met to deliberately interpret your **observations** about how much time it took students to complete the tasks, you reinterpreted their behavior in a way that has an internal attribution, or something you yourself are responsible for addressing. Instead of viewing their behavior as procrastination, you interpreted it as students being confused about the structure of the project which you can address by changing how the task is organized."

Now that Mr. Lee had identified the initial domain of his dilemma and they had sharpened how he was engaging the habits of mind, it was time to focus further on the domain of curriculum and instruction to identify whether there were other issues happening in that domain that he had not yet recognized. His current dilemma statement, *When students are placed in heterogeneous groups for projects, they do not know how to collaborate effectively*, helped him determine he was situating his dilemma in curriculum and instruction, but it did not provide a specific focus on what it is about the group projects that affected students' collaboration. For that, Ms. Brown introduced Mr. Lee to an additional list of guiding questions about each domain to help spur his thinking and asked him to keep his entire **dilemma description** in mind as they proceeded. As they discuss his dilemma, they will refer to information about instructional formats that you first saw in Chapter 6 (Table 6.6). We suggest reviewing that table before proceeding.

Ms. Brown began, "Although this is called the 'frame shifting approach,' we're going to remain focused within this frame a little bit longer before we shift it to the other domains because there are often issues in our original framing of the dilemma that we haven't yet considered. Please look at the handout called Using the Zoomed in Frame (Key Figure 4, see p. 304), which shows the process we'll go through for each domain of teaching. First, we'll generate new dilemma statements in the domain of curriculum and instruction that are more specific than the current one we have. This will be helpful because from these new and more specific dilemma statements we will create focus questions that will help us identify teacher moves that will help solve your dilemma. And all along the way, regardless of which domain we are framing, we'll always be working toward answering your driving question. I know it seems like a lot right now but once we get started, you'll see how it works. And more importantly, you'll come out of this frame shifting process with a host of teacher moves you can implement that will help your future group projects be more effective.

"To help you brainstorm ways that curriculum and instruction may be impacting your dilemma more than you originally realized, let's look at the Guiding Questions for Reframing to the Domain of Curriculum and Instruction (see Handout 7, also Table 3.8). These questions are versions of the indicators you looked at when assessing the original domain of teaching, but they are reworded using the habits of mind to focus on what's in the teacher's control and to avoid subjective language. As you examine these questions, keep in mind the detailed description of your dilemma that you shared when we first met."

Mr. Lee read through the guiding questions and shared, "I'm starting by focusing on the guiding questions that relate to instruction. One of the things we've talked about is how the students needed more structure in order to complete the projects on their own, which relates to scaffolding supports for students to be successful." Ms. Brown replied, "For sure. We can work on identifying a specific dilemma statement related to that in a moment. Let's look through this list just to see if anything else comes up related to your dilemma. For example, I'm thinking about the grouping strategy you used for forming the groups and wondering if the random nature of the groups may have contributed to the dilemma. What do you think? What did you notice?" "Well, I wanted to have heterogeneous groups and for students to work with people other than their friends," Mr. Lee explained, "so I thought counting off would be an easy way to do that, but in the end I'm not sure that resulted in groups that worked well together. Where would that problem show up in this list of guiding questions?" "Grouping is an issue related to interdependent collaboration and social learning, so it definitely belongs in the domain of curriculum and instruction. Good thinking."

Handout 7 *Guiding Questions for Reframing to the Domain of Curriculum and Instruction*

Curriculum

How might the dilemma involve:

- ☐ Conceptual connections from one part of the lesson to another?
- ☐ Content that interests students?
- ☐ Content that builds upon students' funds of knowledge?
- ☐ Content that taps into students' frames of reference?
- ☐ Hidden curriculum that the teacher has not considered?
- ☐ An appropriate level of difficulty in content knowledge?
- ☐ An appropriate level of difficulty in reading comprehension and writing requirements?
- ☐ Development and maintenance of students' knowledge about their own and other cultures?
- ☐ Opportunities for students to develop critical thinking and social consciousness and take social action?
- ☐ Other: _____

Instruction

How might the dilemma involve:

- ☐ The necessary/appropriate amount of direct instruction?
- ☐ Gradual release for students to receive scaffolded support that leads to successful independent work?
- ☐ Meaningful and equitable participation among students?
- ☐ Interdependent collaboration and/or social learning?
- ☐ A variety of activities and ways for students to demonstrate knowledge and skills?
- ☐ The proper amount of feedback?
- ☐ The accessibility of sufficient assistance?
- ☐ Other: _____

Ms. Brown then turned to the guiding questions that focused on curriculum within the domain of curriculum and instruction. She said, "Let's look at the list of guiding questions focused on curriculum. Do you see any topics there that relate to the issues you observed during your group project?" Mr. Lee scanned the questions and some of them stood out to him. He said, "In our previous meeting we talked about how some students complained that they didn't get the topic they wanted. Although I originally thought that was a little entitled of them, I came to recognize through our conversation that they were complaining because they wanted a topic that interested them." Ms. Brown responded, "Great point. We will examine that further in the next step."

By zooming further in to the domain of curriculum and instruction, Mr. Lee was able to identify particular issues that contributed to his overall dilemma of students not collaborating effectively during the group project. Next, Ms. Brown worked with him to create additional dilemma statements that described the issues he raised. After identifying dilemma statements, they generated focus questions from each statement that would help them as they considered relevant teacher moves.

Ms. Brown explained the next step, "Okay, so now we have some more defined issues related to curriculum and instruction. Let's start with the last issue you mentioned, which focused on curriculum within the domain of curriculum and instruction, and let's work on a dilemma statement that captures the dilemma you described. You mentioned that students were frustrated because they wanted to select their topic. Talk through why that created a dilemma for you." Mr. Lee responded, "Well, it can be tricky because I have standards I have to address, so students can't just do a project on whatever they want to study. I had designed the project on environmental issues in the rainforest because I needed to address the life science standard related to human impact on the earth's systems. It's frustrating because I know many of my students like animals, so I had thought that focusing on the rainforest would pique their curiosity, but I guess I missed the mark for students who complained they didn't like the topic they were assigned. I even had one student ask how the rainforest is relevant to a student living in the southwestern US. It annoyed me at the time if I'm being honest, but after having some time to think about it I have to admit that I kind of see his point. It's just hard sometimes to meet my requirements and make the content matter to the students at the same time." Ms. Brown empathized with Mr. Brown's predicament, "That can definitely be a challenge sometimes." Together they decided that this dilemma could be stated as, Students do not feel connected to content. They continued by discussing his other two dilemmas and came up with new dilemma statements for each of them: Students struggled with a lack of structure and delineation of tasks and Random grouping led to groups that did not work well together. Ms. Brown commented, "These new dilemma statements are helpful for us as we work towards addressing the root of your dilemma."

Generating additional dilemma statements will help provide more specificity in response to Mr. Lee's driving question, "How can I structure group projects to help students work together effectively?" Next, they turned to developing focus questions that would guide the teacher moves that he would make.

"Okay, now we have three new dilemma statements within the domain of curriculum and instruction that help us see more clearly what the issues are related to why students were not working effectively in the group project. Let's develop these into focus questions which ultimately will lead us to the teacher moves you can make so that you don't have this problem with group work again. When coming up with these focus questions, we need to be sure to engage the habits of mind. In particular, be sure that the focus question is something you have control over, not something you are expecting students to do differently. Let's practice first with the dilemma statement, Students do not feel connected to content. What specific question do you want to answer to address this dilemma?" After a couple minutes of wordsmithing, together Mr. Lee and Ms. Brown developed the focus question, "How can I provide choices for students that connect to their lives and interests while also meeting my required standards?" This focus question narrows in on a core aspect of Mr. Lee's curricular dilemma as he described it to Ms. Brown earlier in the conversation. They developed two other focus questions to complement the new dilemma statements (see Table 8.2).

Notice that the resulting focus questions all still serve to answer Mr. Lee's driving question, "How can I structure group projects to help students work together effectively?" There are countless ways that teachers could respond to this driving question and the lack of precision in the question can be a stumbling block when

TABLE 8.2 *Mr. Lee's Additional Dilemma Statements and Focus Questions in the Domain of Curriculum and Instruction*

Additional Dilemma Statements in the Domain of Curriculum and Instruction	Focus Questions
Students do not feel connected to content.	How can I provide choices for students that connect to their lives and interests while also meeting my required standards?
Students struggled with a lack of structure and delineation of tasks.	What structures can I implement to support students' completion of group projects?
Random grouping led to groups that did not work well together.	What grouping strategies can I use to create groups that work well together?

it comes to determining the teacher moves that will address the problem(s) at hand.

> "This is great. We have new dilemma statements and focus questions that really zoom in on what needs to change in the domain of curriculum and instruction to have effective group projects. Let's look again at the handout with the zoomed in frame (Key Figure 4, see p. 304). You'll see that the final step is to answer each focus question with teacher moves you can make. Let's start with the focus question, 'How can I provide choices for students that connect to their lives and interests while also meeting my required standards?'" Together Mr. Lee and Ms. Brown discussed how the life science standard related to the human impact on earth's systems did not dictate the specific human impacts students should study, which meant that Mr. Lee had a fair amount of leeway in how he approached the content. Instead of assigning students to similar topics related to the rainforest, he could have chosen topics from a wide variety of environmental concerns faced by humans across the globe.
>
> In order to draw on his students' **frames of reference**, he could also have had students research environmental issues related to human activity in their own communities or region. For example, Mr. Lee told Ms. Brown that last year there was a community-wide protest about coal ash from a nearby power plant threatening the safety of the community's drinking water. Many of his students also had older siblings who were involved in the local high school's environmental club who got involved. This topic would meet the science standards while also helping students develop **critical consciousness** as they learned about how they could advocate for more just policies that positively impact their communities.
>
> Ms. Brown suggested that the element of choice could also be introduced when assigning the project, as we know learners are more motivated to learn when they

care about the topic. Mr. Lee could have designed a brief online survey (e.g., Google form) asking students to rank their choices among topics such as the impact of light pollution on wildlife, fossil fuels' effect on air quality, or water pollution caused by agricultural runoff and then arranged students into groups based on the topics they selected. After talking through these potential teacher moves, Mr. Lee realized that it was possible to increase student interest and motivation while still meeting his science standards, which could ultimately improve learning and productivity.

Next, they turned to his focus question, "What structures can I implement to support students' completion of group projects?" He and Ms. Brown agreed that his students would benefit from more structure, and they brainstormed a variety of teacher moves he could make that could support future projects. They discussed that he could take the action of providing explicit guidance for the skills and steps students need in order to succeed at group projects. For example, he could create a timeline for completion which includes tasks that should be completed each day of the project. Then, each day of the week he could begin class with a brief mini-lesson outlining the core components of the day's tasks before students get together in groups to work. If day two focuses on internet research, for example, he could briefly model how he would go about an internet search, noting information he learns, and how he would use it in the project. He could conduct mini-conferences with each group throughout the week to check on their progress and mitigate any issues that arise.

Last, they discussed what instructional moves Mr. Lee could make to respond to the focus question, "What grouping strategies can I use to create groups that work well together?" Mr. Lee grouped students by having them count off because he wanted them to be in groups with people they were not already sitting beside. Ms. Brown explained the importance of grouping students intentionally based on instructional goals, which would also meet Mr. Lee's desire for students to not group themselves so they can be with their friends. He could purposely group students so that they are in **heterogeneous groups** with mixed abilities and perspectives, or he could create **homogenous groups** in which students share skill levels or interests. By making such changes in his instruction, Mr. Lee could help students effectively manage their projects in the future. Ms. Brown took notes for him about all the teacher moves they discussed.

The collection of teacher moves that emerged from Mr. Lee's focus questions in the domain of curriculum and instruction will help increase students' learning and productivity in his future group projects.

Next, Ms. Brown and Mr. Lee will examine each of the other two domains of teaching. In Part II we first presented the domains in the order of relationships, classroom management, and curriculum and instruction because this is the order in which solid teacher practices can first be built. However, at the point you are having a persistent dilemma, these domains may grow or shift in importance as you work on addressing it. We saw that Ms. Nash's dilemma was first positioned in the domain of classroom management, so we started our frame shifting process there. For Mr. Lee, the first domain of focus was curriculum and instruction. In his case, the dilemma very readily relates to classroom management as well, so that is the domain to which Ms. Brown guided him next as they shifted his frame.

Frame Shifting Mr. Lee's Dilemma to the Domain of Classroom Management

Increasing students' learning and productivity in the classroom is also a goal of the **domain of classroom management**. As a review, the domain of classroom management includes the **rules**, **routines**, and teacher behaviors that structure teaching and learning. In Chapter 5 we emphasized that classroom management should always focus on maximizing the conditions in which students learn and should never be about control. We return to Mr. Lee and Ms. Brown as they begin their conversation about the domain of classroom management.

Ms. Brown pointed at the diagram showing the zoomed in frame (see Figure 8.1) and said, "Now we're going to shift our frame to help us focus on a different domain of teaching: classroom management. If you look here at the diagram where we've positioned the frame around the domain of curriculum and instruction, you can imagine that we are now sliding the frame over so that it surrounds this circle that represents classroom management. We will now use this framing to focus on what the domain of classroom management might have to do with your dilemma." Mr. Lee was curious what was going to come of this conversation with Ms. Brown and shared with her, "You know, I've never had a problem with classroom management. Maybe it's because I'm so tall and have a deep voice, but students generally do what I ask them to do." Ms. Brown thought about how to respond, "That is a gift that you do not have any trouble getting students' attention when you need it. As a much shorter woman, I definitely do not have the physical presence you do in the classroom! But classroom management is about more than students doing what we ask. Much of classroom management actually has to do with structures we can use in the classroom to help the class run efficiently and smoothly so that students are spending most of their time learning. I know you do not have a lot of the behavior issues some of your colleagues have, but let's see if there are other elements of classroom management that may play a role in your group project dilemma. Let's look at the guiding questions that can help us recognize the role that the domain of classroom management might be playing in the dilemma (See Handout 8, also Table 3.4)."

> **Handout 8** *Guiding Questions for Reframing Using the Frame of Classroom Management*
>
> **How might the dilemma involve:**
>
> ☐ Procedures for how and when students should move through the classroom?
> ☐ Procedures for how and when students should use materials?
> ☐ Procedures for how and when teachers distribute and collect assignments?
> ☐ Procedures for how and when students should interact with each other and the teacher?
> ☐ Procedures for how and when students should demonstrate respect?
> ☐ Procedures for how and when teachers and students give and receive feedback?
> ☐ Explicit timing for tasks and behaviors?
> ☐ Teacher behaviors, including nonverbal behavior, movement, and tone of voice?
> ☐ Clear expectations and consistent (re)enforcement?
> ☐ The need for teachers to de-escalate conflicts?
> ☐ Other: _____

Ms. Brown reviewed the notes she took the previous time they met. She said, "I'm looking back at my notes and when we were practicing the **Habit of Deliberate Interpretation** you mentioned that one of your **observations** was that students took too much time to complete tasks in the project. Looking at the guiding questions for reframing to classroom management, do you see any questions there that might relate your observation to classroom management?" Mr. Lee scrolled through the list of questions and stopped when he got to the question about whether the dilemma involves explicit timing for tasks and behaviors. "This question right here seems like it could be relevant," he said, "because students really were dragging out the tasks and then at the end of the week many of the assignments were incomplete." Ms. Brown was pleased that Mr. Lee caught this classroom management issue. "Definitely! The way we structure the time in a class really can have a big impact on students' productivity. Do you see any other guiding questions that relate to your dilemma?" Mr. Lee responded, "Yeah, I'm also noticing as I look at this list that students moving around to talk with their friends in other groups has to do with procedures for how they move through the classroom, when they should talk with each other, and also my lack of clear expectations about that because I really didn't anticipate that it would be a problem." Ms. Brown was pleased that Mr. Lee was able to see on his own how his dilemma did, indeed, have some roots in classroom management challenges.

This interaction demonstrates how the guiding questions can reveal aspects of a teacher's dilemma that they had not previously considered. Mr. Lee had the notion that classroom management related to whether students complied with his requests, but through a closer examination he was able to see that classroom management has many other facets related to how the rules and routines were organized. Next, Ms. Brown next prompted Mr. Lee to come up with **dilemma statements** in this domain.

Ms. Brown returned to Key Figure 4, see p. 304, "So now we've zoomed our frame in to the domain of classroom management and have identified some key ways that your dilemma is affected in this domain. Remember that the next step is for us to write new dilemma statements that summarize the issues related to this domain. Let's talk about the dilemma related to how students used their time. How might you phrase this dilemma in the domain of classroom management? And again, you want to write your statements using **internal attribution**." Mr. Lee ventured a new dilemma statement, "How about, *Students were not provided with a structure to help them budget their* *time wisely."* Ms. Brown nodded in agreement that this statement worked well. He then stated his dilemma related to students moving around between groups as, "Classroom structures do not support students staying in their assigned groups." Ms. Brown commented on these new dilemma statements, "These are really useful, Mr. Lee. They are related to your **driving question**, but with a zoomed in focus on classroom management issues that are impeding your students' success in collaborative tasks.

"Speaking of focus, our next step is to develop **focus questions** that will help direct our attention to selecting relevant teacher moves." Mr. Lee said, "I guess a question I could focus on related to class time would be something like, 'How can I structure class time to maximize student productivity?'" Together he and Ms. Brown worked on a focus question for his second dilemma related to classroom management and arrived at, "What proactive strategies can I use to ensure that students stay working in their own groups? (See Table 8.3)"

Shifting the frame to the domain of classroom management allowed Mr. Lee to consider how routines and teacher behaviors could help him structure group projects so that students could be more productive. As a result of this reframing, Mr. Lee and Ms. Brown discussed actions he could take to respond to his new focus questions.

TABLE 8.3 *Mr. Lee's Dilemma Reframed to the Domain of Classroom Management*

Additional Dilemma Statements in the Domain of Classroom Management	Focus Questions
Students were not provided with a structure to help them budget their time wisely.	How can I structure class time to maximize student productivity?
Classroom structures do not support students staying in their assigned groups.	What proactive strategies can I use to ensure that students stay working in their own groups?

Ms. Brown said, "Now let's respond to these focus questions by discussing what you can do to address these classroom management issues." They came up with a variety of ways Mr. Lee could structure class time to maximize productivity. In conjunction with his plan to divide future group projects into discrete tasks during instruction, he could use **explicit timing** to indicate to students how long they have to work on tasks each day. Using explicit timing rather than providing an open-ended task provides structure that helps the class run efficiently and with purpose. He would then reinforce the explicit timing and hold students accountable for completing the task within the allotted time by asking students to report back to the class what their progress was at the conclusion of the set time.

Next, they discussed Mr. Lee's second focus question, "What proactive strategies can I use to ensure that students stay working in their own groups?" Mr. Lee shared, "This one is a little harder for me because I believe my students should be trusted to behave like young adults. In general, I do not think I should have to spell out behavioral expectations for a group project." Ms. Brown replied, "Seventh graders—and heck, even eleventh graders—benefit from knowing what is expected of them and having that expectation reinforced. Now that you've noticed some consistent off-tasks behaviors, you could possibly prevent them by using **precorrection** to explicitly describe your expectations. For instance, you noticed that some students were frequently away from their groups and visiting with their friends in other groups. Knowing that socializing is very important to many middle school kids, you can anticipate that students may want to talk with their friends instead of their group members and could share your expectations with students ahead of time that they need to stay with their group and only get out of their seat to get materials." They also discussed how Mr. Lee could use verbal and nonverbal behaviors to reinforce this expectation, such as **proximity** and eye contact if a student is socializing outside of their work group. If the behavior were to continue, he could use **redirection focused on instruction** to get the student back to working in their own group.

Each of the teacher moves Mr. Lee and Ms. Brown identified in the domain of classroom management will contribute to the resolution of Mr. Lee's driving question. In the end, Mr. Lee wants his students to be able to work together effectively during group projects and making these moves will provide structures that can support his goal.

Frame Shifting Mr. Lee's Dilemma to the Domain of Relationships

Next, Ms. Brown guided Mr. Lee to shift the frame to the final **domain of relationships**. She pointed to their diagram of the zoomed in frame (see Figure 8.1) and pantomimed the moving of the frame over to the circle of the Venn diagram that represented this domain. The domain of relationships was not as easily identifiable as a source of the dilemma or answer to his **driving question**, but nevertheless Mr. Lee was getting the hang of the approach and was able to make some connections.

> As Mr. Lee considered the work he and Ms. Brown had done up to this point, he knew that some aspects of his dilemma would still not be addressed even if he enacted new teacher moves related to **curriculum, instruction,** and **classroom management**. He shared, "I know the last domain is relationships and I definitely think we have some issues there when it comes to group projects because it was clear that some students did not enjoy working together." Ms. Brown recalled their conversation from the previous week, "Yes, I remember you mentioning that students were in random groups with students who weren't necessarily their friends." Mr. Lee added, "Yeah, and then some students kept leaving their groups because they wanted to be with their friends

instead of working with others. A skill young adults need for their future is being able to work with anyone in their future employment context." Ms. Brown asked, "Do you think students felt uncomfortable with their group members?" Mr. Lee replied, "I thought they all knew each other because we've been in school for a few months already, but yeah...maybe that's part of it. Maybe they weren't comfortable with their group members." "That's definitely an issue in the domain of relationships," Ms. Brown said. "Let's look at the guiding questions for reframing to this domain to see if there are any other issues you haven't thought about yet related to relationships (See Handout 9, also Table 3.6)."

Handout 9 *Guiding Questions for Reframing to the Domain of Relationships*

How might the dilemma involve:

- ☐ How much the teacher knows about students' lives outside of school?
- ☐ The teacher's understanding of students' cultural communication?
- ☐ The teacher's appreciation for who the students are as people?
- ☐ The teacher's understanding of, and ability to respond to, each student's social, emotional, and academic needs?
- ☐ The teacher's understanding of how students' developmental phases impact students' lives and learning?
- ☐ Students' knowledge about each other's backgrounds and current lives?
- ☐ Students' appreciations for each other's unique characteristics, abilities, and talents?
- ☐ Students' and teachers' patience with each other's limitations?
- ☐ Teachers' relationships with students' families?
- ☐ Teachers' knowledge about, and involvement in, students' communities?
- ☐ Other: _____

Mr. Lee read through the list of guiding questions, "Honestly, Ms. Brown, I'm not seeing anything else that jumps out at me related to my dilemma. Do you?" She thought for a moment then replied, "Okay, let me know if I've gone out on a limb or not, but I've noticed a few times that you've mentioned that you expect students to act like young adults. Of course, we should always have high expectations of our students, but sometimes I wonder when middle school teachers say things like that if they embrace where young adolescents are in their development." Mr. Lee agreed that he did not know a lot about young adolescents' developmental phases and asked how that connects to the domain of relationships. Ms. Brown explained that appreciating the importance of social dynamics in many early adolescents' lives might help him be more mindful of group dynamics in collaborative projects. "Hmm," Mr. Lee pondered, "I would never have considered that, but you're right. I was expecting to be a high school science teacher and never really learned about young adolescents and that probably does create a blind spot for me when it comes to understanding my students."

Although Mr. Lee's dilemma was initially framed in the **domain of curriculum and instruction**, when he shifted the frame over to the domain of relationships it was evident that part of why the group project did not go as well as he had hoped had to do with students' relationships with one another. Further, knowing how important social dynamics are to many twelve-year-olds could lead to different teacher moves that could benefit the overall success of group projects.

Mr. Lee said, "By now I think I know the process for **frame shifting**. Is it okay if I focus on one dilemma at a time and do all of the steps together? That's sort of how my brain works." Ms. Brown said, "Sure, give it a try!" Mr. Lee started, "Okay, my first dilemma has to do with students' discomfort with each other." He thought for a moment because he wanted to choose his words carefully.

"I will state this new dilemma as: Students' lack of comfort among one another impacts their ability to work effectively in groups and the **focus question** related to this statement is…'How can I help students get to know one another without sacrificing a lot of class time?'" (See Table 8.4.) Mr. Lee continued, "Can we go ahead and talk about possible teacher moves for this focus question before we talk about the other dilemma in the domain of relationships?" Ms. Brown agreed that was a good idea, and Mr. Lee continued. He explained that he spent a few days during the first week of school doing "icebreakers," but that some students in his class still did not know others' names by the middle of the year. He and Ms. Brown discussed that he would need to plan intentional opportunities for students to learn about each other throughout the school year, not just during the first week of school. He talked with Ms. Brown about how to do this and still feel like himself; he said he would never be the "touchy feely" kind of teacher. They came up with some small activities he could incorporate a couple times a week to nurture students' relationships and knowledge about one another. Mr. Lee could also facilitate **teambuilding activities** during group projects to help group members identify commonalities among one another.

Last, he and Ms. Brown talked through a **dilemma statement** related to his appreciation of students' developmental phases. He decided on the statement, I do not

TABLE 8.4 *Mr. Lee's Dilemma Reframed to the Domain of Relationships*

Dilemma Statements Reframed to the Domain of Relationships	Focus Questions
Students' lack of comfort among one another impacts their ability to work effectively in groups.	How can I help students get to know one another without sacrificing a lot of class time?
I do not know the unique characteristics of young adolescents.	How can I be responsive to the needs of young adolescents when structuring group activities?

know the unique characteristics of young adolescents, and the resulting focus question, "How can I be responsive to the needs of young adolescents when structuring group activities?" They discussed various ways he could learn more about young adolescents, and she shared resources with him such as the Association of Middle Level Educators website that includes a host of information about appreciating middle school students and meeting their varying needs. They agreed this was a longer-term project for him and that she would work with him to use his knowledge of his students when designing and structuring activities such as group projects.

Review of Mr. Lee's Case

Ms. Brown wrapped up their meeting, "I have to say, Mr. Lee, I am very impressed with how you've approached the dilemma and our conversation. Teaching is such a vulnerable act and it takes courage to stick your neck out there and venture the risk of realizing that maybe something you did contributed to the problems you're encountering. I really do want to applaud you for your openness! Now, today we talked about a *lot* of different ideas for how you can tackle your dilemma to avoid a repeat problem in the future. I've jotted down all of the different teacher moves we've identified in the three domains (see Figure 8.2). Of course, you can't do everything all at once—you're only human! The nice thing about this list of moves is that all of them have the potential of helping you answer your driving question, so you can't go wrong in choosing where to start! But remember that some of the teacher moves will affect more than one domain because relationships, classroom management, and curriculum and instruction are all **interdependent**. Think about the different moves we've identified and when we meet next, we will narrow down the list to a couple immediate doable moves to try. Then, if you'd like, we can find a time for me to visit your classroom to see you in action and to give feedback."

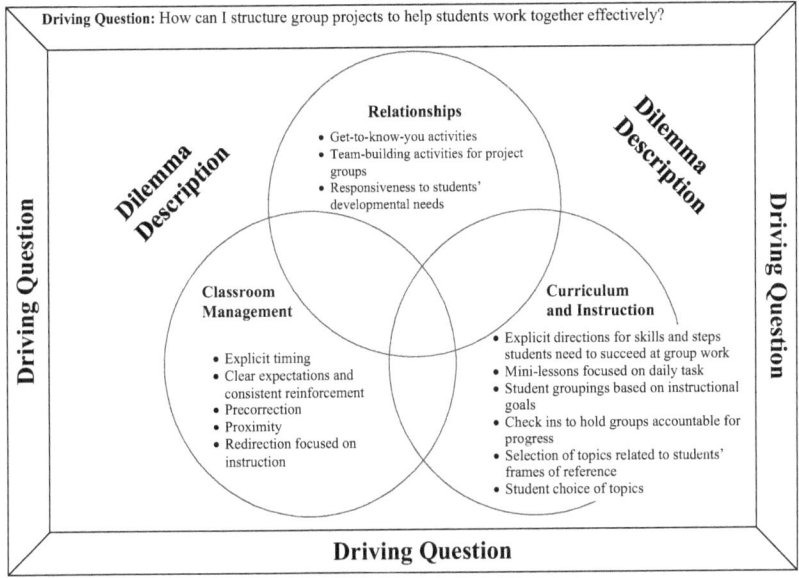

Figure 8.2 Teacher Moves Generated by Mr. Lee's Frame Shifting.

In this case study, Mr. Lee initially blamed students for not being able to handle group work. But after engaging all three **habits of mind** by taking personal responsibility for solving the dilemma, slowing down his judgmental process about what was going on, and committing to build more intentionally on students' assets, he was able to restate his dilemma, zoom in his frame, and shift it to all three domains of teaching to see how each one was relevant for answering his driving question. In the online Study Guide we return to Ms. Cohen's dilemma related to students talking during her second-grade literacy lesson and Ms. Ortega's dilemma with a student's use of technology in her high school Spanish II class. We use the **gradual release of responsibility model** again as we did in Chapter 7 by providing exercises for you to complete with Ms. Cohen's case followed by our explanation of how we might have answered the exercises. Then with the final case we present the exercises with suggested answers. As you work through the practice of reframing each of the teacher's dilemmas to the different domains of teaching, bear in mind that the fundamental practice of **frame shifting** is the same across age levels; the difference comes in selecting and implementing teacher moves. We encourage you to imagine how challenges similar to Ms. Cohen's and Ms. Ortega's dilemmas might be resolved in your own context. After these final exercises, we anticipate that you will have mastered the frame shifting approach and be able to apply it not only to the persistent dilemma you worked on as you read this book, but also to future dilemmas you encounter.

For Discussion and Practice

Before completing the discussion and practice activities for Chapter 8, we recommend completing the exercises for the additional two practice cases provided in the Study Guide, where you will also find additional discussion and practice activities related to these cases.

1. In Chapters 4–6, you completed Exercises 4.2, 5.5, and 6.5, where you identified which teacher moves that were discussed in the chapter could be relevant for you to try when answering your focus questions and addressing your driving question. Compile these teacher moves on Handout 10 (available in the online Study Guide), just as Ms. Brown did for Mr. Lee in Figure 8.2.
    a. Circle the teacher moves you would like to start with.
    b. Explain how the teacher moves might affect other domains of teaching than the one in which they are currently placed.
    c. Explain how the interdependence of the domains of teaching will affect how effective your teacher moves are.
2. As we discussed in Chapter 4, it is important for teachers to be their authentic selves when they interact with students. For example, one teacher might use humor when practicing precorrection and another teacher might be more cut-and-dry and list out the expectations on a chart paper. Revisit the suggested teacher moves we provided throughout this chapter and describe how you might enact similar teacher moves, but in your own personal teaching style. How is what you would say or do different from the examples provided?

Glossary

Below are key terms that appear throughout the book. The number after each definition indicates the page where each term is first defined.

Active Supervision: Continuously checking on students' progress by walking around the classroom, scanning the room, or interacting with students. (169)

Activity Component: Discrete part of an instructional activity, such as the directions or steps students take to complete it. (229)

Affective Statements: Comments that focus on the social and emotional impacts of different behaviors in order to support students' self-regulation and create collaboration and community. (188)

Asset-Based Thinking: Identifying characteristics, dispositions, or resources of students, caregivers, and communities as beneficial and necessary for resolving the dilemma. (35)

Backwards Design: Instructional design that begins with identifying learning objectives, followed by creating assessments to evaluate students' performance on the objectives, and then designing the instructional activities required for students to meet those objectives. (230)

Centers: Instructional format in which different activities targeting the same content are set up in the classroom and small groups of students move at designated times from one activity to the next. (246)

Class-Running Routines: Procedures that students will need to use throughout the class period during each lesson. (151)

Classroom Management: Rules, routines, and teacher behaviors that structure teaching and learning. (69)

Conclusion: See Decision.

Content Knowledge: Knowledge of the teacher's subject area, how subject-specific knowledge and skills deepen and build upon each other, and how the subject relates to other subjects. (207)

Critical Consciousness: The ability to recognize and analyze social systems that systematically disadvantage certain groups and to commit to try to change these. (223)

Curriculum: Content taught both explicitly and implicitly in the classroom through physical materials, verbal exchanges, and classroom activities. (69)

Decision: Conclusion about whether to take action and which actions to take in response to a judgment. This is the fourth step in the Habit of Deliberate Interpretation. (41)

De-escalation: Preventing a loaded moment from becoming a conflict or preventing a current conflict from getting worse. (181)

Deficit Thinking: Identifying the cause for a dilemma as due to something that is wrong with students, caregivers, or communities. (35)

Dilemma Description: Overview of the teaching dilemma including context information and all other information relevant to the dilemma. (14)

Dilemma Statement: The narrowing down of the dilemma into one sentence that describes the core of the issue. (14)

Direct Instruction: Teacher-led exposition on a topic. (p. 241)

Distal: A dilemma caused by circumstances or conditions beyond the educator's control. (p. 27)

Domains of Teaching: Three categories of activities that are always present at every moment during class. These domains are: relationships, classroom management, and curriculum and instruction. (69)

Driving Question: The question that summarizes the dilemma description and drives the teacher to persist towards a solution The frame shifting approach is designed to answer the driving question. (14)

Empirical: Facts that are directly experienced using our senses, such as the actions we see and the words that we hear. (43)

Explicit Curriculum: The facts and messages that are directly communicated when students encounter the materials. (201)

Explicit Timing: Letting students know exactly how much time they have to complete a certain task and providing reminders throughout the task of how much time is left. (162)

External Attribution: Positioning the responsibility for solving a dilemma outside of, or beyond, the educator and/or expressing a sense of hopelessness about being able to solve it. (29)

Focus Question: A question that derives from the dilemma statement and leads to the identification of teacher moves that address the driving question. (14)

Frame Shifting: The act of focusing on how each of the domains of teaching may affect a teaching dilemma and also provide strategies for a solution. (70)

Frames of Reference: Objects, events, or experiences shared by a particular group of people, such as those belonging to a particular cultural group, generation, or geographical location. (215)

Funds of Identity: "Significant people, institutions, cultural artifacts, geographical spaces, and meaningful practices, passions, and interests embedded in a learner's definition of themself" (Esteban-Guitart, 2021, p. 4). (215)

Funds of Knowledge: Mastery of facts, processes, or ways of being based on cultural upbringing that is embedded in family histories and circumstances. (215)

Gradual Release of Responsibility Model: An instructional sequence that begins with teacher modeling followed by activities in which the student has increasing autonomy in, and responsibility for, completing the task. (237)

Group Work: Instructional format in which students work together on a shared activity or project. (245)

Habits of Mind: The beliefs and ways of thinking that play a key role in how teachers view, characterize, and respond to classroom dilemmas. (24)

Habit of Asset Identification: Basing the deliberation about a dilemma on the assets and positive attributes (as opposed to deficits) of students, caregivers, or their communities. (25)

Habit of Deliberate Interpretation: Breaking down the process of diagnosing the source of one's dilemma by exploring alternative interpretations before making judgments or drawing conclusions. The steps in the habit of deliberate interpretation are *observation, interpretation, judgment, conclusion*. (25)

Habit of Personal Attribution: Focusing teaching dilemmas within the realm of the educator's control. (25)

Haptics: The strategic use of touch to focus attention or connect with students. (173)

Heterogeneous Groups: The teacher forms groups of students with differences that are important for the goals of the activity. (245)

Hidden Curriculum: The messages that are communicated but not explicitly stated within the materials or as part of the lesson or classroom interactions. (201)

Higher Order Thinking: Analyzing, evaluating, and creating. (224)

Homogeneous Groups: The teacher forms groups of students with similarities that are important for the goals of the activity. (245)

Human Agency: The resources and power necessary to fulfill one's purpose or potential. (112)

Independent Work: Instructional format in which students work alone to learn new content, develop an idea or product, or practice a skill. (247)

Induction: A process of critical thinking in which we develop different theories or conclusions as we are presented with new information. (45)

Instruction: Formats, activities, and teacher moves designed and used to support the students' learning of the curriculum. (69)

Instructional Agency: Active leadership that members of the classroom community take in directing class activities. (112)

Instructional Design: The overall process of thinking through, planning for, implementing, and evaluating instruction. (229)

Instructional Format: Task, experience, or activity through which students access curriculum. (229)

Instructional Sequence: A set of instructional formats or activities in which one activity leads to the next. (229)

Interaction Routines: Procedures for how, when, and with whom to interact; used across lessons as indicated by the teacher. (151)

Interdependence: The connected relationship that each domain of teaching has with each of the other domains such that a teacher's practices in each domain impacts the other domains. Also, a dilemma in one domain impacts, and is impacted by, issues related to the other domains. (71)

Internal Attribution: Positioning the responsibility for solving a dilemma within the educator and expressing efficacy at being able to solve it. (29)

Interpretation: The theory or explanation we create to make sense of an observation. This is the second step in the Habit of Deliberate Interpretation. (41)

Invisible Funds of Identity: Norms that people engage in and re-create that shape their thinking and behavior often without them realizing it. (223)

Judgment: Internal response to an interpretation. This is the third step in the Habit of Deliberate Interpretation. (41)

Kinesics: The intentional use of body positioning and gestures to help manage a class. (172)

Lesson-Running Routines: Procedures specific to each lesson that help the lesson run smoothly. (151)

Loaded Moment: The moment of friction when the teacher and student(s) have conflicting needs and must negotiate their different needs before the friction becomes a full-fledged conflict. (181)

Lower Order Thinking: Remembering and understanding. (224)

Model of Pedagogical Reasoning and Action: Steps teachers take to determine, plan, implement, and evaluate the content of a lesson. These steps include: 1. Comprehension, 2. Transformation, 3. Instruction, 4. Evaluation, 5. Reflection, 6. New Comprehensions. (230)

Observation: Empirical description of a situation, behavior, or circumstance. This is the first step in the Habit of Deliberate Interpretation. (41)

Pedagogical Knowledge: The general principles and skills of teaching. (207)

Pedagogical Content Knowledge: The blending of pedagogical knowledge and content knowledge that allows the teacher to organize and adapt curriculum and instruction to their particular students. (207)

Personal Agency: The ability to act on an object or situation and see an impact of one's actions. (112)

Planned Ignoring: When the teacher is aware of a student's disruptive behavior but intentionally ignores it in order to keep the focus on the learning. (170)

Precorrection: When the teacher anticipates ways that a transition or activity could descend into students' inattention, unruliness, or other behaviors that distract from the teacher's instructional priorities, and the teacher uses that anticipation to prevent those behaviors from occurring. (159)

Privileged Knowledge: Topics, perspectives, facts, and skills that are included in the explicit curriculum and selected for instruction and assessment. (211)

Progressive: Perspective about curriculum that focuses on the role of teaching and learning as creating a foundation of thinking skills or capabilities that students can apply within various contexts. (203)

Prosody: The tone, rhythm, and volume of one's voice; how one stresses words and phrases. (170)

Proximal: A dilemma, or consequence of a distal dilemma, that is within the educator's control to change. (27)

Proximity: Moving close to a particular student or students in order to redirect behavior. (172)

Redirection by focusing on the instructional task: Shifting students' attention away from a distraction and back to the task at hand by referring to or emphasizing instructional activities, goals, or learning benefits. (164)

Relationships: Sustained patterns of interaction between the teacher and the whole class, the teacher and each individual student, and the students themselves. (69)

Restorative Practices: Practices aimed to restore any damage a student causes to the classroom community through their behavior and then to maintain that community by also supporting the student. (186)

Routines: Procedures used to guide student behaviors in particular situations. (147)

Rules: General expectations for behavior. (147)

Scaffolding: Supports students need to accomplish a certain goal. (232)

SIMMER Down Method: A method for de-escalating a situation that encompasses the slowing down of a heated interaction to notice and respond to the meaning of the message the other is trying to send. The acronym stands for Slow down, Ignore the manner, focus on the Message, respond to the Meaning, Examine the outcome, Repeat or Resolve. (181)

Structures: Interaction sequences that have different applications but are designed to maximize student engagement. (241)

Teacher Efficacy: A teacher's sense of confidence and responsibility for motivating and teaching all students. (30)

Time-out: A non-punitive break during which a student and teacher disengage from interaction for an agreed-upon amount of time in order to compose themselves. (185)

Traditionalist: Perspective about curriculum that focuses on the role of teaching and learning as creating a foundation of factual knowledge upon which students can continue to build throughout their educational careers and lives. (203)

Warm Demanding: Maintaining a positive classroom climate and good relationships with students while insisting that students reach academic mastery. (113)

Whole-Class Cooperative Learning System: Physical and interactional design of all class activities using intentional and consistent student groupings in which all students are equally responsible and accountable for task completion, and group and class success. (241)

Whole-Class Discussion: Instructional format in which students contribute ideas one at a time about a given topic. They listen to each other and build upon the ideas and arguments of those who spoke before them. (243)

Withitness: Conveying a sense that the teacher knows what is happening in all areas of the classroom at all times ("having eyes in the back of your head"). (168)

Key Figures

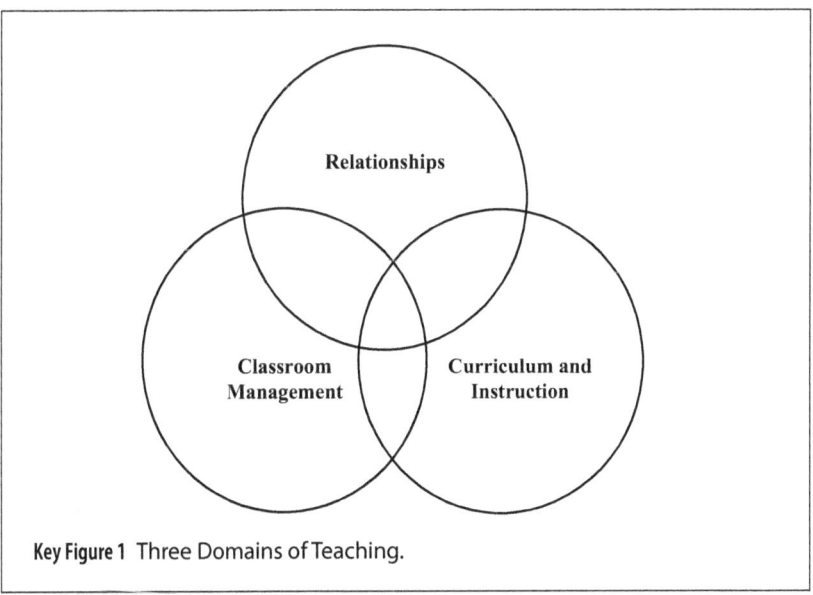

Key Figure 1 Three Domains of Teaching.

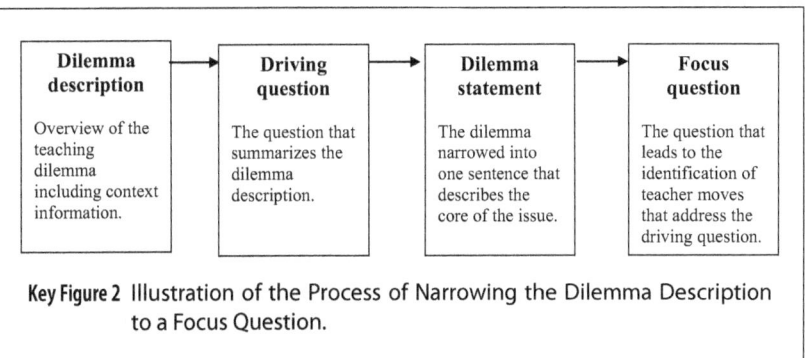

Key Figure 2 Illustration of the Process of Narrowing the Dilemma Description to a Focus Question.

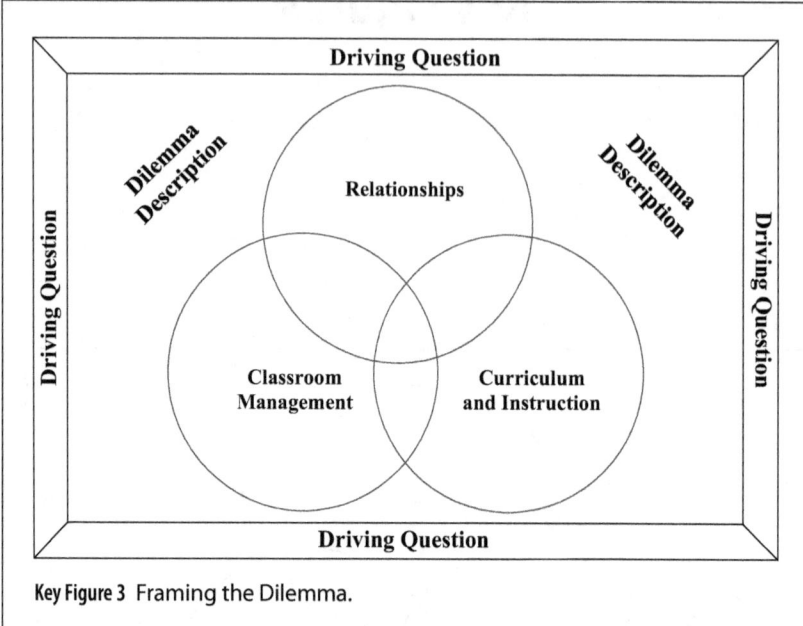

Key Figure 3 Framing the Dilemma.

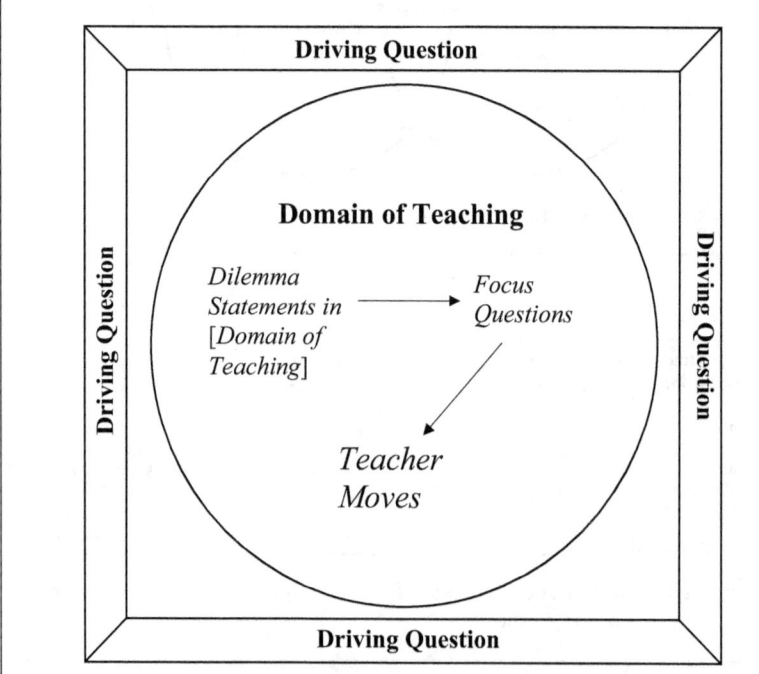

Key Figure 4 Using the Zoomed In Frame as a Focus for Generating Dilemma Statements, Focus Questions, and Teacher Moves Within Each Domain.

Recommended Readings About Cultural Differences in the Classroom

Corbett, D., Wilson, B., & Williams, B. (2002). *Effort and excellence in urban classrooms.* Teachers College Press.

Delpit, L. (2012). *Multiplication is for white people: Raising expectations for other people's children.* New Press.

Fisher, D., & Frey, N. (2021). *Better learning through structured teaching: A framework for the gradual release of responsibility* (3rd ed.). ASCD.

Gorski, P. (2008). The myth of the "culture of poverty". *Educational Leadership, 65*(7), 32–36.

Lareau, A. (2011). *Unequal childhoods* (2nd ed.). University of California Press.

Lewis, A. E., & Diamond, J. B. (2015). *Despite the best intentions: How racial inequality thrives in good schools.* Oxford University Press.

Milner, H. R. (2010). *Start where you are, but don't stay there.* Harvard Education Press.

Milner, H. R. (2013). Analyzing poverty, learning, and teaching through a critical race theory lens. *Review of Research in Education, 37*(1), 1–53. https://doi.org/10.3102/0091732X12459720

Morris, M. W. (2022). *Cultivating joyful learning spaces for Black girls: Insights into interrupting school pushout.* ASCD.

Nieto, S. & Bode, P. (2012). *Affirming diversity: The sociopolitical context of multicultural education* (6th ed.). Allyn & Bacon.

Sensoy, O. & DiAngelo, R. (2017). *Is everyone really equal?* (2nd ed.). Teachers College Press.

Toshalis, E. (2015). *Make me! Understanding and engaging student resistance in school.* Harvard Educational Press.

Valenzuela, A. (1999). *Subtractive schooling: U.S.–Mexican youth and the politics of caring.* State University of New York Press.

Watson, D., Hagopian, J., & Au, W. (Eds.) (2018). *Teaching for Black lives*. Rethinking Schools.

Weinstein, C., Curran, M., & Tomlinson-Clarke, S. (2003). Culturally responsive classroom management: Awareness into action. *Theory Into Practice, 42*(4), 269–276.